How Should We Live?

How Should We Live?

Everyday ethics in Aotearoa New Zealand

EDITED BY STEPHEN CHADWICK

MASSEY UNIVERSITY PRESS

MASSEY UNIVERSITY PRESS

First published in 2017 by Massey University Press
Private Bag 102904, North Shore Mail Centre
Auckland 0745, New Zealand
www.masseypress.ac.nz

Design by Kate Barraclough

A catalogue record for this book is available from the National Library of New Zealand

Printed and bound in China by Everbest Ltd

ISBN: 978-0-9941473-2-5

Contents

Foreword

Philosophy is sometimes criticised as having no practical use, and indeed philosophy contrasts with disciplines in areas such as the social sciences, where the assembling and analysing of empirical data is a significant part of the work. Philosophy is about what to do with the data when you have it. In particular, the empirical data alone will only tell you how things *are*, not how they *ought to be*. Philosophers have for centuries worried about the nature of claims about what ought to be, and about the role of empirical data in determining what ought to be. To take an example from an issue discussed in one of the chapters of this book, a person may believe it is acceptable to eat meat because they are unaware of the processes used in its production — or they may be well aware of how meat is produced but believe that such facts have no moral implications. These are very different reasons, and disentangling what is involved in such differences is why philosophy, as undertaken here, is needed.

This anthology contains chapters written by philosophers currently working in New Zealand and addressing questions which concern every New Zealander. Although the questions are universal, the application to twenty-first-century New Zealand society makes the volume a unique contribution, both to scholarship and to the encouragement of clear thinking about some of the most difficult questions which face us all.

Professor Max Cresswell
Fellow of the Royal Society of New Zealand
Victoria University of Wellington

Introduction

Without necessarily realising it we make ethical decisions every day of our lives. In many situations our actions are simply directed by the rules that our society lays down in law — I may not speed, or lie about my income on my tax returns, simply because I do not want to get caught and face the legal consequences. But there are many situations in which we have to decide what is the right and wrong thing to do irrespective of what the law requires. Telling lies is an obvious example. We are taught as children that it is wrong to tell lies but we soon realise, as we grow older, that this is not necessarily true and that the issue is much more complicated.

A distinction is often drawn between three related and interconnected areas of ethics (or moral philosophy). At the deepest level there are questions that are concerned with the fundamental nature of morality, including whether such a thing exists at all. This is often referred to as *meta-ethics*. In a book of this nature we will simply assume that there is something called morality, without enquiring as to its exact nature. The second area, known as *normative ethics* (or ethical theory), attempts to discover whether there are any fundamental moral principles that underpin ethical decision making. Lastly, questions in *applied* or *practical* ethics consider the moral status of particular actions that humans can and do perform in their everyday lives. These questions are the main focus of this book, although normative principles and theories will be discussed where and when they are useful and informative.

All individuals face everyday ethical dilemmas, wherever they happen to live in the world, but given the particular circumstances that they find themselves in, some may seem more relevant than others. For example, the ethics of over-population might seem of little relevance to someone living in New Zealand, with a population of only 4.5 million, but of great relevance to someone living in the Philippines, a country of comparable size but with a population of over 108 million. However, in a highly interconnected world, with a global economy and with instant access to world news and social media, it is less easy to simply dismiss such issues as being irrelevant. Like never before in human history, all ethical issues are relevant to everyone.

That being said, some ethical issues are more pressing to some people than to others, and this book concentrates on dilemmas that seem particularly immediate to the lives of New Zealanders. Some of the questions raised may be relevant to individuals on a day-to-day basis, including: should I eat meat, download copyrighted music, hire a prostitute, use pornography or have an abortion?

Other issues we face collectively, as members of New Zealand society are: how we should treat the environment, protect online data, deal with inequalities of wealth, treat those who commit murder, or use our armed forces. Although these may seem more distant from our everyday lives, it is only through the actions of individuals that such ethical decisions can be made at a societal level, for in a democratic and relatively free society we can engage in the decision-making process to ensure that they are not simply made for us. Given that New Zealand is a multicultural society it is also crucial that we all acknowledge the importance of different world views and perspectives, particularly those of Māori, and ensure that these inform and help shape our responses to the ethical debates in which we engage.

It is true to say that many people derive their ethical beliefs from religious teachings. However, the number of people in New Zealand who profess to have no religious belief equals those who do, and even of those who do, only a minority regularly engage in religious activity. Furthermore, the wide variety of religious organisations in this country often proclaim conflicting ethical doctrines. In recognition of this, this book does not address comparative religious ethics. Rather, it examines the moral issues from a secular point of view. But it must be acknowledged that secular arguments for moral positions often rely on factual claims, and such facts are easily disputed. Facts as well as arguments must, therefore, always be scrutinised for impartiality and accuracy.

It is important to stress at the outset that everyday ethical questions are controversial, and this is what makes them so interesting to engage with. We have all had different experiences in our lives, and may have been directly confronted with difficult ethical decisions, and so certain readers might find some of the issues this book tackles uncomfortable to consider. This is, however, an unavoidable aspect of considering such questions from a moral point of view.

The views, arguments and ideas presented here are simply a few among many. Although they may be presented clearly and rigorously, it is likely that the reader will disagree with some of them. While the authors are mostly professional philosophers, these issues are central to all our lives and so everyone has an equal right to advance their own opinions. It is hoped that presenting the issues in this way will challenge the reader to think more critically about them. In an ever-changing world it is important that we all consider everyday ethical issues critically, and this book is intended to assist New Zealanders on their journey to discover *how we should live.*

1

Capital Punishment

GERALD K. HARRISON

Introduction

Capital punishment was abolished in New Zealand in 1941. It was brought back in 1950, and then abolished once more for all crimes bar treason, in 1961. It was removed for treason, too, in 1989. Nevertheless, there have been regular calls ever since for capital punishment to be reinstated (although not by any of the major political parties). And according to a 2013 poll conducted for TV3's *The Nation*, 38 per cent of respondents were in favour of its reintroduction. As I hope to show in what follows, this ambivalence about the morality of the death penalty is a fair reflection of the weight of the arguments on either side. This chapter is not an attempt to settle the matter one way or the other, but rather to consider some of the arguments and highlight their strengths and shortcomings.

After describing New Zealand's first and last cases of capital punishment, I will go on to outline one of the most common kinds of objection to such a policy: the absolutist case. I will then go on to consider the possible beneficial social consequences of capital punishment, such as its possible deterrence, educative and incapacitating values. These considerations lie at the heart of utilitarian approaches to punishment that focuses exclusively on outcomes. However, probably the most popular and influential objection to capital punishment is that it inevitably carries with it the risk of irreparable mistakes being made. Since 1842, New Zealand has capitally punished a total of 83 people (one for treason, the rest for murder). It is highly likely that at least some of these people were innocent.

For many, this possibility — which cannot realistically be removed — is sufficient to render capital punishment morally unacceptable. Although a weak objection, it does draw our attention to something of moral significance: a person's deservingness of harm. This is at the heart of a retributivist approach to punishment. Many of those who argue for the reinstatement of capital punishment in New Zealand, as elsewhere, do so partly — sometimes exclusively — on retributivist grounds. While it may be argued that if a person freely commits a sufficiently grave wrong they can become deserving of capital punishment, it is far more questionable whether this makes it right for others to kill them.

First and last

The first person to be officially capitally punished in New Zealand was 17-year-old Maketu Wharetotara. He was charged with murdering five people, including a child, Isabella, the granddaughter of the Ngāpuhi leader Rewa. Maketu Wharetotara had, it seems, been subject to a diet of physical and verbal abuse by Thomas Bull, and one night killed him with an axe. He then murdered Bull's employer, Elizabeth Roberton, her two children and Isabella. Although he pleaded innocent, he was found guilty and publicly hanged in Auckland in 1842.

The last person to be executed was a Whanganui farmer, Walter Bolton. Bolton was accused of murdering his wife, Beatrice, by repeatedly poisoning her tea with arsenic, culminating in her death from an especially large dose on 11 July 1956. Beatrice and Walter had been married for 43 years and had six children. However, according to the prosecution Walter had been conducting an illicit affair with his sister-in-law Florence Doughty and had fallen in love with her. It was this, they alleged, that motivated him to cold-bloodedly murder his wife. Bolton also pleaded innocent, but was found guilty. He was hanged at Mount Eden Prison on 18 February 1957.

Many today believe that these executions, and the 81 others in the intervening years, were wrong, not necessarily because they think that there is a reasonable doubt about the guilt of the parties; but rather because they have a fundamental objection to the whole policy of capitally punishing people, guilty or not.

Absolutism

Many of those who oppose capital punishment do so on what can be termed 'absolutist' grounds. An absolutist is someone who believes that there are some kinds of act that are wrong whatever their consequences. The intentional killing of another person is maintained to be such an act. Capital punishment involves the intentional killing of another person. Therefore, capital punishment is wrong, whatever its consequences. Intentional killing was absolutely wrong when Maketu Wharetotara engaged in it; absolutely wrong when Walter Bolton engaged in it; and absolutely wrong when the State engages in it.

Why might someone think intentionally killing another person is wrong whatever the consequences? Some people appeal to religious injunctions against killing. Others think that it is intuitively obvious that such acts are absolutely wrong. That is, it is just a self-evident truth of reason that intentional killing is immoral. Yet others argue that capital punishment is absolutely wrong because it treats the value of a person's life as if it was a function of its social utility, whereas it is clear that a person's life has intrinsic value. That is, our lives are valuable in and of themselves, rather than because of their usefulness, and the absolute wrongness of intentional killing reflects that.

How credible are these claims? We should, I think, put aside appeals to religious authorities and texts. The credibility of these putative sources of moral insight is going to be hotly contested, plus any argument that rests on an appeal to them will only be persuasive to those convinced of the truth of a relevant religious view (although this is not to deny that religious views have played a significant role in shaping attitudes towards capital punishment).[1]

What about the claim that it is self-evident that it is wrong intentionally to kill another person, whatever the consequences? Any argument for anything eventually appeals to self-evident truths of reason, so if it really is an apparent self-evident truth of reason then this should be allowed to count for something, especially if such an appearance is widely confirmed. However, there is a whole range of cases in which it appears self-evident to most of us that we may intentionally kill another.

For instance, imagine a stranger is engaged in an unprovoked attack on you of such violence that it is reasonable to believe you will die if the attack continues. The only way you can stop the attack is by doing something that you know will almost certainly kill your attacker. It seems clear enough that you are morally permitted to kill your attacker under these circumstances and others like them. Our reason, then, seems to tell us that intentionally killing another *is* sometimes morally permissible. Even if your attacker is not to blame for their attack on you — perhaps they are non-culpably insane, for instance — it still seems clear that you may kill them under these circumstances. It may be — and I think *is* — worse to kill an innocent who is posing a life-threatening danger to you than it is to kill someone who is morally responsible for posing a life-threatening danger to you. Nevertheless, killing an innocent is something you are sometimes permitted to do.

It is, perhaps, possible that our reason is corrupted by our self-interest when our own lives are at stake. But we can test for this easily enough by imagining that our roles are reversed and seeing whether our reason delivers a different verdict. So, imagine that it is *you* who has lost your mind and is attacking someone else. Does your reason tell you that the other person is now morally entitled to kill you? Mine does. If yours does, too, then it is hard to see how these deliverances are a product of bias.

A committed absolutist might respond that all this teaches us is that the absolutist prohibition on intentional killing has a self-defence clause: we are morally prohibited from intentionally killing another person unless our own lives are in immediate danger. Otherwise, the absolutist prohibition stands. Capital punishment cannot very credibly be construed as a form of self-defence. Walter Bolton, as he stood waiting for the trapdoor to open, was not posing an immediate danger to anyone. Thus, capital punishment still violates this slightly revised absolutist principle.

In reply, it is easy to imagine counter-examples to the revised principle. Here is one from philosopher Stephen Law:

> You have been sent into space on a rescue mission. Two astronauts are trapped in different sections of a spaceship, their air running out. You reach the ship with minutes to spare but the oxygen supplies to the two parts of the ship are connected in such a way that it is possible to rescue only one of the astronauts by shutting off the air supply to — and thereby killing — the other. Do you allow both astronauts to die? Or do you save one of the two astronauts? Surely the right thing to do is to save one of the two astronauts, even though you can do so only by killing the other. Here is a case in which it seems very clear to most of us that the right course of action is to kill an innocent person so that a life might be saved.[2]

My reason concurs. And here is another case: a crazed gunman is holding a gun to the head of an innocent, and it is clear that unless he is shot stone dead he will almost certainly pull the trigger. A police marksperson has him in her crosshairs and can kill him instantly. It seems clear enough, at least to many of us, that the marksperson is morally permitted to kill the gunman.

Foresight and intention

Absolutists might argue that we have been overlooking a subtle distinction between an act's intended outcome and its merely foreseen outcome. The absolutist could point out that none of the cases described above necessarily involves any intention to kill another person. In every case it is possible that the death of the other person was merely foreseen, not intended. As such, none of the cases constitutes a genuine counter-example to the absolutist principle.

The distinction between intended and foreseen consequences is a notoriously slippery one.[3] But it is useful to note that what you intended by an action cannot, at the same time as you undertook the action, be something you hoped would not occur. So, if I do X knowing that it will cause P, yet at the same time hope that somehow P will not occur, then I have foreseen P rather than intended it.

To illustrate, imagine a tall building is on fire and someone is trapped on the top floor. She jumps out of a window to her almost certain death. Has she committed suicide? Well, it depends on what, exactly, she was intending to achieve. Suicide involves an intention to die. So, did she intend to die? Possibly, but probably not. More likely she jumped out of the window in order to escape the rising heat and smoke. Given how high she was, she must have known that the fall would kill her. Nevertheless, she could have hoped — by some miracle — to survive the fall. (Note, hoping you will survive a fall is not the same as believing that you will — I hope to win the lottery tonight, but I do not believe I will.) And if she did survive the fall, she would not consider her act a failure. That is, she would not think 'well, that didn't work!' Her death was therefore a foreseen consequence, rather than the intended end, of her action.

Now return to the case in which another person is attacking you. If you kill your attacker, did you intend their death or merely foresee it? It depends on your state of mind at the time, but it is possible that you merely foresee it. Your intention is just to save your life; you merely foresee that to save yourself, your attacker will almost certainly die. Your attacker's death is therefore a foreseen consequence of your action but is not strictly intended.[4]

Likewise, in Law's astronaut case your intention could have been to save one of the astronauts by performing the act of shutting the door. You merely foresaw that in doing this the death of the other would result. And in the marksperson case, it is possible the police marksperson intended to stop a trigger from being pulled by firing a bullet through the gunman's head; she merely foresaw that doing this would result in the assailant's death. So in each case it is possible that no intention to kill lay behind any of the actions.

There are at least two problems for the absolutist, however. The first is that in all of these cases the distinction between intention and foresight does not seem to make any moral difference. Return to the scenario in which you are subject to a life-threatening attack. Imagine that it occurs to you that the only way to stop this attack is to kill your attacker. Now the death of your assailant is intended by you, not merely foreseen. Yet the act is just as morally permissible as before. That is, it seems just as morally permissible to think 'I can stop this attack by killing my attacker — so I will kill them' and to act on that intention, as it is to think 'I can stop this attack by doing X to my attacker — something I foresee will kill them — so I will do X to my attacker' and act on that intention instead.

The same applies to all of the other cases: we can imagine that the death of the other was intended as the means, or we can imagine that the death of the other was foreseen, yet either way the acts seem morally permissible. This is not to deny that the distinction between intention and foresight can sometimes make a moral difference to an action. The point is just that it does not seem to do so in these cases and similar instances. As such, they remain telling counter-examples to the absolutist injunction against intentional killing.

The second reason the distinction between intention and foresight will not help the absolutist is that it would mean that capital punishment no longer necessarily violates the absolutist injunction against intentional killing. We would just have to be careful what we intend to achieve when we execute criminals. So long as we hang criminals with the intention that this operates as a deterrent to others and merely foresee that the hanging will kill the criminal, then they would not qualify as acts of intentional killing, and thus would not be prohibited by the absolutist injunction.

What about the claim that the absolutist injunction against intentional killing is somehow entailed by our possession of intrinsic moral value? The idea that we have intrinsic value — that we are valuable in and of ourselves rather than due to our usefulness to others — is, I think, a very credible one. For instance, speaking personally, it is self-evident to my sense of reason that I do not have to be popular or happy or good-looking or useful to be owed respect and goodwill from others. I am owed it by default, in virtue of being the subject of a life — that is, a bearer of conscious states who thereby has a biography, and not just a biology. Nevertheless, when an equally intrinsically valuable, non-culpably insane person is engaged in a life-threatening attack on me, it still seems clear that I may kill that person in order to save myself. And when I imagine that *I* am engaged in a life-threatening attack on another person, that other person is morally entitled to kill me. Clearly, the change of role cannot alter my intrinsic value (or the intrinsic value of the other). Yet it does affect whether a person of intrinsic value may be killed. It seems to be false, then, that possession of intrinsic value entails an absolutist injunction against intentional killing.

What has been said above does not, in and of itself, imply that capital punishment is morally right after all. It does not even mean that absolutism is false, for there may be other kinds of acts that are absolutely wrong whatever their consequences. What it does show, however, is that the absolutist case against capital punishment is not very compelling, as the absolutist principle has little, if anything, to be said for it.

Utilitarian considerations

In stark contrast to the view that some acts are wrong whatever their consequences are views that maintain all acts are right or wrong in virtue of their consequences. These are known as consequentialist moral theories, of which utilitarianism is the most well-known and popular kind. Utilitarianism is the theory that the morally best act is the one that maximises overall utility, with 'utility' normally being understood to be happiness, or the satisfaction of the greatest number of preferences.

It should be noted that utilitarianism does not necessarily deny that we have intrinsic moral value (although it is sometimes accused of this). Rather, it is an attempt to spell out just what respecting our equal intrinsic moral worth involves. According to the utilitarian, we treat others as equals when we treat everyone's happiness and the satisfaction of their preferences as equally important, for they are what make a life worth living. This means not giving priority to any particular person's happiness or preferences, and seeking instead to maximise general happiness, or general preference satisfaction.

This utilitarian way of thinking about morality has been hugely influential. Its golden age was the nineteenth century, when it enjoyed rigorous defences from, among others, the philosophers Jeremy Bentham (1748–1832), John Stuart Mill (1806–1873) and Henry Sidgwick (1838–1900). Although today most contemporary moral philosophers reject it as an all-encompassing moral theory, it continues to attract defenders, such as Peter Singer (1946–). Even those who reject it acknowledge that it is a source of important moral insights, and many of the arguments for and against capital punishment are utilitarian in character.

We should first reflect on what utilitarianism says about the morality of punishment in general, before focusing on capital punishment in particular. If utilitarianism is true, then wrongdoing does not promote happiness or preference satisfaction. The utilitarian therefore wants to minimise wrongdoing in the way that maximises utility the most. A policy of seeking out and punishing those who commit the most serious wrongs seems likely to do this, for three main reasons. First, such a policy will deter people from doing wrong. We can call this the deterrence value of a system of punishments. Second, there is the reformative or educative value of a system of punishments. Punishing serious wrongs teaches people the significance of wrongful deeds and helps cultivate morally good dispositions. Third, punishing serious wrongdoers has an incapacitating value, preventing them from doing any further wrongs.

What does this mean where capital punishment is concerned? Let's start with incapacitation. There is no dispute that capital punishment is very effective on this score. The dead cannot commit wrongs (at least not in this realm). Maketu Wharetotara's execution prevented him from murdering any more families, and Walter Bolton's execution prevented him from poisoning any more wives. By contrast, lengthy imprisonment merely diminishes a person's scope for future wrongdoing. (Although it may increase it, depending on the kind of environment in which the wrongdoer is incarcerated.) But it does not rule it out with total certainty. A serious wrongdoer who is incarcerated could still wrong others, such as other criminals or prison guards.[5] Plus there is always the risk of escape. For instance, in 2014 murderer and child molester Phillip Smith escaped from New Zealand custody and fled to South America.[6] Although he was arrested and deported three days later, the case underlines the reality of the risk. By contrast, capital punishment removes it entirely.

What about the reformative value of capital punishment? Obviously, executing a person puts them beyond reformation. Neither Walter Bolton nor Maketu Wharetotara can any longer be taught the error of their ways. But this does not prevent capital punishment having a powerful reformative influence on others. As Mill put it:

> [T]he efficacy of a punishment which acts principally through the imagination, is chiefly to be measured by the impression it makes on those who are still innocent; by the horror with which it surrounds the first promptings of guilty; the restraining influence it exercises over the beginning of the thought which, if indulged, would become a temptation; the check which it exerts over the graded declension towards the sate — never suddenly attained — in which crime no longer revolts, and punishment no longer terrifies.[7]

It might serve a useful educative function more generally. The State, by taking the life of those who unjustly kill, teaches others about reciprocity. That is, it promotes the idea that although you have a right to life — one the State will go to great lengths to defend — it is conditional upon you respecting that same right in others.

However, we should note that a policy of capital punishment could also have the opposite effect on some. That is, the State could be seen as setting a bad example. Rather than exercising restraint, the State resorts to violence to settle the score. So the lesson some may take from a policy of capital punishment is that violence is a way to deal with problems.[8]

In the case of Maketu Wharetotara's execution in particular, the drawn-out process of a trial and hanging was seen as cold, inhumane and clinical from the perspective of Māori. (It would have been Māori custom swiftly to kill Maketu with a blow to the back of his head.) So, in the context in which it was carried out, Maketu's execution was more likely to have damaged respect for the British State's system of punishment, not enhanced it.

What about the deterrent value of capital punishment? Will having a policy of capitally punishing the gravest wrongs deter would-be wrongdoers from committing them? In the 1950s, the National Party argued for the reinstatement of capital punishment on precisely this basis. The problem is that it is generally agreed that there is no conclusive empirical evidence of a deterrent effect either way.[9] At present, whether capital punishment is more or less effective as a deterrent than lengthy imprisonment remains an open question.

Nevertheless, many assume that in the absence of hard evidence either way, the moral default is not to have capital punishment. That is, the burden of proof is on those who are arguing for capital punishment, not on those who are arguing against it. But upon reflection it is not clear that this is the right assumption, especially not if we are taking a purely utilitarian approach.

First, in the absence of hard evidence, whichever policy we adopt involves a gamble with people's lives. Other things being equal, isn't it better to gamble with the lives of convicted criminals rather than the lives of innocents? If capital punishment is no more effective than lengthy imprisonment, then some convicted criminals will needlessly have been killed. But if lengthy imprisonment is less effective than capital punishment, then some innocent people will needlessly have been killed.[10]

Second, in the absence of evidence to the contrary, it is reasonable to assume that the more severe a penalty is perceived to be, the more deterrent effect it has. That is, it is reasonable to suppose that a fine of

$1000 has greater deterrent effect than a fine of $100 precisely because most perceive the larger fine to be the more severe punishment. This is not always going to be the case, but the burden of proof is surely on the person who insists that the $100 fine will deter no more effectively than one of $1000. In most people's minds, death is a more severe penalty than lengthy imprisonment. As the American philosopher Louis Pojman says: 'the fact that those who are condemned to death do everything in their power to get their sentences postponed or reduced to long-term prison sentences, in a way lifers do not, shows that they fear death more than life in prison'.[11] If this is correct, then in the absence of hard evidence either way, the reasonable default assumption is that capital punishment will deter more effectively than lengthy imprisonment.

Finally, the deterrent value of capital punishment might reasonably be considered greater than that of lengthy imprisonment, even if they have the same deterrent effect. The deterrent value of capital punishment is going to be determined by its costs and gains in terms of happiness and the prevention of suffering. Lengthy imprisonment causes considerable suffering to the criminal. Killing them may, in fact, cause less harm than would be caused by imprisonment. Capital punishment may be, in many cases, a form of involuntary euthanasia. So even if it has no more deterrent effect than lengthy imprisonment, it could still have greater deterrent value because it achieves the same end at a lower cost in terms of utility.

In summary, when it comes to the justice of capital punishment, the most a utilitarian can say at present is that there is a realistic possibility that it may be a just policy to have. It might serve to teach others about reciprocity. It might shock those who otherwise might have murdered someone into not doing so — something the mere risk of incarceration may not have done. And perhaps murderers themselves might be better off dead than permanently incarcerated. If such claims are true — and it is an open question whether they are — then, based on purely utilitarian considerations, reinstating a policy of capital punishment would be a just thing to do. However, utilitarian considerations do not seem to be the only ones that matter. Indeed, from the perspective of justice, they seem to matter barely at all, as we shall see in the next section.

Innocence

I have been assuming that Maketu Wharetotara and Walter Bolton were guilty of the offences for which they were accused. But what if they were not? Surprisingly, if we are taking a purely utilitarian approach it makes no real difference. So long as they were widely believed to be guilty, executing them would still have exactly the same reformative and deterrent effects. Their actual guilt is irrelevant. Yet our reason tells us that their guilt or innocence is of the first importance. If Maketu Wharetotara and Walter Bolton were innocent, then what was done to them was terribly unjust. That utilitarians will think otherwise is to the discredit of the utilitarians and their theory, surely. As British philosopher Elizabeth Anscombe forcefully expressed it, someone who 'really thinks, in advance, that it is an open question whether such an act as procuring the judicial execution of the innocent should be excluded from consideration — I do not want to argue with him; he shows a corrupt mind'.[12] It is not just the consequences of capital punishment that matter, but the deservingness of those who suffer it.

This brings us to the most common objection to capital punishment, and the one that has probably been more influential than any other in bringing about its abolition. If we have a policy of capital punishment, mistakes will almost inevitably be made. This kind of mistake cannot be rectified. Once someone has been killed we can no longer compensate them or apologise to them (although not all philosophers agree that this is the case — see Davis 1984 for an alternative view).[13]

Despite its popularity and persuasive power, it is not a very good objection. First, it proves too much. For despite initial appearances, it applies to all punishments and not just capital punishment. All punishments carry with them some risk of subjecting innocents to irreversible injustices. To see this, just imagine that Walter Bolton or Maketu Wharetotara were innocent and that advances in technology have meant that we have only today been able to discover this. Even if they had been incarcerated rather than executed, they would both be long dead by now. Thus the injustice of their incarceration would be irreversible. The only way of guaranteeing that no innocents are unjustly and irreversibly punished is to do away with all punishing practices, not just capital punishment.

It might be argued that capital punishment increases the likelihood of irreversible mistakes, because if we incarcerate criminals there is more time in which their innocence can come to light. But this cuts both ways. Having a policy of capital punishment may actually reduce the likelihood of irreversible mistakes being made, precisely because greater efforts will be made to establish innocence, given what is at stake.

The second reason the possibility of irreversible mistakes does not constitute a good objection to capital punishment is that it ignores the irreversible injustice done to murder victims. Imagine, for the sake of argument, that a policy of capital punishment would, in fact, prevent more murders from occurring than a policy of lengthy imprisonment (we have already seen that this may well be the case). Those who oppose capital punishment on the grounds that it carries with it a risk of irreversible mistakes will still oppose capital punishment under these circumstances. Yet the additional victims of murderers that the imprisonment policy will have created have suffered an irreversible injustice.

Nevertheless, our moral horror at the possibility of miscarriages of justice does reflect something of real moral significance, as we shall see in the next section.

Retributivism

Innocent people do not deserve to be killed. It is morally bad when innocents are treated in ways they do not deserve (hence why the possibility of miscarriages of justice worries us so much). But the corollary of this is that it is morally good when people do get what they deserve. That is, if Walter Bolton was innocent, then he did not deserve to be killed and his execution was a terrible injustice. But by the same token, if Walter Bolton was guilty then plausibly he did deserve to be killed and thus his execution was no injustice at all.

Desert — as in 'just deserts' — is at the heart of a retributivist view approach to punishment. On a retributivist view, it is not the social utility of our punishing practices that justifies them. Rather, punishment is all about giving people what they deserve. Those who have committed grave wrongs, such as murder, deserve to come to harm, and thus it is only right and proper that we, as a community, ensure they receive it. Any utility that may come from punishing wrongdoers — that is, any reformative, incapacitating and deterring effects it may have — are moral bonuses.[14]

Proportionality is also central to the idea of desert. The punishment must fit the crime. The graver the wrong a person has committed, the more harm the person deserves to suffer, irrespective of the utility of making them suffer it. So, when it comes to capital punishment there are two main questions we need to ask. First, are there wrongs so grave that one can, by committing them, deserve to die? Second, if someone deserves to die, is it morally just for the State to kill them? However, before we answer these questions, something should be said about our intrinsic moral value and our free will, as both are important components of a retributivist view.

When it comes to our intrinsic moral value, we can distinguish two views a retributivist might take (although combinations are possible, too). A retributivist might hold that we are born with equal intrinsic value. However, as we develop, most of us acquire free will and thus become subject to moral obligations. That is, we become moral agents (those who owe moral obligations) and not just moral patients (those to whom moral obligations are owed). If we subsequently use our free will to do wrong, this can affect our moral value, which in turn affects our deservingness of goodwill and respect from others. So, although we are born moral equals, our free will allows us to become morally unequal. This, in turn, explains why capitally punishing the most serious of wrongdoers may be morally permissible. Those who have committed the gravest wrongs have, plausibly, blotted out or radically reduced their intrinsic value to such an extent that killing them now is, or may be, morally permissible.

A different view is that our intrinsic moral worth is inviolable. Nevertheless, what we freely do can affect how others ought to respect our intrinsic moral worth and the intrinsic worth of others. If I have acted well, then respecting my intrinsic worth involves praising and rewarding me. If I have acted badly, then respecting my intrinsic worth — and those whom I have wronged — involves blaming and punishing me. And if I have murdered, then killing me may be what respecting the intrinsic worth of my victims involves. So, on this view our intrinsic value does not vary, but how we ought to honour that value does.

Free will

The idea that by our actions we can come to deserve harm — including the harm of death — presupposes that we have some kind of free will. Some find this to be a questionable assumption. For, so the reasoning goes, plausibly everything we do is the product of antecedent causes

— things that precede and bring about something. Antecedent causes, such as heredity and environment, lie outside our ultimate control. Thus, if everything we do is ultimately a product of such matters, then we are all victims of our circumstances, and the idea that any of us could truly 'deserve' harm for anything we do is misguided. Blaming and punishing us for our decisions is as unjust as blaming or punishing us for our height, or sex, or skin colour.

The argument is a powerful one, and it is at the heart of the problem of free will. There is not space here to enter it, for it is one of the most complicated and thorny debates in philosophy. What we can do instead is just note a couple of things. First, despite its surface appeal, the above argument has actually persuaded few who have carefully reflected on it. Some agree that if everything we do is a product of antecedent external causes, then we would indeed lack free will, but conclude that as we manifestly do have free will, not everything we do traces to external causes. Others believe that even if everything we do is the product of antecedent external causes, this is compatible with our exercising the kind of free will presupposed by retributivism. These are radically different viewpoints, but both acknowledge that we have free will and are morally responsible in the retributivist sense.

By contrast, nihilists about free will — those who conclude that we lack free will — are a minority. This is because our possession of free will is more self-evident than either the assumption that everything we do is a product of external causes, or the assumption that free will is incompatible with everything we do being the product of external causes. To conclude that we lack free will would allow weaker evidence to overrule stronger evidence.

Hence most philosophers conclude that we have free will, but concede that exactly what it involves remains a matter of investigation. Note, the fact that we may not be able satisfactorily to explain how we have free will should not be allowed to overturn our evidence that we have it. That would be akin to me concluding that because I am unable to explain how my computer is working, it must not be working. Similarly, because exactly how we could have free will remains something of a mystery does not, in and of itself, constitute positive evidence that we lack it.

The second observation we can make is that free will is presupposed not just by retributivism, but by the very idea that we have any moral obligations. Given that the topic we are considering here is whether it is morally right or wrong to have a policy of capital punishment, this entire discussion — and not just the retributivist part of it — presupposes that we possess free will (the necessity of free will is simply clearer in the context of retributivist views). So, rejecting a retributivist approach to punishment on the grounds that we lack free will would, on pain of inconsistency, commit us to rejecting all approaches to justifying punishment.

Inhumanity and burdens

Returning, then, to the issue of capital punishment: are there wrongs so serious that if we freely commit them we deserve to die? Many, myself included, have the intuition that there are. Horrendous deeds, such as maliciously torturing and killing an innocent, are plausibly among them. No doubt not everyone gets such intuitions. But enough of us do for them to be taken seriously.

Assuming, then, that a person who has freely performed one of these deeds deserves to die, does it follow that it is morally permissible for us to execute them? Not necessarily. For instance, I once witnessed, at some distance, a teenager hurl abuse at a passing old man. The teenager was standing on a low wall and shortly after shouting the abuse he lost his footing and fell heavily onto the ground, winding himself. It seemed to me that he got what he deserved; it was good that he was in some discomfort. Be that as it may, it seemed equally clear that if he had not fallen off the wall I would not have been morally permitted to go and shove him off it. So, though he deserved to come to harm — and it was good that he did — I was not morally permitted to harm him.

This, I think, is important to recognise. The relationship between desert and moral permissibility is not a straightforward one. It is clear enough that the norms of moral decency place real limits on what one can do to others, including limiting what one can do in terms of giving someone what they deserve. The limitations may vary according to circumstances (there may be circumstances under which it would be morally permissible to shove a rude teenager off a wall). But one cannot conclude that as a person deserves to die, it is morally permissible for us to kill them.

The relevant question, then, is whether the norms of moral decency allow execution. And here I think it is plausible that they do not. Many of those who have witnessed an execution report that there seems something undignified and unseemly about the act.[15] That, I think, is good prima facie evidence that there is indeed something morally questionable about it.

Something else should be noted as well. There are moral limits on what we can demand from people. If there is a child drowning in a pond and I am standing nearby, then no doubt I ought to wade in and help her out, even if that will inconvenience me somewhat. But what if another child falls in, and then another, and another? It goes on and on. How long do I have to stay at the pond rescuing children? All day? All week? What if (bizarrely) people bring me food and water and the other necessities of life — do I have to dedicate the rest of my life to rescuing children from this pond, given that there is an endless stream of them plopping into it? No, of course not: there is going to come a point at which I am entitled to walk away and live my own life, even though that will mean some children will drown. That is terrible of course, and the children do not deserve to drown, and my life is no more important than theirs. But the truth of these claims just underlines the point: we are not morally required to do all we can to give others what they deserve. Morality does not demand that from us. Spending one's entire life saving drowning children from a pond is, no doubt, a good and praiseworthy thing to do. But it is praiseworthy precisely because it is not morally demanded. It goes well beyond the call of duty. Morality is not that demanding; not in the main, anyway.

Returning to capital punishment: is it reasonable, then, to demand of morally decent people that they coldly and clinically bring about the death of others? In some settings it may be, of course. But when it is merely to give a guilty person what they fully deserve, then I would say that plausibly it is not reasonable at all. After all, what is being asked is considerable, especially given the morally unseemly nature of the act and the emotional hazards that attend it. For instance, when capital punishment was restored in New Zealand in 1950, the staff who had to take part in the execution processes suffered considerably. As the pace of executions sped up during the late 1950s, two of the three staff experienced post-traumatic stress disorder, alcoholism and duodenal haemorrhaging.[16]

We can note something else as well: there seems to be a significant asymmetry between the moral importance of preventing bad things happening to innocent people versus the importance of ensuring bad things happen to guilty people. Consider: it seems significantly worse, morally speaking, for an innocent to receive a harm that they do not deserve, than it does for a guilty person to fail to receive the harm that they do deserve. For instance, if the only way I can prevent an innocent from being harmed unjustly is to do something that will prevent an evil person from receiving the harm they deserve, then it seems — at least to me — morally right and proper for me to do that thing. Whereas if the reverse were true — that is, if the only way I could ensure that an evil person received their just deserts was to do something that would result in an innocent person receiving a harm that they did not deserve — then I ought not do that thing. So, even if some of the worst criminals in New Zealand deserve to be executed, it may be better that they do not receive their just deserts if the alternative means that innocent people will have to be asked to engage in morally unseemly and unduly burdensome acts of killing.

Conclusion

When it comes to the issue of the morality of capital punishment, one side does not have obviously better arguments than the other. None of the arguments surveyed above are conclusive. And I have purposefully tried to leave open what degree of moral importance the various kinds of considerations I have drawn attention to possess. The social consequences of a policy of capital punishment matter morally. But it is extremely hard to make any reliable judgement about what they will be. It also matters that people, including wrongdoers, get what they deserve. However, it is important that we preserve our moral decency and not make unreasonable demands of people. These considerations can pull in different directions. But how much pull one consideration exerts versus another is something we must trust our judgement to discern. That, I think, is exactly as it should be. Our best moral theories and principles should ultimately operate as guides to judgement rather than replacements for it.

---

1 Pauline Engel, *The Abolition of Capital Punishment in New Zealand* (Wellington: Department of Justice, 1977); Maureen Garing, '*Lex talionis* and the Christian Churches: The Question of Capital Punishment in New Zealand,' in *To Strive and Not to Yield: Essays in Honour of Colin Brown*, ed. James Veitch (Wellington: Victoria University Department of Religious Studies, 1994), 112–122.

2 Stephen Law, *The Philosophy Gym: 25 Short Adventures in Thinking* (London: Headline Book Publishing, 2003), 187.

3 Jonathan Glover, *Causing Death and Saving Lives* (London: Penguin Books, 1977), 88.

4 G. E. M. Anscombe, 'War and Murder,' in *Nuclear Weapons, A Catholic Response*, ed. Walter Stein (London: Sheed and Ward, 1961), 44–52.

5 Thomas Mappes, 'The Death Penalty,' in *Social Ethics: Morality and Social Policy*, ed. Thomas Mappes and Jane Zembaty (New York: McGraw-Hill, 2002), 110.

6 ABC news, 'Fugitive killer deported back to New Zealand and returned to prison after escaping to Brazil,' accessed June 6, 2017, http://www.abc.net.au/news/2014-11-29/fugitive-killer-escapee-phillip-smith-back-behind-bars/5927692.

7 John Stuart Mill, 'Speech in Favour of Capital Punishment,' in *Applied Ethics*, ed. Peter Singer (Oxford: Oxford University Press, 2002), 99–100.

8 Stephen Nathanson, 'An Eye for an Eye?' in *Social Ethics: Morality and Social Policy*, ed. Thomas Mappes and Jane Zembaty (New York: McGraw-Hill, 2002), 139.

9 Louis Pojman, 'Deterrence and the Death Penalty,' in *Social Ethics: Morality and Social Policy*, ed. Thomas Mappes and Jane Zembaty (New York: McGraw-Hill, 2002), 141.

10 Ernest van den Haag, 'On Deterrence and the Death Penalty,' *Ethics* 78 (1968): 287.

11 Pojman, 'Deterrence and the Death Penalty,' 143.

12 G. E. M. Anscombe, 'Modern Moral Philosophy,' *Philosophy* 33 (1958): 16–17.

13 Michael Davis, 'Is the Death Penalty Irrevocable?,' *Social Theory and Practice* 10 (1984): 143–156.

14 Igor Primoratz, 'A Life for a Life,' in *Social Ethics: Morality and Social Policy*, ed. Thomas Mappes and Jane Zembaty (New York: McGraw-Hill, 2002), 127.

15 George Orwell, *Decline of the English Murder and Other Essays* (London: Penguin, 1965).

16 Redmer Yska, *All Shook Up* (Auckland: Penguin, 1996), 165.

2

Freedom and the State

STEPHEN CHADWICK

Introduction

Freedom, or liberty, is an important concept in our lives. By 'freedom' we mean the absence of constraint, and a constraint is that which prevents us from doing something. Here are some examples: having a migraine will prevent me from playing soccer, a lack of formal qualifications will prevent me from becoming a high-school teacher, and having a flat car battery will prevent me from getting to work on time. In all of these cases I lack the freedom to do what I desire — to play soccer, become a high-school teacher and to get to work on time, respectively. We can extend this to cover things that we do not desire. I might actually be pleased that I cannot play soccer, because it is raining and I do not want to get muddy. But it is still the case that I am not free to play soccer, because, even if I did want to, I would be unable to because, having a migraine, I do not have the potential to play.

There are two particular types of freedom that are extremely important in our everyday lives, and they raise many important moral questions. These are social and political freedoms. The sort of constraint that limits these forms of freedom is known as coercion, and it involves humans constraining each other from doing things. With respect to social freedom, we might say that I am not free to keep my smartphone if a gunman demands that I hand it over to him. Of course, in one sense I am still free — it is, after all, my free choice whether to give him the phone or have my head blown off. But it seems reasonable to claim here that, given the extreme consequence of this choice, the gunman is limiting my freedom by putting me in this situation. However, the sort of freedom that we are concerned with in this chapter is political freedom.

Political freedom

Political freedom concerns humans constraining each other's behaviour through the institutions of the State — such as the legal system, the law enforcement agencies and the prison service.

Political freedoms are constrained by laws that we have to obey unless we are willing to face negative consequences — for example, receive fines, be imprisoned, have our driving licences revoked. As with the gunman example, in one sense we are free to break these laws, but the sanctions that exist for lawbreakers are coercive, in that, in general, most of us are not happy if we are subjected to them. Given this, most of us are coerced into obeying the law whether we want to break it or not. Most people who do wish to act contrary to the law only do so if they think they will not get caught — if they know they will get caught, then the coercive pressure of the law usually prevents them from breaking it.

It is appealing to think that political freedom is always a good thing, and perhaps the more of it we have the better. After all, if I am a rational adult then why should I not be allowed to choose to do as I please? Surely, if the State tries to curtail my freedom it is treating me like a child, and is thus acting paternalistically. However, it does not take much thought to realise that a lawless society, one that grants unlimited freedom to all, is actually senseless. For example, in such a society I would be free to burn down your house, but then if I do, you would no longer be free to live in it. So, even in a lawless society, there would not actually be unlimited freedom for everyone. Maybe in an ideal utopia, where everyone voluntarily respected everyone else's freedom, that would be possible. But for real human beings, to be able to live collectively in cohesive societies there do have to be some laws to protect basic freedoms.

So, given that human society does require coercive laws, what political freedoms should people have? In New Zealand, we are legally free (with some conditions) to vote for whichever political party we choose, drive cars that pollute the environment, eat meat, use some types of recreational drugs (such as alcohol, nicotine and caffeine), read certain forms of pornographic magazines, and so on. At the same time, we are not legally free to do such things as assault our spouses, have underage sex, drive while drunk, steal other people's property, or urinate on the steps of parliament. Furthermore, the law prescribes that we must wear seat belts when driving on a State highway, must undertake jury service when summoned, and pay income tax.

How are we then to decide which freedoms the State should be entitled to restrict and which freedoms it should not be?

Prudence, morality and the law

Before addressing this question, an important distinction needs to be drawn. We need to distinguish between moral, prudent and legal actions, and, conversely, immoral, imprudent and illegal actions. We also need to recognise that actions that fall into one of these categories do not necessarily fall into any particular one of the others. For example, you may consider that not wearing a coat when walking up a snowy mountain is imprudent (i.e. not in your self-interest), because you might die of hypothermia. But it does not appear to be immoral, and it is not illegal.

Likewise, you might consider that stealing food from a wealthy person, if you are starving, is prudent and not immoral, but it is illegal. Furthermore, you might consider that lying to your spouse about having an affair is prudent, and it is not illegal, but you still might consider it immoral.

This distinction raises interesting moral questions regarding the way we run our society, and the laws that should govern the behaviour of its citizens. For we can ask: should all immoral actions be illegal? Should all imprudent actions be illegal? Does the fact that an action is illegal make it immoral to perform? In this chapter we are going to discuss whether there is any moral principle that can help us to decide whether or not a particular action should or should not be illegal — i.e. whether there should or should not be a law constraining the freedom to perform that action.

John Stuart Mill and the harm principle

In 1859 the English philosopher John Stuart Mill wrote a long essay, titled 'On Liberty', in which he outlined a theory of political freedom formulated to answer this very question. His purpose was to discover which actions it is morally acceptable for the State to prevent us from performing. In his essay he makes an important distinction between two sorts of actions: self-regarding actions and other-regarding actions. Other-regarding actions are those which affect the person performing the action and also other people directly. Self-regarding actions, on the other hand, are those which affect only the person performing the action 'directly, and in the first instance', and only affect other people indirectly 'through' the agent.[1]

Some actions seem to fall nicely into these categories. For example, singing in the shower, watching TV, eating food, picking your nose alone in bed, and smoking in your own back garden do not appear to directly affect anyone else, and so are self-regarding actions. On the other hand murder, buying food, stealing, and having adult consensual sex do directly affect other people, and are therefore other-regarding actions.

Mill then proposes a moral principle, often referred to as the harm principle, which is at the heart of his theory. He says:

> The only purpose for which power can be rightfully exercised over any member of a civilised community, against his will, is to prevent harm to others.[2]

So, for Mill, legal restrictions on our freedom to perform an action are legitimate only if that action has the potential to harm other people.

He continues:

> The only part of the conduct of anyone for which he is amenable to society is that which concerns others. In the part which merely concerns himself, his independence is, of right, absolute. Over himself, over his own body and mind, the individual is sovereign.[3]

What exactly Mill means by harm is a matter of debate, but he seems to equate harming others with interfering with, or injuring, their interests.[4] So, for example, one of my interests is that I possess the phone that I have purchased. If you steal it, you interfere with that interest. It is, therefore, acceptable for the State to restrict your freedom by outlawing theft.

Mill also thinks that the harm principle applies when the failure to perform an action can directly lead to other people being harmed. As he says, a 'person may cause evil to others not only by his actions but by his inaction, and in either case he is justly accountable to them for the injury'.[5] So, for example, I have an interest not to die if I have a car crash. If you find me in this situation, injured, and fail to call an ambulance, you interfere with this interest and harm me. In this instance, according to the harm principle, it is acceptable for the State to compel you to assist me where possible.

Both self-regarding acts and other-regarding acts can cause harm. For example, chopping my own wood without wearing safety glasses is a self-regarding act that has the potential to cause me harm; after all, I might get a splinter in my eye. But this is a self-regarding harm, and Mill claims that a person 'cannot rightfully be compelled to do or forbear because it will be better for him to do so, because it will make him happier, because, in the opinions of others, to do so would be wise, or even right'.[6] So, although chopping wood as described might not be in my own interest (i.e. it is imprudent), the potential harm is only to me, and so the State has no right to compel me to wear safety glasses.

If Mill is right, then in order to justify restrictions on freedom we have to decide which actions are self-regarding and which ones are other-regarding, and, furthermore, which actions cause harm to other people and which ones do not.

In New Zealand we find that many laws do in fact accord nicely with the harm principle. We find that there are no laws prohibiting singing in the shower, watching TV, eating food and picking your nose alone in bed (all harmless, self-regarding actions). Likewise, there are no laws banning potentially harmful self-regarding actions either, such as tramping up a mountain without a coat, or chopping your own wood without wearing safety glasses. Furthermore, there are no laws prohibiting attending rugby matches, having adult consensual sex and buying food (all non-harmful, other-regarding actions). But there are laws prohibiting harmful other-regarding actions, such as murder and theft.

Mill does add some important restrictions to the applicability of his harm principle. First, he states that:

> this doctrine is meant to apply only to human beings in the maturity of their faculties. We are not speaking of children, or of young persons below the age which the law may fix as that of manhood

> or womanhood. Those who are still in a state to require being taken care of by others, must be protected against their own actions as well as against external injury.[7]

So he acknowledges that children are not old enough to fully understand the consequences of their actions, or the nature of civil laws, and so should not, therefore, be directly subject to the harm principle. He holds the same to be the case for adults with intellectual disabilities, and also adults with severe mental illnesses. In these three cases, society needs to care for them in different ways, as is the case in New Zealand.

It is also important to realise that Mill's principle states a necessary, but not a sufficient, condition for governmental interference with people's actions.[8] As we saw in Chapter 1, Mill is a utilitarian, and so believes that the morally right action is that which maximises overall happiness in society. This means that, when we consider the justification of legal restrictions on freedom, we have to consider not only the harm that an action may cause to other individuals, but also the harm it may cause society as a whole. For example, suppose you are a shopkeeper and you lower the cost of your products. This action could force me out of business, and so harm me, my family and my employees. However, allowing such economic competition may benefit society as a whole. And so society overall may be better off if it allows the freedom to perform some actions which can potentially harm others. (This will be important later.)

It must, however, be appreciated that Mill is not promoting a selfish, uncaring society that is not concerned about its citizens so long as their actions only harm themselves and no one else. He says:

> Human beings owe to each other help to distinguish the better from the worse, and encouragement to choose the former and avoid the

> latter. They should be for ever stimulating each other to increased exercise of their higher faculties, and increased direction of their feelings and aims towards wise instead of foolish, elevating instead of degrading, objects and contemplations.[9]

Essentially, he thinks that society has a duty to persuade or educate its citizens not to harm themselves. What society should not do is compel or coerce them not to do so.

Another important point Mill makes is that harm to others *is* acceptable if it occurs 'with their free, voluntary, and undeceived consent and participation'.[10] Thus, a boxer can harm his opponent in the ring and, assuming they are both consenting adults, this harm is acceptable. On the other hand, except in self-defence, it is unacceptable for the boxer to punch someone in the face in a bar, because the victim has not consented.

So is the harm principle, along with these caveats, the perfect moral principle that can help us determine the rightful extension of the State's prohibitive laws? One way to answer this question is to examine controversial examples and see whether it helps settle the debates. We could discuss freedom of speech, sexual prohibitions, religious expression, paying taxes and many more. In all of these cases there are laws regulating our actions, and the existence or extent of these laws is highly contentious. Furthermore, Mill's theory is frequently used (often implicitly) by politicians, commentators and activists to justify their various stances.

We could also examine pursuits that we undertake in our spare time. Everyone does different things for fun and enjoyment. Some play rugby, sing in choirs and watch TV. These sorts of pursuits do not, in general, seem controversial, and this is because they do not really harm the individual or affect anyone else. However, there are other pursuits that do cause controversy. Playing video games, having sadomasochistic sex, and eating vast amounts of unhealthy food all cause controversy because of their potential harmful effects on the individual and/or others. For Mill, the harm principle 'requires liberty of tastes and pursuits; of framing the plan of our life to suit our own character' so long as we do not harm others.[11] So, as we can see, it could be very useful to apply it to all of these aforementioned debates.

There is, however, one very common pursuit that is particularly controversial, and is subject to severe government regulation — the use of recreational drugs — and it is this issue that we will discuss in this chapter. Mill himself discusses the application of his theory to alcohol use, but we shall see whether the points that he raises can be extended to cover all forms of recreational drug use. We will consider whether or not his theory can help us decide if the extent of the New Zealand government's interference in this form of recreational pursuit is morally justified.

We are not going to consider the moral status of recreational drug use itself — i.e. whether taking drugs recreationally is a morally acceptable way to live our lives. Given how central the use of alcohol is in our culture, it seems that most people do not think that consuming at least some recreational drugs is, in itself, morally problematic. Rather, what we will discuss is whether it is morally permissible for society to prohibit recreational drug use, irrespective of its moral status. As mentioned earlier, just because something is moral does not necessarily mean it should be legal and, conversely, just because something is immoral does not mean it should be illegal. What we are interested in here is whether recreational drug use should be illegal or regulated, and, if so, why.

Recreational drug use

Before we can begin, it is important that we have an adequate understanding of what is meant by 'recreational drug use'. Humans consume a range of different drugs. Many of them are for medicinal purposes, some of which are prescribed by doctors, whereas others, such as paracetamol, are freely available in supermarkets. These drugs are produced by pharmaceutical companies and have undergone years of research and development to ensure their safety. In New Zealand such drugs are legal, so long as they are administered appropriately.

Other drugs are not taken for medicinal purposes, but are rather used for 'recreation'. By 'recreational drugs' we will use the definition put forward by philosopher Douglas Husak, who says they are drugs that are consumed in order to 'promote the pleasure, happiness, or euphoria of the user. The more specific purposes that are encompassed under this broad umbrella include sociability, relaxation, alleviation of boredom, conviviality, feelings of harmony, enhancement of sexuality, and the like.'[12] Recreational drugs, therefore, include nicotine, 'legal highs', alcohol, cannabis, caffeine, methamphetamine ('P'), cocaine, 'magic mushrooms', LSD, ecstasy and heroin. Some pharmaceutical drugs are also sometimes used recreationally, such as diazepam and phenobarbital. What all of these drugs have in common is that they are psychoactive — they alter an individual's mental state. Thus, 'recreational drug use' could also be called 'recreational psychoactive substance use'.

What is immediately apparent from this list of recreational drugs is that some of them can be legally possessed and consumed in New Zealand, and some cannot. In 1975 the Misuse of Drugs Act became law, with the purpose of prohibiting the manufacture, possession, supply and importation of many drugs, some of which are used recreationally. It classifies drugs into three categories — A, B and C — 'based on the risk of harm the drug poses to individuals, or to society, by its misuse'.[13] Class A drugs are deemed the most harmful, and include cocaine, heroin, LSD and methamphetamine. Class B includes cannabis preparations (such as hashish or oil) and morphine.

Class C includes the cannabis plant, diazepam and phenobarbital. The Act also sets out the penalties attached to the possession, importation and dealing of these substances. Three recreational drugs that are not included in this classification system are alcohol, nicotine and caffeine. These three therefore remain legally available, whereas cannabis and methamphetamine are outlawed.

We need to consider why this is the case, and whether Mill's harm principle is useful for deciding what the legal status of all, or some, recreational drugs should be. In order not to prejudice the debate we shall not distinguish between 'drugs' and 'alcohol', as is often done by the media, government, health services and the police. Given our definition, alcohol is just as much a recreational drug as the others thus far mentioned, and in this chapter it will be treated as such.

So we need to examine the arguments for why some recreational drugs, such as cannabis and methamphetamine, are prohibited, whereas others, such as alcohol and nicotine, are not. Given that the possession of cannabis can lead to a three-month prison sentence, and in the case of methamphetamine a six-month sentence, there have to be good reasons for why such penalties are not received in the case of alcohol, nicotine and caffeine.

Two important caveats need to be stressed before we begin. First, with all recreational drugs the psychoactive effect they induce can differ when they are combined. When more than one substance is consumed at the same time to induce a unique psychological state, it is called polydrug use. The problem this can cause is that it can be difficult to draw concrete scientific conclusions about the potential harms and health risks of specific drugs, because polydrug use has to be controlled for.

Second, we need to acknowledge that data gathered for illegal drugs, and their harmful effects, is often biased because users are less forthcoming about their usage; there is a huge 'hidden population' of illegal drug users. Data regarding the use and effects of illegal drugs is often gathered from individuals who have become involved in the criminal justice system or the health service (such as rehabilitation clinics). Such users tend to be experiencing the greatest drug-related problems, and it is therefore tempting to infer that illegal drug use is actually more dangerous than it necessarily is.

CAFFEINE

The most popular recreational drug consumed in New Zealand is caffeine. Found in tea, coffee, fizzy drinks and chocolate, it is regularly consumed by over 70 per cent of the population.[14] It is true to say that it is not always consumed directly for its psychoactive effect, and in many cases is in such low doses that such effects are negligible. In many cases the products that contain caffeine, such as chocolate, are consumed purely for their taste on the palate.

However, many people consume caffeine as a 'pick-me-up', and this psychoactive effect is, for them, often more important than the taste of the product in which it is found. As there is rarely any debate concerning its legal status, we will not discuss caffeine here. Rather, we will consider the next four drugs in terms of decreasing popularity in New Zealand — alcohol, nicotine, cannabis and methamphetamine. We will examine the arguments that have been raised that have affected their legal status, and see whether they accord with Mill's theory of political freedom.

ALCOHOL

After caffeine, the most popular recreational drug used in New Zealand is alcohol, the consumption of which has been legal throughout the whole country since 1999.[15] As with caffeine, people often consume alcohol because they enjoy the taste of the products in which it is found. There are hundreds of different wines and beers in New

Zealand alone, and competitions, both national and international, are testament to the importance of their effect on the palate. However, it cannot be denied that, however sublime the beverages may taste, an extremely important factor is that the alcohol they contain has a psychoactive effect; and for many people this is the main reason for their consumption.

In terms of Mill's theory, the consumption of alcohol is not, in itself, a harmful other-regarding act, because it is only the consumer who partakes of the substance. Although the majority of users consume in moderation, it can, however, be a harmful self-regarding act, because 'directly, and in the first instance' long-term use can cause damage to the heart, brain and liver, as well as lead to stomach bleeding, reduced fertility, malnutrition and breast cancer. It can also precipitate mental and emotional problems.[16] Furthermore, as it can lead to dependence, it can be particularly difficult for some people to avoid these health problems and, in New Zealand, it is estimated that up to 10 per cent of the population have alcohol use disorder.[17] Alcohol can even be dangerous to the casual user, as it can lead to death by overdose if a sufficient quantity is consumed in a single sitting. Although all of these potential harms of alcohol are undesirable, they are all self-regarding harms, and so it might seem that Mill's harm principle should dictate that there should be no legislation limiting its use.

However, depending on where and how much is consumed, it can also be harmful to other people 'through' the individual, due to the fact that it can lower inhibitions; it can lead to inter-personal violence, antisocial behaviour, familial neglect and risky sexual behaviour. It is also the most common 'date-rape' drug.[18] Furthermore, if a driver is intoxicated, it can increase the likelihood of their causing a traffic accident. Given these indirect harms to others, it does seem that, although drinking alcohol is a self-regarding act, there is at least prima facie justification for prohibition.

NICOTINE

The third most popular recreational drug in New Zealand, used by approximately 18 per cent of the population, is nicotine.[19] Historically, the delivery of this drug has been through the use of tobacco, although this is now changing since the introduction of 'e-cigarettes'. As the difference between these delivery methods may be of relevance to the debate, we shall distinguish between 'smoking', when nicotine is administered via tobacco products, and 'vaping', when it is administered via e-cigarettes.

As with alcohol, smoking has the potential to be a harmful self-regarding act, as it can cause harm to the individual 'directly, and in the first instance'. It is linked to an increased chance of heart disease, respiratory problems and lung cancer in long-term users. As nicotine is extremely addictive, it has a great propensity to lead to long-term use, which makes the likelihood of users developing these problems extremely high.[20] However, smoking is different from alcohol in that it does not significantly alter the behaviour of the consumer towards other people. Therefore, it does not seem to cause indirect harm to other people 'through' the individual. If smoking is, therefore, only harmful to the smoker, then, with respect to the harm principle, there should be no legislation restricting the activity.

However, by the late 1980s it had been scientifically proven that 'passive smoking' — inhaling second-hand smoke — can be dangerous, because it can lead to third-persons developing smoking-related diseases. As a consequence of this, in 1990 legislation was introduced in New Zealand to prohibit smoking in some public places. The main purpose of this was to 'prevent the detrimental effect of other people's smoking on the health of people in workplaces, or in certain public enclosed areas, who do not smoke or do not wish to smoke there'.[21]

The important point here is that these prohibitions were put in place because smoking in the presence of others can be a harmful other-regarding action.

Legislation to prevent passive smoking is, therefore, in accordance with Mill's harm principle. Yet there is good reason to suggest that New Zealand legislation aimed at preventing passive smoking does not go far enough, as smoking does not occur just in public: it is still legal to smoke in private homes and vehicles, in the presence of non-consenting adults and children. In some countries, such as England and Wales, smoking in vehicles in the presence of passengers under the age of 18 is illegal.[22] For consistency, in order to prevent other-regarding harm, there should be bans in New Zealand on smoking anywhere in the presence of non-consenting adults and children, whether in private or in public.

Recent research actually suggests that things are even more complicated. There is now good evidence to suggest that, while not as dangerous as passive smoking, exposure to 'third-hand' smoke may also be a significant health risk to non-smokers, especially children.[23] Third-hand smoke is the chemical residuals and toxins that linger on clothes, hair, furniture and carpets, long after the cigarette has been extinguished. If such smoke is, in fact, dangerous, then in accordance with the harm principle there should be legislation to prevent it occurring. This could take the form of excluding smokers from having contact with children and non-consenting adults, even when they are not actually smoking. This would seem very difficult to enforce. There is, therefore, as with alcohol, a prima facie justification for the total prohibition of smoking.

Earlier it was acknowledged that smoking tobacco is not the only way to deliver the recreational drug nicotine. It can also be delivered by vaping. Although illegal, e-cigarettes have been available in New Zealand since 2007, and many scientific studies suggest that vaping is 95 per cent less harmful than smoking.[24] There is still much scientific debate surrounding this issue, and, as it is a relatively new phenomenon, no conclusive proof through longitudinal studies can be provided.

However, it is widely accepted by the medical profession that vaping is much less harmful than smoking tobacco, and so from 2018 the New Zealand government has made it legal. At present it is being promoted as a smoking-cessation method, rather than as an acceptable recreational activity in itself. However, if it turns out that the risks of vaping (and 'passive vaping') are minimal, then it causes no self- or other-regarding harm and, to accord with the harm principle, there should be no legislation to limit its use, or prevent its promotion as a recreational activity in itself. Legislation restricting vaping, even in public spaces, would then appear to be paternalistic and run contrary to the harm principle.

CANNABIS

Cannabis is the fourth most popular recreational drug in New Zealand, and has been tried by over 500,000 citizens.[25] (We will not discuss the use of medicinal cannabis here, as such use is not for recreation.)

As with alcohol, the majority of users partake of cannabis in moderation. Casual use seems to pose few health risks, and, unlike alcohol, cannabis use cannot lead to death in a single sitting. But there is evidence, albeit less conclusive, that there are health risks associated with heavy, long-term use. It certainly seems to be the case that, as with nicotine, the mode of administration has an effect on these risks. The long-term smoking of cannabis can certainly lead to respiratory problems, but this risk can be lowered significantly by using a vaporiser, which, somewhat like an e-cigarette, releases the active substance as vapour.[26] These harmful respiratory effects can be avoided completely by administering the drug orally.

There is evidence, though, that other physical health problems are associated with the heavy, long-term use of cannabis, however it is administered, including the likelihood of developing certain forms of cancer.[27] Furthermore, there is now good evidence that heavy, long-term use can cause mental health issues and lead to cannabis use disorder. Overall, it does seem reasonable to conclude that the long-term, heavy use of cannabis can cause self-regarding harm.

If we just consider the potential self-regarding harm 'directly, and in the first instance' that may result from consuming cannabis, then, like alcohol, to accord with Mill's harm principle the State should not legislate against its use. However, if heavy, long-term use of cannabis can cause harm to others indirectly 'through' the user, then the matter is more complicated. Unlike alcohol, there is little evidence that its use makes individuals aggressive, and thus leads to violent or anti-social behaviour.[28] But significant psychological dependence may result in familial neglect, and it does seem to increase the likelihood of risky sexual behaviour.[29] There is, however, conflicting evidence as to whether driving under the influence of cannabis increases the likelihood of causing accidents.[30]

Given the indirect harms to others 'through' the user, it does, therefore, seem that, as with smoking and the consumption of alcohol, there is at least prima facie justification for legislation outlawing its use.

METHAMPHETAMINE

Methamphetamine ('P') became openly available in New Zealand only in the 1990s. Its popularity is much lower than that of the other drugs discussed here, but, due to its illegal status and its highly stigmatised image in the media, data regarding its use is less conclusive. A study undertaken for the Ministry of Health, called The New Zealand Drug Harm Index 2016, estimates that less than 1 per cent of the population uses amphetamine-type stimulants,[31] and of these, 94 per cent are short-term, casual users.[32] However, like alcohol, methamphetamine can be physically dangerous even to the casual user and can even lead to death.[33]

As with nicotine it is highly addictive and is, therefore, more likely to engender long-term use, which can lead to premature tooth loss, psychosis, paranoia, insomnia, confusion, hallucinations, depression and brain damage, even long after the individual has stopped using it. Its use can, therefore, cause self-regarding harm 'directly, and in the first instance' to the consumer. There are also many indirect harmful effects on others 'through' the user, for it can lead to violent behaviour and familial neglect. Furthermore, it increases the tendency to have unprotected sex.

There is also good evidence that 'passively' smoking the substance can cause health issues to those exposed to it.[34] There is, therefore, at least prima facie justification for legislation outlawing its use for both self- and other-regarding reasons.

Recreational drug use and harms to society

We have seen that, in all cases of recreational drug use, heavy, long-term use can cause harm directly to the user. If this were the full extent of their harm, then the harm principle would suggest that, to protect freedom and liberty, all recreational drug use should be legal. However, we have also seen that, to a greater or lesser extent, all of these drugs can cause harm to others either indirectly 'through' the individual or, in the case of the passive smoking of tobacco and methamphetamine, directly. Due to this, there is at least a prima facie reason to concede that the freedom to engage in all recreational drug use *is* a candidate for governmental interference.

However, the issue is much more complicated than this. Earlier we saw that, for Mill, the harm principle is a necessary but not a sufficient condition for governmental interference with people's actions. In order to decide whether interfering in people's lives is acceptable, we have to take into account not only the harm that individuals can potentially cause each other, but also the harms that their actions can cause society in general. Once we do this, we realise that all recreational drug use causes a lot more harm than has been outlined so far, and this may seriously affect the outcome of the debate.

The social harm caused by recreational drug use is difficult to quantify, and is value-laden, as it depends on what is considered to be a harm. Harms that can be assessed in monetary terms include things like health service use, lost output, law enforcement costs and the wider effects of crime, morbidity and motor vehicle accidents. In attempting to put a monetary value on the overall harm caused by some recreational drugs, the New Zealand Drug Harm Index 2016 study considered the cost of personal harm, the cost to the community and the cost of intervention (such as health, education and law enforcement).[35] However, this is of limited use to this debate, as it only attempts to estimate the costs that arise as a result of the use of illicit recreational drugs. It therefore ignores the costs associated with the use of alcohol and tobacco.

A more useful study, for our purpose, was undertaken in the United Kingdom by the Independent Scientific Committee on Drugs, and it attempted to estimate the harm that all common recreational drugs cause to the individual user, to other people and to society as a whole. In order for meaningful conclusions to be drawn, it took into account the fact that it used broader criteria and did not put a monetary value on harms. It scored the drugs using 16 different criteria, seven related to the harms that a drug produces in the individual, and nine to the harms to others, including society. The criteria were weighted to indicate their relative importance.[36]

The criteria of harm to the self were: drug-specific mortality (intrinsic lethality of the drug); drug-related mortality (the extent to which life is shortened by the use of the drug); drug-specific damage to physical health; drug-related damage to physical health; the extent to which the drug creates dependency; drug-specific impairment of mental functioning; and drug-related impairment of mental functioning.

The criteria of harms to others and society were: loss of tangibles (such as income and housing); loss of relationships; chance of injury; chance of involvement in crime; environmental damage; family adversities (such as the extent to which the drug affects emotional wellbeing and future prospects); international damage; economic cost; and costs to social cohesion.

As the findings of this study were similar to those undertaken in other countries, such as the Netherlands, it seems reasonable to apply these findings, albeit with caution, to the case of New Zealand.

The study found that, regardless the number of users, the drug that is by far the most harmful to others and society as a whole is alcohol, followed by tobacco, cannabis and lastly methamphetamine. In terms of harm to the individual user, the most harmful was methamphetamine, followed by alcohol, tobacco and lastly cannabis.

HARMS RESULTING FROM THE ILLEGAL STATUS OF RECREATIONAL DRUGS

The study points out that 'many of the harms of drugs are affected by their availability and legal status . . . Ideally, a model needs to distinguish between the harms resulting directly from drug use and those resulting from the control system for that drug.'[37] Earlier we saw that alcohol and nicotine are not controlled under the 1975 Misuse of Drugs Act, whereas cannabis and methamphetamine are, and this very fact greatly affects the harm caused to the individual user, to others and to society as a whole. For example, in 2014 the approximate cost to the New Zealand criminal justice system of cannabis use was

$305 million, alongside $16 million for methamphetamine.[38] As these drugs are illegal, society has to pay the cost of apprehending and prosecuting users, dealers and producers. Furthermore, society has to pay for incarceration, which from 2007 to 2011 cost $59 million for minor offences alone.[39]

In addition, as the means of production of illicit drugs is often in the hands of criminal organisations, society has to pay for the consequential illegal activity that can arise from the money obtained through this criminal venture. These costs are much lower in the case of alcohol and tobacco because of their legal status.

Furthermore, the use of illicit recreational drugs can criminalise otherwise law-abiding citizens. Those caught in possession can gain criminal records, which can then limit their future employment opportunities. This can negatively affect their dependants and society as a whole. It can also put users into contact with the criminal underclass — something that users of legal recreational drugs do not have to face.

Recreational drug legalisation

We are now in a better position to judge whether, by applying the harm principle, individuals should have the freedom to use all or some recreational drugs, or whether the harm caused to others and society is sufficiently great that the activity should be outlawed, or at least restricted.

We have seen that it is naïve to think that outlawing the use of a substance will remove all potential harms. Having seen the harm caused by the illegality of some recreational drugs, there is every reason to believe that others, and society, would still face great harm even if all recreational drugs were prohibited. So we need to assess whether the harm caused by the consumption of recreational drugs is outweighed by the harm caused by restricting their use. If the harm caused to others and society by an action being legal is equal to, or outweighed by, the harm of it being illegal, then, to accord with Mill's theory, the freedom to perform the action should not be curtailed.

Whether more harm would be caused by all recreational drugs being legalised or not is, of course, difficult to assess. But some useful data can be obtained by examining the experiences of other countries that have experimented with different forms of restrictions on the freedom to partake. There have been occasions where alcohol prohibition has been enforced, such as in the United States between 1920 and 1933, and it seemed to increase harm to individuals and society.[40] Furthermore, there is now evidence that the legalisation of cannabis in many states in the United States has not significantly increased harm to others and society as a whole.[41] So, in the case of these two drugs we do have at least a prima facie reason to accept that the freedom to partake of them should be respected by law.

In the case of methamphetamine, there is no society that has actually legalised its use, but Portugal has attempted to introduce some policies of decriminalisation — a strategy that has largely changed its use from a criminal to a healthcare issue. How successful this has been is, however, debatable.[42]

Smoking tobacco has not been outlawed in any country, so it is difficult to know whether the harm to society and others would decrease to such an extent that the freedom to partake should be curtailed. With the rise in popularity of vaping, which seems much less harmful, the demographics of smoking may change over time anyway.

For the sake of argument, let us suppose that harm to others and society would not increase significantly if the use of all recreational drugs were legal. Then, according to the harm principle, the freedom and liberty to partake of the substances should be rightfully protected. Would this mean that there should be no restrictions on their use?

Harm reduction

We have seen that, for Mill, society has a duty to care for its citizens. If we accept this, then, even in a society in which all recreational drugs were legal, society would still have a duty to introduce policies to minimise the harm that they may cause. The majority of recreational drug users do not cause harm to themselves, to others or to society. But there are still ways in which regulation may help to minimise the harm caused by the minority that do. To this end, Mill himself makes some interesting suggestions.

HEALTH

Given that all recreational drugs can cause serious health issues for a minority of users, as a caring society harm-reduction strategies need to be implemented to minimise these. At present alcohol can only be produced and sold by registered companies, and they are legally bound to declare what their products contain. Due to this, consumers are aware of the level of alcohol their drinks contain, and can therefore make a free, informed choice as to the level of intoxication they wish to experience. In the case of illegal recreational drugs, users have no guarantee that what they are consuming is what they actually desire, and this can amplify serious health problems. If all recreational drugs were legalised, production would have to be in the hands of registered companies only, thus ensuring effective quality control.

Furthermore, as possessing and using illegal drugs can lead to a criminal conviction, it is understandable that many users shy away from publicly acknowledging that they are experiencing drug-related problems. Removing prohibitive legislation might help to ensure that users receive medical attention, counselling support and rehabilitation as early as possible. It would also assist social services in implementing early intervention strategies designed to protect the user's children and families.

Health warnings could also be suitably added to the packaging of all recreational drugs, as is currently the policy with tobacco products (although, interestingly, this is not the case with alcohol, even though it is legal and potentially just as harmful to the user's health).[43] Providing education and advice to users to minimise potentially harmful effects on their health, and thus keep associated healthcare costs down, should also be a priority. (This may involve the distribution of clean needles and condoms.)

LICENSING

Harm can also be reduced by restricting who sells recreational drugs, and from where they are available. Mill says, with respect to alcohol:

> it is fit to confine the power of selling . . . to persons of known or vouched-for respectability of conduct; to make such regulations respecting hours of opening and closing as may be requisite for public surveillance, and to withdraw the licence if breaches of the peace repeatedly take place . . .[44]

So, according to Mill, licensing regulation is legitimate as a way of reducing harm to society, and thus laws such as restricting the consumption of recreational drugs in public places are justified. However, restricting access to recreational drugs for the express purpose of making fewer people partake of them, just because a small percentage of the population does cause harm through their use, is paternalistic. For a freedom that you legally possess, but is so restricted that you can rarely express it, is not really a freedom at all.

TAXATION

There are currently extremely high taxes on alcohol, and this goes some way towards paying for the harm it can cause society (over

$5.8 billion a year).[45] Mill accepts that society has to raise taxes in order to operate effectively, and so, as long as taxes exist for this purpose, then it is acceptable. If all recreational drugs were legal, it seems reasonable, therefore, that such taxation should be applied to all of them. It is estimated that in 2016 cannabis and methamphetamine raised $630 million for their producers and dealers, of which $70 million was reinvested in other criminal activity. It is thought that if this money had been legally earned, declared and invested, society would have raised approximately $240 million in tax, as well as reducing the criminal activity that the profits from the illegal drug trade caused.[46] This money could go towards paying for the societal harm that the drugs' use can cause.

With the tax on tobacco things are a little different. In 2011 the New Zealand government announced an initiative called 'Smokefree Aotearoa 2025', which is a commitment to reduce the consumption of tobacco products to zero by 2025. In order to achieve this it introduced highly subsidised smoking-cessation programmes. But it also adopted a policy of increasing the tax on tobacco, year on year, as a means of encouraging people to stop smoking.[47] Mill says to tax recreational drugs 'for the sole purpose of making them more difficult to be obtained, is a measure differing only in degree from their entire prohibition; and would be justifiable only if that were justifiable'; for 'every increase of cost is a prohibition, to those whose means do not come up to the augmented price'.[48] The proportion of smokers who live in the most-deprived areas is much higher than those who live in the least-deprived areas (32 per cent and 8 per cent, respectively).[49] Thus high taxation on tobacco, a drug that is highly addictive, is extremely harmful to the dependants of poor people.

So it does seem reasonable that recreational drugs should be taxed, to offset the cost to society that their use can produce. However, it is important that, in order to reduce harm to society, and thus accord with the harm principle, the level of taxation should not be set to a point where it actually causes more harm than good. When recreational drugs cost too much, it can lead to acquisitive crime to fund supply (which, for those recreational drugs that are currently illegal, stands at $140 million a year), as well as familial neglect.[50]

AGE LIMIT

Legislation stipulating a minimum age at which recreational drugs can be consumed is clearly not, according to Mill's theory, an abuse of freedom. All drugs can cause self-regarding harm if used to excess, but, as Mill points out, it is only those 'in the maturity of their faculties' who can truly make the free choice as to whether such risk of harm is worth taking. So there should be a minimum age, set by society, at which all recreational drugs are available. At what point people become mature enough is of course arbitrary, and a matter for society to decide. But, whichever recreational drugs are legal, it seems reasonable that the same age limit applies to them all.

The current age restriction for buying and selling tobacco products and alcohol is 18. But, of course, having a minimum age limit does not prevent those who are underage from acquiring the drug. Approximately 57 per cent of 15–17-year-olds consumed alcohol in 2015;[51] 90 per cent of them obtained it from their guardian or a family member.[52] And it is actually legal for parents to supply alcohol to children of *any* age, so long as it is done in a 'responsible manner'. (What constitutes a 'responsible manner' is, of course, open to interpretation.)[53] Mill says, of children, 'society has had absolute power over them during all the early portion of their existence: it has had the whole period of childhood and nonage in which to try whether it could make them capable of rational conduct in life'.[54] Whether the legal supply of alcohol, the most harmful recreational drug, to children of any age promotes this ideal is surely a matter for serious debate.

DEALING WITH OFFENDERS

Mill also makes an interesting point regarding the minority who do cause harm to others through recreational drug use. He says:

> drunkenness, for example, in ordinary cases, is not a fit subject for legislative interference; but I should deem it perfectly legitimate that a person, who had once been convicted of any act of violence to others under the influence of drink, should be placed under a special legal restriction, personal to himself; that if he were afterwards found drunk, he should be liable to a penalty.

He goes on: 'the making himself drunk, in a person whom drunkenness excites to do harm to others, is a crime against others'.[55] So, showing a propensity to harm others, while under the influence of any recreational drug, is a reasonable ground for having restrictions placed on the freedom to obtain access to the drug in the future.

INTOXICATION IN THE WORKPLACE

As recreational drugs are psychoactive, it also seems reasonable that there be legislation designed to prevent intoxication in the workplace, in order to reduce harm. Mill says, 'when a person disables himself, by conduct purely self-regarding, from the performance of some definite duty incumbent on him to the public, he is guilty of a social offence'. He goes on to say, of alcohol, 'no person ought to be punished simply for being drunk; but a soldier or a policeman should be punished for being drunk on duty'.[56] So, while using recreational drugs is not, in itself, to be prohibited, if the state of mind that the drugs induces negatively affects the public duty one has as a worker, then the freedom to get intoxicated should be curtailed while at work.

PREGNANCY AND DRUG USE

The use of recreational drugs while pregnant raises an interesting philosophical point. It is often argued that a fetus is not a person,[57] and, if so, then surely the harm principle does not apply to it. If this is true, then you should be allowed to consume recreational drugs while pregnant and any legislation curtailing this freedom is paternalistic. However, if you do intend to bring the fetus to term, then surely you have a moral duty to ensure that the resultant baby will be as healthy as possible. All recreational drug use while pregnant has the potential to cause damage to the developing fetus.

Thus, even if you believe that such an activity does not directly harm an actual person, it can directly harm a future person, and it is the mother who has the capacity to minimise this. It could therefore be argued that, in accordance with the harm principle, this potential indirect harm to a future person demands legislation prohibiting the consumption of all recreational drugs while knowingly pregnant (something which is not the case with alcohol and nicotine in New Zealand).[58]

Conclusion

The writer John Donne famously wrote 'no man is an island entire of itself; every man is a piece of the continent, a part of the main'.[59] Fundamentally, the distinction between actions that affect only oneself, and those that also affect others and society as a whole, may be impossible to draw. Mill's theory may, therefore, be inadequate as a means to settle debates in which there is a clash between the freedom of the individual and the State.

His theory has, however, been very influential over the past 150 years, and has been used to justify why the State should and should not interfere in many different aspects of our lives. Here we have examined one particular controversial case in which its application is potentially useful. We have seen that in terms of recreational drug use the majority of people who partake do not cause harm to themselves or to others directly. So, given this, is it reasonable that the freedom of the majority should be curtailed because of the actions of the minority?

To answer this we have concentrated on the harms caused by recreational drug use. There are of course many benefits of such use, in terms of both the enjoyment they bring to the majority of users, as well as the rewards that they do, and could, bring to our economy. Many enjoyable activities can cause harm to the self, others and society. For example, the enjoyment gained from eating too much unhealthy food is estimated to cost society $800 million a year through associated healthcare expenditure and loss of productivity.[60] But maybe these harms are just a burden that society has to shoulder so that its citizens can express their freedom to enjoy their lives in whatever way they choose?

As Mill says, 'mankind are greater gainers by suffering each other to live as seems good to themselves, than by compelling each to live as seems good to the rest'.[61] This does not mean, however, that as a caring society we should not do all we can to minimise the harms that can arise through the expressions of these freedoms, through advice, education and effective regulation.

---

1 John Stuart Mill, 'On Liberty,' in John Stuart Mill, *Utilitarianism, Liberty and Representational Government* (London: J.M. Dent and Sons, 1910), 75.

2 Ibid., 73.

3 Ibid., 73.

4 Ibid., 142.

5 Ibid., 74.

6 Ibid., 73.

7 Ibid., 73.

8 Michael Lacewing, 'Mill's Harm Principle,' 1, accessed May 12, 2017, http://

documents.routledge-interactive.s3.amazonaws.com/9781138793934/A2/Mill/MillHarm.pdf.

9 Mill, 'On Liberty,' 133.

10 Ibid., 75.

11 Ibid., 75.

12 Douglas N. Husak, 'Liberal Neutrality, Autonomy, and Drug Prohibitions,' *Philosophy and Public Affairs* 29, no. 1 (2000): 66.

13 Parliamentary Counsel Office, Misuse of Drugs Act 1975, accessed May 5, 2017, http://www.legislation.govt.nz/act/public/1975/0116/latest/DLM436190.html.

14 Jamie Morton, 'That Coffee Craving Could Be Hurting You,' *New Zealand Herald*, October 1, 2016, accessed May 30, 2017, http://www.nzherald.co.nz/lifestyle/news/article.cfm?c_id=6&objectid=11719535.

15 Bruce Murray, *A History of Tawa* (Wellington: Tawa Historical Society, 2014), 229.

16 Ministry of Health, 'The Effects of Alcohol,' accessed February 22, 2017, http://www.health.govt.nz/your-health/healthy-living/addictions/alcohol-and-drug-abuse/alcohol/effects-alcohol.

17 Kirsty Johnston, 'One in 10 Kiwis Now Alcoholic,' *Stuff*, October 27, 2013, accessed February 19, 2017, http://www.stuff.co.nz/national/health/9331572/One-in-10-Kiwis-now-alcoholic.

18 University of Ulster, 'Alcohol is Most Common "Date Rape" Drug,' *Science Daily*, October 22, 2007, accessed May 10, 2017, https://www.sciencedaily.com/releases/2007/10/071020113144.htm.

19 Ministry of Social Development, 'The Social Report 2016 — Te Pūrongo Oranga Tangata,' June 2016, accessed June 1, 2017, http://socialreport.msd.govt.nz/health/cigarette-smoking.html#socio-economic-differences.

20 Ministry of Health, 'Health Effects of Smoking,' accessed February 18, 2017, http://www.health.govt.nz/your-health/healthy-living/addictions/smoking/health-effects-smoking.

21 Parliamentary Counsel Office, Smoke-Free Environments Act 1990, accessed March 10, 2017, http://www.legislation.govt.nz/act/public/1990/0108/latest/DLM223921.html.

22 BBC News, 'England Bans Smoking in Cars with Children,' February 11, 2015, accessed June 15, 2017, http://www.bbc.com/news/health-31310685.

23 Coco Ballantyne, 'What Is Third-Hand Smoke? Is It Hazardous?' *Scientific American*, January 6, 2009, accessed May 3, 2017, https://www.scientificamerican.com/article/what-is-third-hand-smoke.

24 Public Health England, 'E-cigarettes: An Evidence Update,' August 2015, accessed April 2, 2017, https://www.gov.uk/government/uploads/system/uploads/attachment_data/file/457102/Ecigarettes_an_evidence_update_A_report_commissioned_by_Public_Health_England_FINAL.pdf.

25 Ministry of Health, 'Cannabis Use 2012/13: New Zealand Health Survey,' May 28, 2015, accessed April 8, 2017, http://www.health.govt.nz/publication/cannabis-

use-2012-13-new-zealand-health-survey.

26 Mitch Earleywine and Sara Smucker Barnwell, 'Decreased Respiratory Symptoms in Cannabis Users Who Vaporize,' *Harm Reduction Journal* 4, no. 11 (2007), accessed June 16, 2017, https://www.ncbi.nlm.nih.gov/pmc/articles/PMC1853086/pdf/1477-7517-4-11.pdf.

27 Adam J. Gordon, James W. Conley, and Joanne M. Gordon, 'Medical Consequences of Marijuana Use: A Review of Current Literature,' *Current Psychiatric Reports* 15 (2013): 1–11.

28 Michael K. Ostrowsky, 'Does Marijuana Use Lead to Aggression and Violent Behaviour?' *Journal of Drug Education* 41, no. 4 (2011): 369–389.

29 C. S. Hendershot, R. E. Magnan, and A. D. Bryan, 'Associations of Marijuana Use and Sex-Related Marijuana Expectancies With HIV/STD Risk Behavior in High-Risk Adolescents,' *Psychology of Addictive Behaviors* 24, no. 3 (2010): 404–414.

30 R. Andrew Sewell, James Poling, and Mehmet Sofuoglu, 'The Effect of Cannabis Compared With Alcohol On Driving,' *American Journal of Addictions* 18, no. 3 (2009): 185–193.

31 Ministry of Health, 'The New Zealand Drug Harm Index 2016,' 34, https://www.health.govt.nz/system/files/documents/publications/nz-drug-harm-index-2016-2nd-ed-jul16.pdf.

32 Ibid., 34.

33 Eugene A. Kiyatkin and Hari S. Sharma, 'Acute Methamphetamine Intoxication: Brain Hyperthermia, Blood-Brain Barrier and Brain Edema,' *International Review of Neurobiology* 88 (2009): 65–100.

34 Lisa Spellman, 'May 4 Omaha Science Cafe Focused on Secondhand Exposure to Meth,' UNMC Newsroom, April 28, 2010, accessed May 16, 2017, https://www.unmc.edu/news.cfm?match=6829.

35 Ministry of Health, 'The New Zealand Drug Harm Index 2016,' 9.

36 David J. Nutt, Lesley A. King, and Lawrence D. Phillips, 'Drug Harms in the UK: A Multicriteria Decision Analysis,' *The Lancet* 376, no. 9752 (2010): 1558–1565, 1559.

37 Ibid., 1564

38 Ministry of Health, 'The New Zealand Drug Harm Index 2016,' 1.

39 NZ Drug Foundation, 'The Cost of Our Convictions,' *Matters of Substance* 24, no. 1 (2013), accessed May 4, 2017, https://www.drugfoundation.org.nz/matters-of-substance/february-2013/cost-of-our-convictions/.

40 Alcohol Problems and Solutions, 'Negative Effects of Prohibition: Do You Know These Facts?' accessed February 17, 2017, https://www.alcoholproblemsandsolutions.org/effects-of-prohibition.

41 Angela Dills, Sietse Goffard, and Jeffrey Miron, 'Dose of Reality: The Effect of State Marijuana Legalisations,' *Policy Analysis* 799 (2016), accessed May 19, 2017, https://object.cato.org/sites/cato.org/files/pubs/pdf/pa799.pdf.

42 Caitlin Elizabeth Hughes and Alex Stevens, 'A Resounding Success or a Disastrous Failure: Re-examining the Interpretation of Evidence on the

Portuguese Decriminalisation of Illicit Drugs,' *Drug and Alcohol Review* 31, no. 1 (2012): 101–113.

43 Nutt et al., 'Drug Harms in the UK,' 1563.

44 Mill, 'On Liberty,' 156.

45 Alcohol Health Watch, 'Alcohol Harm in New Zealand,' September 2009, accessed June 1, 2017, http://www.ahw.org.nz/resources/Toolkit%202009/Fact%20Sheet%20Alcohol%20Harm%20in%20New%20Zealand%20final%202009.pdf.

46 Ministry of Health, 'The New Zealand Drug Harm Index 2016,' 34.

47 Smokefree, 'What is Smokefree 2025?' accessed June 10, 2017, http://www.smokefree.org.nz/smokefree-in-action/smokefree-aotearoa-2025.

48 Mill, 'On Liberty,' 156.

49 Ministry of Social Development, 'The Social Report 2016'.

50 Ministry of Health, 'The New Zealand Drug Harm Index 2016,' 34.

51 Ministry of Health, 'Annual Update of Key Results 2015/16,' 17, December 15, 2016, accessed June 2, 2017, http://www.health.govt.nz/publication/annual-update-key-results-2015-16-new-zealand-health-survey.

52 Health Promotion Agency, 'Alcohol and Your Kids,' March 2015, accessed June 5, 2017, http://www.alcohol.org.nz/sites/default/files/field/file_attachment/AL801%20March2015_%20update_Online%20LR.pdf.

53 Health Promotion Agency, 'Supply of Alcohol to Under-18s — FAQS for Parents,' 1, accessed May 10, 2017, http://www.hpa.org.nz/sites/default/files/documents/FAQs_Parents_FINAL-1.pdf.

54 Mill, 'On Liberty,' 139.

55 Ibid., 153.

56 Ibid., 155.

57 Mary Anne Warren, 'On the Moral and Legal Status of Abortion,' *The Monist* 57, no. 1 (1973): 43–61.

58 Chantelle Murray, 'Cross Examination: Drinking While Pregnant — A Woman's Choice?' accessed May 30, 2017, http://equaljusticeproject.co.nz/2015/05/cross-examination-drinking-while-pregnant-a-womans-choice.

59 John Donne, *Complete Poetry and Selected Prose*, ed. John Hayword (London: John Nonesuch Press, 1962), 538.

60 Anita Lal, Marj Moodie, Toni Ashton, Mohammad Siahpush, and Boyd Swinburn, 'Health Care and Lost Productivity Costs of Overweight and Obesity in New Zealand,' *Australian and New Zealand Journal of Public Health* 36, no. 6 (2012): 550–556.

61 Mill, 'On Liberty,' 75.

3

The Treatment of Animals

VANYA KOVACH

Introduction

The topics presented in this book show us the diverse ethical issues that may confront us as we try to work out how we should live our lives, both as individuals and as communities. One of the most challenging of these issues is our treatment of other animals. We might never have to deal personally with abortion or internet porn, but we cannot avoid the ethical issues surrounding what we must all do every day — eat.

Let's start our thinking about our treatment of other animals by acknowledging that nearly all of us are the inheritors of the ethical issues in this area, rather than the initiators. We have been born into a country where the farming and consumption of other animals is a given, and is the mainstay of our national economy. We are surrounded by the intensive marketing of meat, eggs and dairy products that advertises and also normalises their consumption. Animal-based foods are constantly promoted as being essential to health, providing invaluable sources of protein, calcium and iron. The consumption of milk and lamb, in particular, is often subtly portrayed as patriotic behaviour. Although 10.3 per cent of New Zealanders eat a vegetarian or mostly vegetarian diet, and plant-based diets are on the rise, especially among the 14–34-year-old age group,[1] most of us haven't made this choice, and most of our parents and grandparents ate animal foods as a matter of course.[2] To quote psychologist Melanie Joy, most of us see eating animal products as 'normal, natural and necessary'.[3] But one of the most important tasks of philosophy, as Peter Singer claims, is to question the assumptions of the age, and to think through 'critically and carefully what most people take for granted', and that is what we will do in this chapter.[4]

Here are some unpalatable facts about the animals we use for food.

Chickens: In New Zealand, we eat 90 million chickens a year, and around 1 billion eggs, 82 per cent from caged hens.[5] Even colony-caged hens have only a space the size of an A4 page to live in, and battery hens are worse off. Many chickens have their beaks trimmed to reduce the incidence of cannibalism, which is brought on by the confined conditions. Male chicks are gassed or 'macerated' — minced alive. Chickens destined to be meat are forced to slaughter weight in huge, concrete-floored barns in just six weeks.

Cows: The milk we drink comes from cows that are kept perpetually in lactation, requiring a pregnancy every year and forced separation from their young when they are four days old. The male calves are either slaughtered immediately, for pet food, or raised for veal and killed after a few months. Dairy cows live for about 25 per cent of their natural lifespan, and suffer a range of health problems caused by constant milk production.

Pigs: Most of the 700,000 pigs eaten in New Zealand each year are raised in small concrete pens, and never see the sunlight. Sows kept in farrowing crates can only stand up and lie down, and their piglets are taken away at four weeks of age, after which the sow is impregnated again, to continue the cycle. Pigs, which are intelligent and highly social animals, can live as long as 15 years, but pigs killed for meat die at four to six months old.

Of course we don't just *eat* animals. Most people wear shoes made of animal skins. We use imported cosmetic products that are tested on rabbits and other mammals. We use drugs that have been tested on mice, rats, cats, dogs and guinea pigs, and most animal testing in New Zealand is aimed not at making safer drugs but more profitable agriculture. Some of us hunt deer, and catch fish for food or sport, and 58 per cent of us have dog or cat companion animals. Some of us kill possums for a living, or to protect the environment. A few of us have had porcine cartilage transplanted into us, and now a small number of diabetics are having insulin made inside them by pancreatic islets which have been taken from newborn pigs.

How should we view these various uses of other animals? And who should be the ones to make decisions about these uses — individuals, according to their own consciences? Or governments?

Why might other animals matter?

Many people perceive a huge gulf between human beings and other animals, and some may even have difficulty with the term '*other* animals'. It is understandable that this perceived gulf exists, as there are many characteristics of human beings that we see as valuable and defining of humanity that other animals do not share. Humans have the capacity for abstract thought, for moral reasoning, for creating art and sophisticated comedy, and for inventing the complex technology that is so much part of human life today. Of course, there is much evidence that other animals also have a wide range of capacities: for example, dolphins have a sophisticated communication system, chimpanzees can deceive, cows have friends, and the humble chicken can recognise up to 100 other chickens and practise self-control![6] It is true that there is debate about whether dolphin language is really like human language, with grammar and syntax, and we could ask ourselves whether what cows do — hanging out with particular other cows, exhibiting lethargy when they are parted, and liveliness when they are reunited — is enough to properly call them 'friends'.

But it is important to see that we do not need to argue that other animals are like humans in all ways. No animal activists are calling for art classes for chickens or tertiary education for guinea pigs. The question that we need to answer is: are other animals like humans in ways that are relevant to how we treat them? If the treatment in question is close confinement, then is the capacity for complex language, or humour, relevant? If we are considering whether to run a caged hen factory or a free-range chicken farm, should we be thinking about chickens' lack of law-based social equality or their natural tendencies to roam, forage and fly?

What makes a non-human animal's capacity morally relevant is whether the ways in which we propose to control and use them affect the exercise of that capacity. Other capacities, or lack of capacities, are morally irrelevant to our treatment of those beings. So now we can see why it is important to ask about the ways in which humans and other animals are similar. If the similarities are morally relevant ones, in the context of our proposed treatment of animals, then to fail to take their interests into account may count as a kind of discrimination, unless we have other reasons for excluding them from our consideration.

Identifying the morally relevant ways in which other animals are like humans is sometimes described as establishing the 'moral status' of other animals. If they have this status, then they are part of our moral community, and that entitles them to have their interests considered, or their rights respected, for example. Two views we will look at in detail are (a) that it is other animals' capacity for suffering that requires us to take their interests into account, and (b) that it is their being a 'subject of awareness' that requires us to recognise their rights. We will also consider the view that an animal's moral status does not determine how we should treat it, before we go on to examine some arguments against ascribing moral status to animals, and then finally to thinking about who can and should be making decisions in the area of animal ethics.

Animal interests and their capacity to suffer

A much-quoted passage from the philosopher Jeremy Bentham, in 1781, brings together the ideas of discrimination and morally relevant similarities between humans and other animals:

> The French have already discovered that the blackness of skin is no reason why a human being should be abandoned without redress to the caprice of a tormentor. It may come one day to be recognized, that the number of legs, the villosity of the skin, or the termination of the *os sacrum*, are reasons equally insufficient for abandoning a sensitive being to the same fate. What else is it that should trace the insuperable line? Is it the faculty of reason, or perhaps, the faculty for discourse? . . . the question is not, Can they *reason*? nor, Can they *talk*? but, Can they *suffer*?[7]

Here, Bentham is suggesting that if we fail to take into account the interests of other beings purely on the grounds of morally irrelevant characteristics — such as the colour of human skin — we are doing something wrong. And he is also claiming that it is the capacity for suffering that is the important characteristic that humans share with other animals.

Animals' capacity for suffering, their ability to feel both pleasure and pain, we will label 'sentience'.[8] The scientific evidence of the sentience of all of our common food animals — cows, pigs, sheep, chickens and fish — has been well documented;[9] but a simple way to see this for yourself is to ask how you know that other humans feel pain. You will probably say: because I see them behave the same way I do when I am in pain, because they have a nervous system like mine, and because I know that pain plays an important role in keeping us safe from injury. All of these things are true of all vertebrates, and clearly so in the case of mammals and birds.

Various scientific tests back up this common-sense conclusion. One test of the capacities of other animals to experience pain, as well as fear and anxiety, is to give them drugs that reduce these experiences in humans. That these have clear behavioural impacts, and that the animals tested have the appropriate receptors for these drugs in their central nervous systems, is a telling result.[10] The detection of increased levels of cortisol — the stress hormone — in a range of different situations is further evidence of other animals' ability to experience pain and even emotional distress.

However, we can agree that animals are sentient, but still ask: why should we consider that fact in our decision making, and exactly how should it figure in our decisions? These are two questions answered in a particular way by one of the most famous writers in the area of animal ethics, the philosopher Peter Singer. For Singer, the reason why we should consider other animals' abilities to feel pleasure and pain is that if we do not, we are guilty of a kind of discrimination that he calls 'speciesism'.

Other discriminatory 'isms' — sexism and racism — are wrong, because when we engage in them we give greater weight to the interests of our own sex or race than we give to the similar interests of the members of another sex or race. If, as an employer, John gives greater weight to the claims to the job of a man, just because he is a man, and not because of his qualifications, John is a sexist. If I give greater weight to the needs of a person begging on the street, for no other reason than that she is of the same race as me, then I am a racist.

Singer claims this wrong occurs in the case of humans and other animals, too. He thinks we routinely give greater weight to the pains of humans over the pains of other animals, most obviously when we buy and consume intensively farmed animal flesh. He thinks we do this on no other ground than that we are of one species and they are of another: merely on the basis of group membership. If we reject discrimination purely on this basis in the cases of sexism and racism, then we should do the same when the group in question is species. To formalise this idea, Singer proposes the 'Principle of Equal Consideration of Interests', which he takes to be the core of our idea of equality. Equality is not a fact, he stresses, it is an ideal about how we treat others, and in particular how we take their interests into consideration. According to this principle, we must give like weight to like interests, no matter who or what has those interests. For example, all aspiring artists have an interest in having art materials, no matter what their gender, race or age, and all young people have an interest in quality education, no matter what their socioeconomic background.

One vital interest that humans and most other animals share is the interest in not suffering. Applying his principle, Singer points out that satisfying our taste for meat most often comes at the cost of tremendous suffering for factory-farmed animals — and in doing this we are, to use his words, sacrificing the fundamental interests of other animals for the trivial interests of our own. Other uses of animals violate Singer's principle as well. The testing of a new shampoo might involve sacrificing the interests that rabbits have in not being restrained and having shampoo dripped continuously into their eyes, for the interests that we might have in another shampoo that offers more bounce to our curls.[11] What follows from Singer's 'Principle of Equal Consideration of Interests' is that any use of other animals which causes them significant suffering cannot be justified if the human interests it serves are trivial — arguably all of those connected to taste, fashion, sport or entertainment.

There are a number of objections that could be made to Singer's position, which focus on the claims that our use of other animals, especially for food, is 'normal, natural and necessary'. We will come to these later. What is important to note now is that Singer's principle does not obviously rule out *all* uses of other animals. This principle of equality does not require that everyone be treated equally, only that all similar interests be given equal weight. Perhaps there are fundamental, rather than trivial, human interests that are served by our use of other animals. If you were marooned on a rock in the middle of the ocean with a goat, no food at all and no chance of rescue, the principle would not forbid the sacrifice of the goat to keep you alive. Here your especially human capacities are relevant — they make your life overall worth more than the goat's. Singer's principle can allow us to weigh up interests, even like interests, and sometimes justify sacrificing some in order to protect others. This is because Singer is committed to a view about what makes all actions right or wrong — the ethical theory called utilitarianism.

We encountered this theory in Chapter 1. We saw that it is a variety of a more general theory, called consequentialism. Consequentialists hold that the rightness and wrongness of human actions depends solely on the consequences of those actions. We should decide what to do on the basis of what we can reasonably predict will be the outcomes of the options we are considering. People's rights, their character and their intentions are relevant only insofar as they have certain consequences or outcomes; they have no special value in and of themselves. Utilitarianism is also committed to (a) creating the maximum good consequences for all affected, (b) allowing that some bad consequences may be outweighed by good consequences to get the greatest net result, (c) doing so impartially, and (d) taking 'good consequences' or 'utility' to be the promotion of pleasure and the avoidance of pain, or, in a more modern version, the satisfaction of preferences.

From this quick summary, we can see how Singer's position on our treatment of other animals is connected to his underlying commitment to utilitarianism. As a utilitarian, he must impartially consider the pleasures and pains of all affected, and so he must include consideration of all beings that are sentient when he decides how to act. He must also be willing to sacrifice the pains of the few for the pleasures of the many — but only, again, if this is done impartially. This has a number of implications for our treatment of animals, but let us note first that it is not only utilitarians who will be committed to Singer's Principle of Equal Consideration of Interests. Any person who holds that equality is a fundamental value will have to consider this principle seriously, and ask themselves on what grounds they exclude other animals from its application, if they do.

What are the implications of being a utilitarian for our use of other animals? First, we may not trade the serious pains of animals for trivial pleasures of our own. But, second, there may be situations where some kind of trade-off is justified. As mentioned at the outset, medical advances have now allowed a use of pigs that might pass a utilitarian test, and Singer's central principle, too. A process trademarked 'Diabecell' has been developed which takes pancreatic islets from newborn Auckland Island pigs, encapsulates them, and injects them into the abdomens of people suffering from type 1 diabetes, in order to secrete insulin.[12] Pig islets are used because they are more readily available than human ones. Initial indications show better control of diabetic symptoms, and it is expected that insulin independence may eventually be possible. This use of piglets, most would agree, is not serving a merely trivial interest. Even if we assume that the sows used were treated similarly to those in intensive piggeries, the Diabecell process may count as a justified sacrifice of pig interests. So a question that Singer's approach leaves open is: what uses of animals might be significant enough to outweigh their interests in not experiencing pain? Perhaps some cultural uses of animals would pass this test, too, and other medical uses.

Around 200,000 non-human animals are used in medical experimentation in New Zealand every year, half of which are euthanised afterwards. Singer has an explicit view on the morality of this.[13] It comes in two parts: one obvious, the other very controversial. Singer holds that we may test on non-human animals only if we do all we can to refine experiments in ways that minimise animal suffering, reduce the number of animals used, and replace them with cell cultures or computer simulations wherever possible. The second condition is that we must experiment in a non-speciesist way — we must be equally willing to use humans as experimental subjects if they are of the same level of capacity and awareness as the usual non-human test subjects. Singer is *not* arguing that we use very cognitively disabled humans as test subjects (or as sources of pancreatic islets), but that we reduce our use of other animals to what we would be willing to impose on one of our own kind who had comparable capacities to the animals used. This view challenges its opponents to provide an account of what the morally significant differences are between humans and non-human mammals of the same capacity. Of course Singer will not accept any difference that depends solely on species membership. According to Singer, we can't justifiably say 'but the disabled human is one of us, and that's what counts' any more than a sexist can say 'but the male applicant is one of us men, and that's what counts'.

Let's return to the issue of eating other animals. What about consumption of painlessly killed, ethically farmed animals — what some call 'conscientious omnivory'? In the wake of more awareness about the horrors of factory farming, a new industry has sprung up that produces meat from animals that have been reared in more natural environments, and in some cases killed painlessly without a trip to the abattoir. Is it ethically acceptable to consume animal products sourced from these providers? The answer to this will depend on whether we think cows, sheep and chickens have not only interests in not suffering, but also interests in continued life.

What would ground such an interest? For Singer it is having what he calls a 'personal' rather than an 'impersonal' life — being a creature that has an understanding of itself as continuing through time; that is, being self-conscious, and with a sense of the future, just as most (at least adult) humans are. Singer argues that animals that have 'personal' lives cannot be killed, even painlessly and after a happy life, without sacrificing an important interest, just for a trivial interest of our own. However, animals that have 'impersonal' lives may be killed, as no such important interest is being sacrificed.[14] This argument could be challenged — does a being need to have an understanding of itself as continuing over time in order to have an interest in continued life, or does it merely need an interest in pleasurable life and the possibility of more of this?

But if we adopt Singer's distinction, perhaps we can eat compassionately raised and killed animals. The question then becomes: which other animals have this capacity to experience themselves as beings continuing over time? Singer himself thought that chickens probably did not. Here are some questions to consider: does missing the company of particular fellow cows suggest that cows have this capacity? If a chicken can choose an option that offers more food, at the cost of a longer wait for it, does that suggest that chickens have this ability? Primates, dolphins, elephants and common pigs have been observed to utilise information gained in a mirror — and recognising oneself in a mirror is the classic test of self-awareness. What's more, the possession of 'episodic memory' that 'involves the conscious recollection of unique personal experiences as well as the ability to mentally project oneself into the future' has been detected in birds, rats and mice, monkeys and the domestic chicken![15] Should we conclude that these and similar animals have what Singer calls 'personal lives', and that therefore in killing them we sacrifice more than just the possibility of pleasure?

These questions have relevance well beyond the assessment of Peter Singer's utilitarian arguments, as self-consciousness is the key feature of humans that so many of us point to as the one that marks us off from other animals. Evidence of the self-consciousness of our common food animals then would call us to consistency; we cannot justify the superiority of humans by reference to a capacity that is shared by the animals that we use.

Being a subject of a life, and having rights

The philosopher Tom Regan, like Singer, has views that are rooted in a particular normative ethical theory. Regan is a deontologist. In short, what this commits him to is the application of moral rules, not for the sake of the good consequences they bring about, but because they are the right rules. One such rule, which underpins much of our contemporary emphasis on human rights and self-determination, is the rule proposed by Immanuel Kant that we should never use a person merely as a means to an end.[16] Using people as tools or resources, without their consent, no matter what good can result, is a violation of the inherent value that they have because they possess reason, argued Kant. 'So that rules out food animals' you might think. 'Some may be self-conscious, but they can't reason.'

However, Regan does not accept the capacity to reason as the source of a being's inherent value, and in doing so he issues another call to consistency. He points out that we do not think that people with dementia, and severely cognitively disabled infants, have no rights and require no respect. We take them to have the same inherent value as other humans. What grounds this equal inherent value is not the possession of reason, but the thing that we all share — being aware, no matter how unsophisticated our awareness, being an 'experiencing subject of a life'. If we are conscious, if we have a welfare that is important to us, and if we can 'want, prefer, believe, recall and expect things', then we must not be used as mere resources.[17]

Notice two things about Regan's view that contrast with Singer's.

First, he sets the bar higher — 'being an experiencing subject of a life', as he describes it, seems more than just the capacity to feel pain. It looks much like what Singer calls 'personal' life (and may even rule out some humans, particularly those in persistent vegetative states). Second, because of his commitment to rule-based deontological ethics, he will not engage in utilitarian 'trade-offs' in order to achieve the greatest good. For Regan, both cosmetic and medical testing on animals is immoral, and the wrong we do to animals used for food and entertainment is not just the suffering we cause them, but the very fact that we are using them as resources, when they have inherent value as experiencing beings. All subjects of a life, he thinks, have a right not to be used by others. Regan does not go as far as many vegans, who refuse to use as resources any animals at all, no matter what their capacity to experience. But it is still a radical one, and one clearly at odds with the traditional Christian idea that God put non-human animals on Earth for our use.

For some, his conclusion is too radical. One of the ways in which we assess arguments in ethics is to ask whether those arguments have unacceptable implications. Regan thinks that holding reason or intelligence to be what qualifies a being for moral consideration has unacceptable implications — it commits us to excluding severely cognitively disabled humans from our consideration.

Perhaps you think that Regan's view has unacceptable practical implications; that we should reject it because it implies that we can no longer use other animals for food, even if they are free-range, or for drug testing — surely this is an unacceptable implication of the view! Although an important test for ethical theories, these arguments should be treated with some caution. One reason that slave-owners in the American South gave for rejecting calls for emancipation was that this would have unacceptable practical implications — they would lose their livelihoods, and the economy would suffer. Having implications that are unacceptable for some will not, on its own, settle the matter.

Regan's view raises some interesting questions. Is having a companion animal 'using it merely as a means to an end'? If not, what would count as evidence that we are not using our cats and dogs merely as resources? If we love our backyard chickens, does that show we can escape a prohibition on using their eggs? And, for a peculiarly New Zealand question: is it wrong to kill possums to save the native bush and fauna?

Let us assume that the possums that live in Australia, and those that live in New Zealand as a result of their introduction in colonial times, have sufficient capacities to make them 'experiencing subjects'. Most people probably think that it would be wrong to kill an Australian possum, which is a protected species, but permissible, perhaps even praiseworthy, to kill a possum living in New Zealand. No approach to animal ethics that focuses solely on the moral status of the animal can account for this difference, which is why it is an interesting question.

Focusing away from the moral status of other animals

In the area of normative ethics, a third option is virtue ethics. This approach is characterised by a focus not on consequences or rules and rights, but on the character people have, and the way in which a virtuous character expresses itself in action, through the use of practical wisdom. Practical wisdom is the ability to be compassionate, for example, 'on the right occasions, about the right things, towards the right people, for the right end and in the right way'.[18] Why would we cultivate the virtues? Because doing so is required for living a good life, for being a flourishing human.

The New Zealand philosopher Rosalind Hursthouse is a virtue ethicist who has applied this theory to the topic of animal ethics.[19]

What virtues are relevant to our treatment of animals? Honesty, she says, requires that we do not deny the sufferings of animals in the food industry, and that we acknowledge that we do not need to eat meat. Compassion requires that we care about their suffering. To go on eating animal-based foods and using cosmetic products tested on animals is, she thinks, callous, greedy, self-indulgent and vain. Virtue ethics calls us not to consistency, but to compassion, and to aspire to be better people.

What is interesting about the virtue ethics approach to our topic is that it does not centre on claims about the moral status of animals, because, Hursthouse points out, such status does not determine how we treat other animals. There are multiple factors in each particular context that are relevant, and the attention to these is characteristic of virtue ethics. In the case of the possum in New Zealand, the sentience of individual creatures is surely relevant — we should aim to curtail their impact on the environment in as painless a way as possible. But the value of the native bush, and the other animals in it, is important, too, as are the human interests in conservation. Responding with respectfulness and care towards all of the beings affected can lead the virtuous to try to eradicate the possum. Singer could agree with this decision, as his utilitarian view would allow him also to attend to the context, and to trade off the loss of the happy possums for the wider benefits. Virtue ethicists, however, would require that we feel regret for these animals losing their lives, because the virtue of compassion does not deactivate just because there is occasionally a good enough overall reason to kill.[20]

With regard to eating animals, Hursthouse's view is unequivocal — the honest and compassionate person refrains from doing so. Her view on experimentation on other animals is less straightforward, as she believes that the vast machine of the worldwide pharmaceutical industry, with its researchers and doctors and marketing executives, cannot be changed by people simply refraining from taking the drugs produced.[21] Instead, smaller, persistent action is required of the virtuous — informing, lobbying, voting and joining activist groups.

Some arguments that might justify our use of animals

So far we have seen three approaches to evaluating our treatment of other animals, each of which is inspired by a particular view of ethics. We don't have to buy into any of these views fully to see that they each shine a different light on the issue. None of the views take for granted that eating and using other animals is 'normal, natural and necessary', but they do not tackle these ideas head-on. We will address these now, and a sample of other arguments that might justify our use of animals.

EATING ANIMALS IS NORMAL

There are two things that this might mean: that eating animals is usual, or that it is 'normal' in some value-laden sense, most commonly 'natural'. We will address these claims in turn. What is the significance of a practice being usual? What obviously follows is that the majority of people find it at least acceptable. Is that fact enough on its own to legitimate our use of other animals? Many things that we now abhor were once usual, and accepted by many in New Zealand: child labour, suppression of te reo Māori, restriction of opportunities for women, to name but a few. Such comparisons do not in themselves show that our current use of animals is something we should abhor, of course, but they do show that something being usual is no guarantee of its moral acceptability.

EATING ANIMALS IS NATURAL

There are three reasons we might think this. First, humans have been doing it for many thousands of years, all the way back to our origin as hunter-gatherers. Of course, the factory farming of animals is a recent practice, and so would not be supported by this argument. More pertinently, recent evidence suggests that we were originally scavengers, not hunters, so an appeal to our natural and original practices might not justify killing after all.[22] We might also want to be cautious about using early human practices as a general guide to current morality.

Second, we might think that it is natural because humans have canine teeth, and digestive systems that can process meat. Certainly this does mean that humans have the option to eat animal flesh. Our grinding molars and our digestive systems also mean we have the option to eat a plant-based diet. Here it is useful to ask: if we can do something, is that sufficient justification for us to do it?

Third, we might think that it is natural for us to eat meat because other animals do it — an interesting move in the context of attempts to show how different we are from them. The common responses to this are: that most meat-eating animals are obligate carnivores, not omnivores like us; that lions and tigers are not moral agents, and so cannot be held responsible for their choice, as we can be; and that, again, factory farming cannot be justified using this argument.

EATING ANIMALS IS NECESSARY

Despite the fact that many of us feel that we just could not do without eating meat, the evidence is now clear that animal-based foods are not necessary for human health. For example, the American Academy of Nutrition and Dietetics in 2009, and the Australian Dietary Guidelines, revised in 2016, both affirm that properly planned vegetarian and fully vegan diets are safe and healthy for all people, at all stages of their lives. Indeed, a number of health benefits go with a plant-based diet — including a reduction in obesity, diabetes, high blood pressure, high cholesterol, heart attack, stroke and some kinds of cancer. But just for the sake of the argument, let's assume that is not true, and that truly optimum human health cannot be achieved without the consumption of some meat. Would that justify intensive farming practices? And in the case of those animals that have a conscious interest in continued life, or an interest in continued pleasurable existence, would the goal of optimum human health justify the taking of their lives?

ANIMALS CAN'T HAVE RIGHTS

Earlier we saw that Tom Regan argues for the rights of all beings that are 'subjects of a life' to not be used as resources. But can other animals really have rights? Regan is arguing that animals have what we might call 'moral rights'. These are not legally recognised rights; they are best thought of as a call for legal rights to be created. Insofar as we are considering legal rights, then animals can of course have rights *if* legislatures confer them. But in New Zealand the Animal Welfare Act 1999 created rights that protect animals without granting that animals themselves have rights. These rights are held by the State, and the duties that owners and people in charge of animals have to, for example, 'ensure that the physical, health, and behavioural needs of the animal are met in a manner that is in accordance with both — (a) good practice; and (b) scientific knowledge' are owed to the State, not to animals.[23]

Could animals have rights themselves, rather than being protected by the rights of the State or of their owners? Some claim that other animals cannot have rights, and that we should not create legal rights for them, because they are not the kinds of beings that can be 'rights holders'. There are two views on what kind of things can have rights. The will theory of rights is based on the idea that rights function to protect the autonomous choices of rational beings. This restricts rights holders to those rational beings that can make autonomous choices — usually taken to exclude non-human animals. The worry this raises is that some humans are not rational and autonomous —

and so, although they may be protected by rights held by the State, or by their families, they do not qualify to have rights themselves. The interest theory of rights is based on the idea that rights function to protect the important interests of beings. This allows that any being that has interests could be a rights holder. The worry this raises is that there are many beings with interests — perhaps even pot plants have an interest in being watered — and moreover that it might be hard to determine which interests are the 'important' ones.

This takes us back to the debates we discussed earlier. Do non-human animals have an important interest in avoiding suffering? Do they have important interests in continued life? If the answer to the latter is 'yes' for some non-human animals, then on the interest theory they may qualify not only to be a rights holder, but also to have a right to life.

THE ECONOMIC IMPACT OF ABANDONING THE MEAT AND DAIRY INDUSTRY

A commonly offered argument for continuing, as a society, to consume animal products is that if we stopped doing this there would be a serious impact on the economy of our country. This would be a pressing issue for any nation with animal agriculture, but for New Zealand, given the heavy reliance of our economy on exports of meat and dairy foods, the impact would be catastrophic. Animal products account for over $20 billion of our revenue each year.

Two comparisons may help us to see the issues more clearly. First, we could note that the advent of the digital camera was not halted on the grounds that it would eradicate the film-development industry. Of course, that was not an industry that underpinned a national economy. The second comparison, one often made in the context of our treatment of animals, is slavery. The abolition of slavery had very serious consequences for the economy of the American South, in part because the value of slaves in 1860, five years before emancipation, has been estimated at $3.5 billion.[24] What this example shows is that economic impact is not sufficient to justify the continuation of a morally abhorrent practice.

The comparison of our treatment of other animals with human slavery is, for some, deeply offensive, for others, highly illuminating. It will be our response to the other arguments surveyed in this chapter that will determine how we see this. Fortunately, at least for most humans in New Zealand, and for our government, no such immediate and momentous change is likely. Change in our national eating habits, if it happens, is likely to be slow.

Who or what should make decisions about our use of animals?

Animal ethics is often portrayed as an issue for individuals, something that is the proper province of conscience and personal commitment. On this view, governments should curb only the worst aspects of farming and experimental practices, leaving their citizens to make their own moral choices, in the spirit of Western liberal ideals. But even a liberal state is justified in interfering with its citizens' choices if doing so prevents a serious harm to others. Of course the central question in this chapter has been: on what grounds do non-human animals count as 'others'?

Let's go back to Hursthouse's point about the vast machine of medical research and pharmaceutical companies that individual decisions can have no impact on. The same seems to be true of the complex web of farming businesses, government-driven exports, ubiquitous advertising, traditions and cultural practices that operates to entrench our use of non-human animals in New Zealand. In this landscape, it would be too harsh to blame individual meat-eaters for the widespread suffering of animals, and too optimistic to tell them that their refraining will make a difference. But surely when individuals make decisions based on their own consciences, they influence the market to make changes that are in line with those values?

To evaluate this claim, let's ask if the market really does respond to individual values. This is obviously true when a significant number of individuals stop buying bacon or dairy products altogether, for a long enough period of time. Production will then have to go down. It is less true in the case of motivating changes to the conditions that animals are kept in. The banning of sow crates in New Zealand in 2012 was not a result of consumer-driven market pressure, but of vigorous lobbying and international influences.[25] Consumer choice has increased the availability of free-range eggs, but is less likely to have motivated the move from battery cages to colony cages.[26] Arguably, we can rely on the market to respond to wholesale conversions to plant-based diets, but not necessarily to the concerns of those who want to consume animals farmed under better conditions.

If the market cannot drive all change, what is the role of government? Does it include constraining, on moral grounds, the activities of businesses? In the case of anti-exploitation and minimum-wage legislation, we do think that it is the government's job to make sure that business owners are prevented from engaging in harmful practices. But, of course, those are activities that impact only on humans, and so some will question the relevance of these examples.

Finally, let us consider the fairly common claim that eating meat is a matter of personal choice. What might this mean? Yet again, there are a few possibilities:

First, as we saw in Chapter 2, according to John Stuart Mill's harm principle there are a range of things that people do which are private matters; they are outside the area that should be legislated about, or even approved or disapproved of by other people. Sexual practices between consenting adults would be one example, at least at this stage in our national history. Since it affects no one else, the activity is not a proper subject for State interference or the moral attention of others. Perhaps eating meat is like this — it is nobody's business but our own. But is it true that eating other animals affects no one but ourselves? Only someone who held that other animals had no interests, or that their interests counted for nothing, could hold this view on meat eating.

Second, this might mean: 'If I choose to eat meat, then eating meat is right for me.' There are two ways we can understand this claim. The first is that when we choose to do something, we are thereby implying that we believe that it is right to do that. This is mostly true, except in the case of weakness of will, when we do something we do not think to be right (for example, cheating vegetarians). The other way we can understand this claim is: if someone believes something to be right, then the fact that they believe it is, is what makes it right, and moreover there is no outside, objective viewpoint from which we can judge this belief to be right or wrong. This is called subjectivism. Subjectivists hold that moral beliefs about anything are made right just by the fact that an individual believes them.

A common way to challenge this is to offer examples that most people would not accept — 'If I believe that torturing puppies is right, then it is right for me, and there is no objective standard against which my view can be assessed.' Insert beliefs about slavery here, for another illustration. Clearly those who owned slaves thought that doing so was right — and we can understand that, given the beliefs about some races that were held at the time — but does it follow from the fact that they believed it to be right, that it *was* right?

Finally, it might mean that only an individual themself can make, and follow through on, a choice of whether or not to eat animals, or to refuse factory-farmed flesh. Of course this is true. Everyone, apart from the young children of vegetarians and vegans, is free to decide to partake or not in the animal foods currently available. And only the person themselves can decide to hold to their commitments, if they make them.

---

1 Roy Morgan Research, released February 2016, accessed April 9, 2017, https://www.roymorgan.com.

2 To find out about the history of vegetarianism in colonial New Zealand, see Catherine Amey, *The Compassionate Contrarians, A History of Vegetarians in Aotearoa New Zealand* (Wellington: Rebel Press, 2014).

3 Read about the results of Melanie Joy's PhD on the psychology of meat eating at carnism.org, accessed March 2, 2017. Note: some of her film clips are very explicit about the harms of intensive farming practices in the United States.

4 Peter Singer, 'All Animals are Equal,' in *Animal Rights and Human Obligations*, ed. Tom Regan and Peter Singer (New Jersey: Prentice-Hall, 1989), 148–62. See also Peter Singer's ground-breaking 1975 book *Animal Liberation* (New York: Random House, 1990).

5 A great deal of information about intensive farming practices is available at www.safe.org.nz, accessed February 4, 2017. If you are not aware of the full extent of suffering caused to other animals in this way, go to the website.

6 See Robert C. Jones, 'Science, Sentience and Animal Welfare,' *Biology and Philosophy* 28 (2013): 1–30.

7 Jeremy Bentham, *An Introduction to the Principles of Morals and Legislation*, 1781, ed. J. H. Burns and H. L. A. Hart (London: Methuen, 1982).

8 The word originally means the ability to perceive things through the senses generally, and some use the term to mean 'self-consciousness', but this term is more commonly used as shorthand for the ability to feel pleasure and pain.

9 See, for example, Mark Rowlands, *Animals Like Us* (London: Verso, 2002), Ch. 1. This is an accessible summary of the science on animal pain and awareness. For a more scientifically sophisticated discussion, see Jones, 'Science, Sentience and Animal Welfare,' 1–30.

10 Rowlands, *Animals Like Us*, 10–11.

11 Cosmetic testing on animals has been banned in New Zealand since 2015, but we import many items that have been tested in this way overseas.

12 This process is the result of the first trial using xenotransplantation of live cells approved in New Zealand.

13 Singer, 'All Animals are Equal,' 148–162.

14 Peter Singer, 'Killing Humans and Killing Animals,' *Inquiry* 22 (1979): 145–156. Defending this difference involves Singer distinguishing between two variants of utilitarianism.

15 Jones, 'Science, Sentience and Animal Welfare,' 1–30.

16 Immanuel Kant, *The Moral Law or The Groundwork of the Metaphysics of Morals*, trans. H. J. Paton (London: Hutchinson, 1948).

17 Tom Regan, 'The Case for Animal Rights,' in *In Defense of Animals*, ed. Peter Singer (New York: Basil Blackwell, 1985), 13–26.

18 Aristotle, *Nicomachean Ethics*, trans. J. A. K. Thompson (London: Penguin Classics, 2004).

19 Rosalind Hursthouse, 'Applying Virtue Ethics to Our Treatment of Other Animals,' in *The Practice of Virtue: Classic and Contemporary Readings in Virtue Ethics*, ed. Jennifer Welchman (Indianapolis: Hackett Publishing, 2006), 136–155.

20 It is worth noting that utilitarians might also require us to regret killing the possum, because failure to do so might well lead to worse consequences in other human/animal interactions.

21 Of course, individuals could refrain, but perhaps that would not be virtuous, if the consequence was death, and others were relying on you.

22 Bob Holmes, 'Man's Early Hunting Role in Doubt,' *New Scientist*, accessed April 7, 2017, https://www.newscientist.com/article/dn3222-mans-early-hunting-role-in-doubt.

23 Parliamentary Counsel Office, Animal Welfare Act 1999, Pt 1, s 10, accessed April 7, 2017, http://www.legislation.govt.nz/act/public/1999/0142/latest/DLM49664.html. Animal activists in New Zealand, such as S.A.F.E., claim that intensive farming practices contravene this Act in a number of significant ways.

24 For information on the monetary value of slaves in the United States, see Samuel H. Williamson and Louis P. Cain, 'Measuring Slavery in 2016 Dollars,' accessed April 9, 2017, https://www.measuringworth.com/slavery.php.

25 The Department of Statistics' Agricultural Production Statistics in 2012 do show a 14 per cent drop in the number of pigs farmed since 2007, which was caused by competition from imported pork, disease and the increased costs of animal welfare — not by a drop in market demand. Imported pork made up 45 per cent of pig flesh consumed in New Zealand; accessed April 18, 2017, http://www.stats.govt.nz/browse_for_stats/industry_sectors/agriculture-horticulture-forestry/info-releases.aspx. The sale of pork did drop, just for a few months, following the Mike King pig-farming TV exposé in 2009 on the *Sunday* programme, accessed February 2, 2017, https://www.youtube.com/watch?v=9fQXhefHdWo.

26 If you care about the welfare of chickens, you won't buy colony-cage eggs any more willingly than battery eggs, and if you buy caged eggs, you probably don't care what kind of cages are used.

4

Cyber-ethics

NICK MUNN

Introduction

As more and more of our daily activities move online, the need for a clear understanding of the norms and practices of behaviour in virtual spaces becomes more pressing. Cyber-ethics is the branch of applied ethics which deals with virtual spaces and online environments. In this chapter, we discuss a range of important topics within the broad field of cyber-ethics, drawing on recent New Zealand examples to illustrate the issues.

There are two easily classifiable major issues in cyber-ethics, and a third important cluster of issues that is harder to define. The two easily classifiable issues are copyright concerns and data protection (privacy) concerns. The cluster of issues revolves around behavioural norms in online spaces, and includes such topics as trolling, harassment, free speech, political behaviour and, at a more abstract level, whether our behaviour in online spaces is relevantly similar to our behaviour in offline spaces — are we doing the same kinds of things when we do them online as we do offline? This chapter will address each of these issues in turn.

We will discuss copyright infringement across a range of industries (music, movies, television, gaming and publishing), considering industry responses to copyright, as well as the responsibilities of both the companies that facilitate copyright infringement, and the users who engage in it. We will look at issues of data protection by examining the need for it, and the problems that robust data protections can avoid and resolve. Finally, we will consider behavioural norms in online spaces by examining the role that various online spaces play as catalysts for protest and social change, in the context of political and social justice issues. This will include an analysis of sexism, racism and objectification, and responses to it via protests against popular songs. We will look at where criticisms were made against the artists (Lorde was subject to such an attack), and where artists have used digital media to draw attention to problematic pieces of popular culture (such as the Auckland Law Revue parody of 'Blurred Lines').

A common thread in these discussions will be an analysis of what role the internet has played in making these situations relevant. The issues themselves are not new. Copyright infringement occurred before the internet, as did bullying and harassment. Privacy as a matter of legal concern has been relevant since the 1800s. But the rise of the internet, and the subsequent changes in the way we interact with each other (and who we interact with), has made the various problems we address in this chapter easier to engage in, and more prevalent.

This is both the power and the weakness of online activity. We have many more connections, and much more scope to influence and engage, than we had without it, but this comes with risks and responsibilities. It is easy when discussing applied ethics to focus on the wrongs that a particular technology (such as the internet) enables, while overlooking the opportunities that technology creates for moral improvement. In an attempt to redress this balance to some degree, the section on behavioural norms investigates the positives as well as negatives of our online interactions.

Copyright

WHAT IS COPYRIGHT?

Copyright is an interesting sort of right. While it is a property right of a kind, it does not exist in a physical object. Property rights are rights to control a thing, and to prevent others from using or changing it without your consent. But copyright attempts to protect ideas, rather than physical objects. This means that, unlike physical goods, the idea (the song, the movie, the easily reproducible digital file) can be copied and redistributed without depriving the original owner of the idea itself.

If I tell you a joke, and you tell someone else the joke, then all three of us know the joke. Your telling the joke doesn't deprive me of it, but it does potentially deprive me of the income I would get from telling the joke, if I am a comedian who relies on jokes to make my living. I cannot make people laugh by telling them jokes they have heard before, even if those jokes were mine in the first place. By comparison, if I were to take your car, or your handbag, you would no longer have those things, and the damage to you would be much easier to track.

Copyright infringement is one of the most discussed issues in cyber-ethics, and to a large degree this is because the internet makes copyright infringement easy. It is very simple to access copyrighted materials online, whether through moral and legal means such as YouTube and Spotify, or through less official channels, such as torrent sites, or various illicit streaming services. However, much of the discussion of copyright infringement in the literature is based on an industry in which the practice of copyright infringement has declined: music. The music industry was one of the earliest to be harmed by rampant copyright infringement, but it has also been willing and able to respond in ways that other industries have not. Industry responses to copyright infringement have been varied.

When file-sharing first became widespread, the primary target was the music industry, because at that stage the internet operated too slowly, with too little bandwidth, to make the sharing of movies and television practical. The music industry responded by attempting to sue individuals providing files online, and the companies operating services that enabled individuals to share those files. As evidenced by the ongoing prevalence of file-sharing, such approaches did not resolve the problem. More recently, the music, movie and television industries have moved away from targeting individual end users, and towards targeting hosting and distribution services. They have at the same time increasingly made material available through legal channels online, thereby attempting to encourage users to use those channels rather than the illegal ones.

Let us briefly consider the trajectory of infringement in the music industry before moving on to discuss industries where the practice of infringement remains commonplace — movies, television and publishing.

COPYRIGHT AND MUSIC

Compare the difficulty of finding a high-quality recording of the new single 'Be Mine Tonight' by Th' Dudes in 1978, to how hard it was to get your hands on Salmonella Dub's album *Killervision* in 1999, to Lorde's album *Pure Heroine* in 2013.

To illicitly access the first of these was almost impossible. In 1978, Sony had yet to release the original Walkman, and the average individual had no means to copy music from the vinyl recording it was sold on to another medium.

By 1999, the internet was operating in a fairly primitive form, and people could, and did, upload MP3s that they had ripped off CDs to services such as Napster, from where others could download them. These services were still comparatively hard to use, and slow to access, and, particularly for local music, it was difficult to find all that you wanted. At this stage, most copyright infringement still operated via peer-to-peer networks. That meant that both parties had to be connected to the internet at the same time, and the file was directly copied from them to you. So by 1999 people could commit copyright infringement, on a much larger scale than in 1978, but it still wasn't easy.

By 2013, when Lorde released *Pure Heroine*, copyright infringement online was as simple as clicking a button. But, at the same time, it was almost unnecessary. The music industry has adapted to the reality of the new media environment, and now makes new releases available, free of charge, via services such as YouTube, almost simultaneously with their initial release. Further, legal streaming services such as Spotify enable end users to freely and legally listen to a vast range of music from all of the major recording companies. So, in the space of 35 years, illegally reproducing music went from practically impossible, to possible but somewhat irritating, to unnecessary because the music you want is now freely available to all. Copyright infringement emerged as the biggest problem faced by the music industry, and then ceased to be an issue.

COPYRIGHT AND OTHER INDUSTRIES

Other industries have not yet replicated the success of the music industry at resolving their problems with copyright infringement. Services such as Netflix are doing for movies and television what Spotify did for music, but they do not have Spotify's advantages. In particular, Netflix does not have a free option, it does not have the breadth of coverage of movies and television that Spotify has of music, and it does not have simultaneous release — there is often a delay between theatrical or television release and Netflix availability. These issues mean that there is still room in the market for illicit services. For the publishing and gaming industries the room is greater again, with no digital subscription library for books or games having close to the impact that Netflix or Spotify have in their respective areas.

For some time one of the most popular illicit services, Megaupload, was run by Kim Dotcom, who has since been the subject of a variety of criminal proceedings in New Zealand, wherein authorities in the United States have argued that he should be extradited to the United States to stand trial for a range of offences, including conspiring to commit copyright infringement. As of February 2017, courts in New Zealand had ruled that he could be extradited to stand trial in the United States, but proceedings were ongoing, as Dotcom's lawyer intended to appeal the ruling.[1]

What, morally, is at stake with services like those provided by Kim Dotcom? His website provided hosting space, in which individual users could upload, store and access whatever materials they liked. As a result, Megaupload was a repository of copyrighted materials, the majority of which were not placed there by those who owned the copyright in them. Most of these materials were accessible by many users, and thus Megaupload enabled individuals worldwide to illegally trade in copyrighted materials. Dotcom has claimed that he did not seek to control what users posted to his site, and that he ought not to be responsible for the decisions of individual users to breach the relevant copyright laws. The authorities have countered that, by not inquiring as to the purposes for which the services he provided were being used, Dotcom facilitated widespread copyright infringement and ought to be held accountable.

But this is all, so far, a legal rather than a moral discussion. The law in New Zealand is quite clear. The Copyright (Infringing File Sharing) Amendment Act of 2011 allows copyright owners to notify internet service providers (ISPs) of infringements. ISPs then warn users that they are in breach of the Act. After three such warnings, the infringer can be taken before the Copyright Tribunal and is liable to a penalty of up to $15,000 for each infringement. To examine the moral status of copyright infringement, we should look at the various ways in which one could, if one was so inclined, acquire copyrighted material. It may be that our moral judgements differ in each of these cases, and that would reflect different morally relevant considerations. That is, it does not seem as though the morality of copyright infringement directly correlates with the law.

MORALITY AND COPYRIGHT

Lawrence Lessig, a professor of law at Harvard University, provides an important analysis of the relationship between copyright law and morality.[2] He argues, first, that the large-scale copying of copyrighted works for sale is immoral. Why? Simply because this is no different in essence from any other property crime. If we allowed people to take whatever they wanted, and sell it as if it were their own, there would be no point to having property rights at all, and no markets. When someone goes to the effort of creating something, whether that thing is a physical object like a pounamu carving, or an ephemeral one such as a song or a movie, they have a legitimate claim to that thing, and no one else ought to profit from it. However, Lessig denies that the kind of issues at stake in internet file-sharing are always of this kind. He argues that there are potential benefits to engaging in file-sharing, and that the purported harms of it are often overstated.

Lessig claims that we can divide file-sharing into four distinct categories. First, material is downloaded or streamed instead of being purchased. Second, material is downloaded or streamed in order to determine whether or not to buy it. Third, copyrighted material that is not being offered for sale is downloaded or streamed, and fourth, non-copyrighted material is downloaded or streamed. The last of these categories is the only one that is currently legal. The second and third of these are, he claims, illegal, but beneficial to all parties, and as such are moral and ought not to be illegal. The first category, he claims, is both illegal and immoral, but much less harmful than is often thought. Let us work through why the law and morality might come apart in these cases.

For case one, where end users replace the purchasing of copyrighted material with streaming or illegal downloading it, there is a direct analogy with theft. The user, who would otherwise have paid for the product, chooses to acquire it without paying for it. Had the illegal (free) version not been available, they would have paid for it, thereby paying the producers of the product for their time and effort. Law and morality agree that in cases like these there is an obligation to in fact buy the product in question. For games, books and the like, much of the material that is illegally shared is available to purchase, and, as such, the downloading often looks to be of this type.

In case two, the analogy is not with theft, but with listening to the radio, or watching a show on free-to-air television. The purpose of downloading is to determine whether the end user wants to spend money on the product, and their enjoyment of the product will determine whether they in fact do so. In the same way that hearing a song on the radio might prompt one to buy a recording of that song, downloading and listening to a song may prompt one to buy it. Note that both intention and practice are relevant to determining whether a particular instance of downloading is of type two rather than type one. Someone may claim to be merely sampling music or movies, and yet never purchase them.

In case three, it is not possible for the end user to purchase the product in question. This may be because it is not released in the jurisdiction (as happens with gated releases for television or movies), or because the product in question has been discontinued (older games often have this issue). Lessig's point in regards to this case is simply that it is disingenuous of the copyright holder to claim that they suffer a loss from infringement of this kind, as it was impossible to pay for the product at the time when it was acquired. The more people who infringe copyright in this way, the stronger the case becomes for doing things like removing region-specific releases and restrictions from movies and television, which would benefit end users and producers. New Zealand often waits weeks or months for shows that are available in other parts of the world, and when a show has been spoiled, or heavily criticised post-release, viewer numbers upon its eventual release are understandably low.

Case four is of course the simplest. There is no copyright claim made on the material, and it being freely available to download is in effect a public service, with no downside. Many older books (both academic and literary) have been made digitally available in this way through providers such as Project Gutenberg. While computer games as a medium are not old enough to have fallen out of copyright, there exists a large class of them that are 'abandonware', games which are no longer produced for sale, and for which the original copyright holders often no longer exist (as the companies which developed the games have gone out of business). These seem to bridge the divide between the third and fourth cases.

SUMMARY

Copyright infringement via online services is widespread, and the majority of it is illegal. However, as we have seen, the law bluntly distinguishes between those works under copyright and those not, and a nuanced analysis of the moral considerations at stake in particular instances shows that it is not always the case that particular instances of illegal file-sharing are immoral. Some, of course, are, but in instances where copyright infringement occurs as a precursor to purchasing the material in question, or in cases where the copyright holder does not make the material available to purchase, the morality of infringing copyright is less clear than the (il)legality.

Data protection (privacy)

The issue of privacy has been morally relevant for a long time, but the rise of the internet has caused renewed interest in it, simply because online activities provide more frequent and more intrusive means for the breach of individual privacy. The issue at stake in discussions of privacy is simply what restrictions there are (or should be) on the access that others (individuals, corporations or the State) have to your person and personal information. The protection of privacy for any given individual requires restrictions on access to, transmission of, and publication of personal information. Whereas historically the kind of information considered was such data as medical and financial records, the technologically mediated version of privacy is concerned in addition with things like browser or search history, and postings on services such as Facebook, which are at best semi-private, but are often considered to be, or used as if they are, 'private'.

Consider the ease with which we share information on Facebook. It is possible to create private Facebook groups, and to restrict access to those groups, so that only certain people can see postings. But it is not clear that there exists a reasonable expectation that the information in those groups remains private. People use Facebook for reprehensible purposes, as occurred in the 'Roastbusters' scandal of 2013,[3] or the similar events that occur periodically, wherein a group of (usually, and unfortunately) young men say or do horrible things online.[4] Their privacy is breached in making public what they are doing and posting, but at the same time the company (Facebook) can argue that it has an obligation not to enable such behaviour in the spaces that it controls. There is a real sense in which a private Facebook group provides only the illusion of privacy.

Compare this kind of case to the court proceedings against Kim Dotcom, which were discussed earlier in the context of data sharing. His defence included the claim that the company didn't want to abuse the trust and privacy of its consumers by inquiring as to what, exactly, they were uploading, storing and trading via Megaupload and Mega. But the position of both the New Zealand and the US governments has been that the company had at least some duty to do just that. If we are to be consistent, then, we ought to accept that Facebook has similar duties, and to accept that in Facebook's online space — and in those of other companies performing similar roles — privacy as a concept is irrelevant.

This, however, leads us to a further question: namely, how worried should we be regarding the information we do make available online? It may be that we can still expect and demand privacy considerations for basic data, even while denying that such privacy exists for more contentious information. This would be possible if we can determine what counts as basic data and requires protection, and what does not.

PERSONAL DATA PROTECTION

There are at least four distinct types of reason for thinking that online privacy is morally important.[5] The philosopher Jeroen van den Hoven prefers to frame these as issues of 'protecting personal data' rather than of privacy, as he claims that the development of technology means that now what is of most concern to us in online domains is that the information we put online can be accessed by the right people in the right kinds of ways, rather than being 'private'. He claims that protecting personal data enables harm prevention, redresses informational inequality, avoids informational injustice and discrimination, and protects us against the encroachment of moral autonomy.[6]

The harm prevention aspect of personal data protection is perhaps the most relevant of the four. If any individual can access your personal information, then if even one person wants to use it against you, you are vulnerable to such attacks. Obvious instances of this arise in cases where bank account details are taken in order to defraud or steal from people, but a variety of less obvious issues also arise.

Consider the following example. If I were to go on holiday, then the stream of photographs of food, ski slopes, fancy beer and fine wines appearing on my social media accounts would instantly alert anyone who saw them that I was no longer in Hamilton. Were they maliciously inclined, this information would enable them to confidently break into my house — after all, they know I'm not there. Such information is much easier to access than it has been in the past. Similarly, Google and Apple both know how long it takes you to walk from your house to your workplace, and what roads and paths you take in doing so, via the location tracking on your cellphone. If someone wished to do you harm, and had access to the data collected by your phone regarding your location and movement patterns, this information would greatly assist them in harming you.

In 2012, ACC records, including the personal details of 250 clients, were accidentally sent to a number of people who had no reason to have access to them. This was at best a terrible mistake on the part of the ACC, and yet its initial response was minimal.[7] In 2014/15 the Privacy Commissioner reported 121 total data breaches in New Zealand, of varying severity. That is, 121 instances where personal information was released that ought not to have been, ranging from the information of a single individual, to cases similar to the ACC one, involving hundreds of affected persons.[8]

We need not address the other components of data protection at such length. In short, informational inequality occurs when one group (business or government) has the ability to collect and track data on the habits and practices of consumers, while the consumers have little or no control over what data on them is collected, nor on how it is used. This can occur as buying patterns are tracked (every time you use a FlyBuys card, for example), or whenever personal details are required to access information online ('sign in to this service using your Facebook login').

Informational injustice occurs when the information that has been collected about you and your habits is used to form judgements about you in domains disconnected from the reasons for which the data was collected. So, for example, if we were to unearth a Domino's pizza record showing that Bill English always orders pineapple on his pizza, we ought not to use this information as part of the electoral campaign against him. A less trivial example would arise if the ACC data mentioned above was used to discriminate against the individuals concerned when making employment decisions, or when deciding whether to offer them a mortgage. In each of these cases, the medical data legitimately collected by the ACC would be illegitimately used, if used in pursuit of these unrelated ends.

Finally, on the issue of moral autonomy, the worry is that there is a temptation — on the part of the State, of companies and of others — to judge the character of individuals from the content of their public profiles. The issue, of course, is that these public profiles are incomplete. One simply cannot adequately represent who one is on a Facebook profile, nor can a good judgement of character be made from the content of a Twitter feed, the avatar a person uses in their MMO of choice, or any combination of these. This aspect will be examined in more detail later.

SUMMARY

Online interactions are a large and growing component of our daily activities. We entrust the State and private corporations with a huge range of data on all aspects of our lives, and it is important that we know how, when and why that data can be used by the organisations that have access to them. It is increasingly implausible to place the burden of data protection on individual end users, as interactions with government services (for example, the Inland Revenue Department) occur online, and as such end users have no choice but to transmit their information in these spaces. As such, the moral responsibility for data protection must also lie in part with the organisations collecting the data, to only use it in appropriate ways, and to take reasonable care in protecting access to it.

Online behavioural norms

Virtual spaces offer many new opportunities for interactions with other people. Whether one is participating in social media channels such as Facebook, Twitter or Instagram, in virtual worlds and game-spaces such as MMOs (*World of Warcraft*, *EVE*), services such as Xbox Live, Steam or Battle.net, or new media spaces like blogs, news websites and forums, participants have a reach far beyond what we are used to. Behavioural norms, whether or how to engage in political behaviour, or when to criticise the actions of others, must adapt to how we now behave online. But doing so requires a significant reimagining of what we are doing online, and of how important it is.

PROTEST AND CRITICISM

The reach of the internet comes with risks. Online, the world is (potentially) your audience. This means that you cannot rely on those who view or hear your work having the same background and sharing the same assumptions as you. At the same time, you should not be too quick to criticise the things you view or hear, as the producer of the material may not be who you expect them to be, and as such your criticisms may be misguided.

In this section, we consider two examples of protest regarding the content of a popular song. One example illustrates the perils of aggressive criticism online, showing how such criticism can be misplaced when it is not sensitive to the diversity of backgrounds and lived experiences that artists have. The other illustrates the success that such criticism can have on a global scale, when it is targeted at behaviour that is condemned across cultures and social backgrounds.

The example of misplaced criticism arises out of a New Zealand success story. In 'Royals', a song off her 2013 album *Pure Heroine*, Lorde sings the following lines:

> But every song's like
> Gold teeth, Grey Goose, trippin' in the bathroom,
> Bloodstains, ball gowns, trashin' the hotel room
> We don't care
> We're driving Cadillacs in our dreams
> But everybody's like
> Cristal, Maybach, diamonds on your timepiece
> Jet planes, islands, tigers on a gold leash
> We don't care
> We aren't caught up in your love affair

They evoke, to a New Zealander, images of excess, populated with musicians and movie stars, probably American, as that is where much of the music and the movies we see come from. They do not, to a New Zealander, have explicitly racial connotations, because the type of conversations Americans have about racial justice issues are not the ones that New Zealanders have. Our environments are different so the imagery in the lines above is not coded 'African-American' to us. As it turns out, it is to at least some Americans.

Verónica Bayetti Flores, a blogger for the website Feministing, called Lorde out, saying that '[w]hile I love a good critique of wealth accumulation and inequity, this song is not one; in fact, it is deeply racist. Because we all know who she's thinking when we're talking gold teeth, Cristal and Maybachs.'[9] What is occurring here is a clash of expectations between artist and consumer or critic. It is generated in this instance by the popularity of the song, and by the relative ease with which a New Zealander can now have exposure in the US music marketplace.

Flores was claiming, in essence, that these lyrics, written by a white American, would be intended to diminish the characters engaged in such behaviour, and to do so, at least in part, on account of their race. But of course, Lorde is not American, and intended no such thing. To judge her lyrics and her intentions by the standards one would apply to a citizen of the United States is to overlook the diversity of origin the internet enables, and to diminish the experience of those who are not from the United States.

By contrast, some criticisms gain force because they come from a diverse range of cultures and backgrounds. Also in 2013, Robin Thicke released a highly successful song and music video, 'Blurred Lines', the lyrics of which played fast and loose with the notion of consent in sexual relationships. Unlike the Lorde case, criticism of the content of this song was able to be consistently made from around the world, and the breadth of that criticism reinforced, rather than diminished, the strength of the objection to the imagery involved. The Auckland Law Revue parody, 'Defined Lines', reversed the gender roles of the original and altered the lyrics in an attempt to draw attention to the problematic aspects of the song. It did so spectacularly, drawing over 5.5 million YouTube views and providing massive exposure to the protest against Thicke's work.

POLITICAL ACTIVITY

In New Zealand, the Internet-Mana Party failed spectacularly to make an impact on domestic politics during the 2014 election, but grassroots movements like the support of 'Red Peak' as an alternative option in the flag referendum have altered our political practice. Red Peak rose out of dissatisfaction with how the process of conducting referenda regarding whether we ought to have a new flag was being run, and, in particular, dissatisfaction with the options being touted. The campaign, fuelled almost entirely by new media such as Twitter and Facebook, stoked public suspicion of the referenda, and within a short timeframe succeeded both in breaking what had hitherto been fairly stable support for one of the other change-options, and in undermining the support for change at all.

This mixed record suggests that there is some potential for the internet to form a deliberative space of the sort envisaged by the German philosopher Jürgen Habermas, who believed that strong democratic institutions required spaces for deliberative communication in which the various risks and benefits of different courses of action could be debated, and the best course of action decided upon.[10] However, it is also clear that not all online spaces display such virtues. People do engage in political discussion online, but, as we will see in the following section, where they self-select the membership of their community the possible advantages of online deliberation are nullified.

A second issue in the political sphere relates to the use of online social activism to attempt to force policy change. This is distinct from the flag referendum case, mentioned above, as in that instance the government intended for there to be meaningful public deliberation, albeit not in the form it ultimately took. Rather, the worry is that online spaces can be used to pressure institutions into acting without going through the process of fact-checking and consideration that would normally be required. Imagine the outcry that would occur today were the news media to report, as they did in 2007, that a professor at a New Zealand university had suggested putting birth control drugs into the national water supply.[11] Whether the professor in fact said just that, or was merely describing the possibility to illustrate a broader claim, is beside the point. The issue is that public perception online drives protest, and there is a risk that in New Zealand, as has happened abroad, vigilante groups of internet activists would demand that people be punished for things that they may not have said or meant.

The solution, of course, is not to act without careful examination of the facts of the case at hand.

ECHO CHAMBERS AND SOUNDING BOARDS

A further consideration within the sphere of communication online is what kind of information one can access, and how one does so. A common concern is that online spaces may operate as echo chambers, amplifying confirming voices and nullifying dissenting ones, until one's understanding of what the population at large believes regarding particular issues is heavily distorted.

To illustrate this concern, consider the following example. If you are a motivated and progressive social liberal, who cares deeply about the environment and wants the benefits of the State to be equitably distributed across all groups within society, you may curate your online environment in the following ways. Those friends and family members who praise the National Government's clean waterway policy change in 2017 are quietly muted on Facebook. The enthusiastic supporters of Cameron Slater, and even those who merely re-tweet him, are blocked on Twitter. The comment threads on the *New Zealand Herald* website go unread (as do many of the *Herald* articles). After some time, your Facebook feed is full of commentary that agrees with you on issues of social justice and environmental considerations. You see positive and supportive Twitter conversations about the new Green Party policies for environmental protection, and only criticism of the National and New Zealand First policy statements. Everyone, it seems, is in agreement that it would be a disaster were the political right to retain power. Clearly, a Labour–Green coalition will win an easy majority at the next election. Not so (at least, not necessarily so). Rather, this process of curation and selective inclusion of online material, which is widely undertaken (in varying degrees), is isolating people within groups of shared interests, and excluding those with different opinions. That is, it is forming echo chambers.

If we operate solely or predominantly within echo chambers, they will shape our expectations regarding political and social practice, and, when these expectations are not met, this may undermine confidence in the institutions of governance. However, it is not clear that this is how online spaces work. Most people do not forget the existence of the elderly relative on Facebook with the reactionary political views, nor do they isolate themselves from those with whom they disagree. In fact, there are a range of domains where disagreement on political and social issues is common — namely, those online spaces whose primary purpose is not the sharing of political and social viewpoints. Where individuals interact for other purposes, be they playing online games or discussing sports, movies or the like, bonds of friendship are formed that arise prior to political and social discussions. They can even do so more easily than in the offline world, as the obvious social markers of difference (race, gender, class) are not so obvious online.[12] So the worry about echo chambers appears to be overstated.

VIRTUAL FRIENDS AND MORAL CHARACTER

In the previous section, we discussed in passing the formation of friendships via online environments. However, these are controversial. Some have argued that such friendships may be fundamentally different from those we create and develop in the physical world.[13] If this is the case, and if the difference is that online friendships are missing something positive that physical friendships have, then a behavioural shift towards online interaction will make our lives worse, insofar as it causes us to get fewer of the benefits of friendships and other close interactions.

Fortunately, it turns out that the early technophobic concerns of those who thought that online friendships necessarily lacked something important have been overblown. Most friendships do not operate purely online, but are what we might call 'mixed-mode relationships' — mediated through both online and offline interaction.[14] Even those friendships that occur solely online do not display the problems that were posited. Instead, they provide alternative means to the goods of friendship.[15]

Current research on the morality of friendship in online spaces now focuses on how online spaces serve to enhance or continue offline friendships when we migrate them online.[16] This area of research is active and rapidly changing, as the nature of online friendships is not stable but is continually evolving.[17] What we do know is that people act as if their online friendships are as real, as close and as important as their offline friendships are, and we would need good reasons to reject people's own testimony regarding who their friends are and which of their friendships are important to them.[18]

If we can make friends online, one might ask, what else can we do? In particular, we might wonder whether our actions in virtual worlds shape our character, for good or for bad. This type of debate arises in the context of video games, where the argument is made that violent games incite violence in the physical world among those who play them. Only recently has the corresponding claim been examined in depth: that pro-social or positive games might incite positive behaviours among those who play them. There has been an abundance of research into questions like these, and two recent meta-analyses (that is, studies of the studies of video games) have found that there is evidence that playing games does affect social behaviour.[19]

It is important to note that there is a distinction between what these findings mean for our actions online in general, and what they mean for our actions in a particular game. It may well be that they provide us with reasons not to play *Grand Theft Auto*, but at the same time the benefits of playing *Civilization*, and thereby learning about world history, or of playing *World of Warcraft*, and thereby collaboratively problem-solving in the company of a diverse group of friends, must not be overlooked. The answer to whether it is good for us to spend a lot of time online will be a function of what it is that we do online.

We ought not to draw from the evidence that playing games alters our social behaviour the conclusion that what we do online is directly analogous to what we do offline. It is clear that there is not perfect symmetry between online and offline actions, whether in terms of what we do, or in terms of the moral content of what we do. So while we can make sense of a notion such as 'virtual murder', we do not think it is punishable in the way that physical murder is. The philosopher Morgan Luck claims that '[a] player commits an act of virtual murder in those cases where he directs his character to kill another in circumstances such that, were the game environment actual, the actions of his character would constitute actual murder'.[20] While virtual murder is clearly wrong, it is not the kind of wrong that physical murder is, not least because the action undertaken in a case of 'virtual murder' does not kill the apparent target (the player), but only their avatar (character).

The opposite thesis — one which posits a perfect asymmetry between online and offline behaviour — ought also to be rejected. This thesis claims that actions committed in virtual worlds can never be wrong. Virtual worlds are not, on this account, the type of spaces where questions of morality arise. So, for example, virtual theft is not actually theft, as one is not taking an actual thing. This, of course, only works insofar as there is no analogue between the virtual thing being taken and any sort of actual thing. If there is an agreed-upon exchange rate between the physical and the virtual, this kind of argument collapses. (So, for example, if a month of game time in *World of Warcraft* costs you 100,000 gold or $15, then a theft of 1,000,000 gold is a theft of $150.)

The asymmetry thesis has been consistently rejected in the law, regarding virtual value and now regarding objects in virtual worlds.[21]

One might attempt to defend the asymmetry thesis regarding the morality (rather than legality) of actions in online spaces by claiming something like the following: that virtual worlds are games in which different rules apply. The game argument, however, only works if we can craft an all-encompassing set of rules for virtual worlds that cannot be breached. This is the idea of the 'magic circle' of game-space, within which alternative rules apply.[22] The claim is that it isn't wrong to bankrupt your friends while playing Monopoly, because Monopoly has a different rule-set in which things which would be immoral if you did them 'for real' are perfectly fine. Similarly, the claim goes, there are all sorts of things that would be immoral 'for real' which are fine in online environments. On this kind of account, if an act follows the rules of the game-space, it is not morally wrong. So, killing in a game is not wrong, if the objective of the game is to kill.

However, virtual worlds are never completely closed. Actions taken within them in fact matter to participants in the worlds; and influence the physical world. Even if the virtual worlds were completely closed, it is possible for rule-following actions to be morally wrong. Some rules are wrong.

Conclusion

Cyber-ethics is a complex and evolving domain. Longstanding ethical issues, such as copyright infringement, privacy, protest and freedoms of expression, gain new dimensions when put into the context of a data-rich, permanently connected world. There are ever fewer domains for which it is not possible to do (at least some of) one's everyday activities online. Correspondingly, where the online world differs from the physical world, we have to ask whether the old rules still function as intended in these new spaces. At the same time, virtual spaces have opened up entirely new areas of moral concern, where things that were not possible without the internet become commonplace, such as worrying about whether your (Australian) bank is adequately protecting the login details of your (New Zealand) bank account from (Russian) hackers based elsewhere (Liberia). Virtual spaces have rules and laws, but these don't always work in the ways we are used to.

---

1 Charlotte Greenfield, 'NZ Court Rules Megaupload Founder Kim Dotcom can be Extradited to U.S. for Alleged Fraud,' February 20, 2017, accessed April 2017, http://www.msn.com/en-us/news/world/nz-court-rules-megaupload-founder-kim-dotcom-can-be-extradited-to-us-for-alleged-fraud/ar-AAn7pTf?OCID=ansmsnnews11.

2 Lawrence Lessig, *Free Culture: How Big Media Uses Technology and the Law to Lock Down Culture and Control Creativity* (New York: Penguin, 2004), accessed April 2017, http://www.free-culture.cc/freecontent/.

3 The Roastbusters case involved a group of young men in Auckland allegedly co-ordinating the abuse and rape of young women via a Facebook page. The police response to these allegations was widely viewed as inadequate.

4 Anastasia Powell and Nicola Henry, 'Blurred Lines? Responding to "Sexting" and Gender-based Violence Among Young People,' *Children Australia* 39, no. 2 (2014): 119–124.

5 J. van den Hoven, M. Blaauw, W. Pieters, and M. Warnier, 'Privacy and Information Technology,' *The Stanford Encyclopedia of Philosophy*, ed. Edward N. Zalta (Spring 2016), May 14, 2002, revised August 9, 2013, accessed April 2017, https://plato.stanford.edu/archives/spr2016/entries/it-privacy/.

6 J. van den Hoven, *Information Technology, Privacy and the Protection of Personal Data* (Cambridge: Cambridge University Press, 2008).

7 Phil Kitchin, 'ACC Apologises Over Privacy Breach,' *The Dominion Post*, March 13, 2012, accessed June 2017, http://www.stuff.co.nz/national/health/6563083/ACC-apologises-over-privacy-breach.

8 John Edwards, *Privacy Commissioner Annual Report, 2015*. (Wellington: Office of the Privacy Commissioner, 2015), accessed April 2017, https://www.privacy.org.nz/assets/Files/Reports-to-ParlGovt/OPC-annual-report-2015.pdf.

9 Verónica Bayetti Flores, 'Wow, That Lorde Song "Royals" is Racist,' *Feministing* blog, October 3, 2013, accessed April 2017, http://feministing.com/2013/10/03/wow-that-lorde-song-royals-is-racist.

10 Jürgen Habermas, 'Further Reflections on the Public Sphere,' in *Habermas and the Public Sphere*, ed. Craig Calhoun (Cambridge, Mass: The MIT Press, 1993): 421–461.

11 New Zealand Press Association, 'Brainier Mums Needed to Maintain

Future Generations' Intelligence, says Professor,' *New Zealand Herald*, July 8, 2007, accessed April 2017, http://webcache.googleusercontent.com/search?q=cache:n5oYIsZ5MNcJ:m.nzherald.co.nz/nz/news/article.cfm%3Fc_id%3D1%26objectid%3D10450313+&cd=1&hl=en&ct=clnk&gl=nz.

12 Elizabeth Mazur and Lacey Richards, 'Adolescents' and Emerging Adults' Social Networking Online: Homophily or Diversity?' *Journal of Applied Developmental Psychology* 32, no. 4 (2011): 180–188.

13 Dean Cocking and Steve Matthews, 'Unreal Friends,' *Ethics and Information Technology* 2, no. 4 (2000): 223–231.

14 Marjolijn L. Antheunis, Patti M. Valkenburg, and Jochen Peter, 'The Quality of Online, Offline, and Mixed-mode Friendships Among Users of a Social Networking Site,' *Cyberpsychology: Journal of Psychosocial Research on Cyberspace* 6, no. 3 (2015), https://doi.org/10.5817/CP2012-3-6.

15 Adam Briggle, 'Real Friends: How the Internet can Foster Friendship,' *Ethics and Information Technology* 10, no. 1 (2008): 71–79. Also N. J. Munn, 'The Reality of Friendship Within Immersive Virtual Worlds,' *Ethics and Information Technology* 14, no. 1 (2011): 1–10.

16 Shannon Vallor, 'Flourishing on Facebook: Virtue Friendship and New Social Media,' *Ethics and Information Technology* 14, no. 3 (2012): 185–199.

17 Robert Sharp, 'The Obstacles Against Reaching the Highest Level of Aristotelian Friendship Online,' *Ethics and Information Technology* 14, no. 3 (2012): 231–239. Also Barbro Fröding and Martin Peterson, 'Why Virtual Friendship is No Genuine Friendship,' *Ethics and Information Technology* 14, no. 3 (2012): 201–207. Also Alexis Elder, 'Excellent Online Friendships: An Aristotelian Defense of Social Media,' *Ethics and Information Technology* 16, no. 4 (2014): 287–297.

18 Katelyn Y. A. McKenna, Amie S. Green, and Marci E. Gleason, 'Relationship Formation on the Internet: What's the Big Attraction?' *Journal of Social Issues* 58, no. 1 (2002): 9–31.

19 Tobias Greitemeyer and Dirk O. Mügge, 'Video Games Do Affect Social Outcomes: A Meta-analytic Review of the Effects of Violent and Prosocial Video Game Play,' *Personality and Social Psychology Bulletin* 40, no. 5 (2014): 578–589. doi: 0146167213520459, accessed June 2017. Also Malte Elson and Christopher J. Ferguson, 'Twenty-five Years of Research on Violence in Digital Games and Aggression,' *European Psychologist* 19 (2014): 33–46, http://econtent.hogrefe.com/doi/abs/10.1027/1016-9040/a000147.

20 Morgan Luck, 'The Gamer's Dilemma: An Analysis of the Arguments for the Moral Distinction Between Virtual Murder and Virtual Paedophilia,' *Ethics and Information Technology* 11, no. 1 (2009): 31–36.

21 Arno R. Lodder, 'Dutch Supreme Court 2012: Virtual Theft Ruling a One-off or First in a Series?' *Journal of Virtual Worlds Research* 6, no. 3 (2013): 1–12.

22 Johan Huizinga, *Homo Ludens: A Study of the Play-Element in Culture* (London: Routledge, 1949).

5

Sex and Intimacy

VANESSA SCHOUTEN

Introduction

When you think of the ethics of sex, you probably think about issues like consent, sexual violence, or perhaps adultery. But philosophers interested in the ethics of sex and intimacy work on a wide variety of issues — the obligations generated by friendship, the morality of open marriage, and the ethics of sadomasochism are just some examples. The common thread is that all of these issues have to do with either our sexual lives or our intimate relationships.

In this chapter, we will be looking at three issues that are both of public interest and have also been widely discussed by academic philosophers. We will canvass the main arguments on each topic, and then summarise the important questions.

First, we will discuss the ethics of sex work (or prostitution), and will consider the following questions. Is there a moral problem with sex work? If so, what kind of problem is it? Is it a problem to do with the very nature of the work itself, or is it a problem to do with our attitudes towards sex work and sex workers?

Next, we will discuss pornography. We will talk about what pornography is, canvass some moral objections to pornography, and consider whether there are good moral reasons for supporting any kind of ban on pornographic material.

Finally, we will discuss gay marriage. We will look briefly at the history of gay marriage legislation in New Zealand, and consider arguments that have been made both for and against gay marriage.

Sex work

WHAT IS SEX WORK?

Sex work is the selling or trading of sexual services for money or other goods, including activities such as trading sexual intercourse for money, stripping or erotic dancing, acting in a pornographic film, webcam or phone sex, working as a dominatrix, and even perhaps work as a therapeutic sexual surrogate. However, the boundaries of what does and does not count as sex work are fuzzy. A person who works as an escort or as a 'sugar baby' (a young person, usually a woman, who trades companionship and sometimes sex for goods or money) may not consider themselves a sex worker. Sex work also may not actually involve anything that we might think of as being 'sexual contact'. For example, someone working as a dominatrix may not physically touch their partner.

'Prostitution' might be a more familiar term for this kind of activity, but it is worth noting that both 'prostitution' and 'sex work' are contested terms. Until relatively recently, 'prostitution' was the most commonly used term for this kind of work, but this terminology has been increasingly replaced with the use of the term 'sex work' (and those who engage in sex work are referred to as 'sex workers'). Why the change? The change has come about because the terms 'prostitution' and 'prostitute' are considered to be stigmatising — the idea is that the terms themselves reinforce the notions that sex work is somehow different from other kinds of work in which people trade labour or services for money, and that prostitutes themselves are therefore engaging in something which means they deserve the stigma associated with that kind of work. But this change has not been universally welcomed — many anti-prostitution advocates reject it on the grounds that the change in terminology has the effect of legitimising an industry which is based largely on the exploitation of those who are, in many cases, already vulnerable.

In this chapter, I will be using the term 'prostitution', simply because the discussion will focus on a certain type of sex work covered by the New Zealand Prostitution Reform Act 2003: commercial sexual services — the physical participation by a person in sexual acts with, and for the gratification of, another person, provided for payment or other reward.[1]

SEPARATING THE LEGAL FROM THE MORAL

Until the Prostitution Reform Act was passed in 2003, certain types of activity surrounding sex work were illegal in New Zealand. It was not actually illegal to provide sexual services in exchange for money, but it was illegal to run a brothel, to live off the earnings of prostitution, and to procure sex by offering payment, or to solicit (offer sex in return for money). The Reform Act decriminalised sex work in New Zealand (so long as the sex worker is over 18), and brothels now operate under a certification system and are required to abide by health and safety regulations.

While it is true that many of the arguments made in favour of reform were moral arguments, we should be careful not to confuse the question 'Should prostitution be illegal?' with the question 'Is prostitution immoral?' There are plenty of things that are illegal, but which aren't clearly immoral — like running a red light at 3am at an entirely deserted intersection. There are also plenty of things which are immoral, but that we don't think should be illegal — adultery may be immoral under most circumstances, but it is not illegal to cheat on your partner.

In this chapter, we will be focusing on the ethical questions, but it will also be helpful to consider the change in law, and the report which followed it, for the following reason. While many of the arguments for the claim that prostitution is immoral rest on the fact that it causes harm to those who engage in it, these harms may not be a result of a moral problem with prostitution, but a result of a *belief* that there is a moral problem with prostitution, or a result of the fact that prostitution is often illegal. So there are two important questions we need to ask: why do people think there is a moral problem with prostitution? And are these problems inherent in the work itself, or a result of outside factors?

WHAT (IF ANYTHING) IS WRONG WITH SEX WORK?

On the face of it, it is not clear why there should be a moral problem with sex work. People engage in all kinds of activities which involve trading their physical and emotional labour for payment that seem morally unproblematic. A ballet dancer uses her body to make money. A therapist talks to people in order to help them feel better and receives payment for it. So why is sex work any different? And if it is different, is it different in ways that are contingent — that is, because of background features to do with legal and social structures that could in theory be changed? Or is it inherently different — is there something about the very nature of trading sex for money that means it is different from other kinds of work?

It might be useful here to distinguish between things that can't be sold, and things that can be sold but shouldn't be. An example of the former might be friendship — it is not possible to sell someone friendship, because of the very nature of this kind of relationship. If I am friends with you only because you pay me, then I am not really your friend. We might have a facsimile of friendship — maybe I help you put your kitset furniture together, or listen uncomplainingly to you whinge about your boss — but real friendship requires that I help you and spend time with you because I care about you as a person, not because

I am being paid to.[2] On the other hand, there are things that can be sold, but shouldn't be — people, for example. It is clear that people can be sold — that is what the institution of slavery is — but the vast majority of us think that it is morally wrong to buy and sell people.

Sex doesn't appear to be the kind of thing that can't be sold. However, some philosophers argue that the good of sex — the reason that sex is valuable — can't be sold, and so selling sex itself is wrong because it undermines the value of non-market sexual relationships. The idea is that the reason that sex is valuable is that it involves a reciprocal offering of the self to another person, and that if sex is commodified it loses the thing that really makes it valuable.[3] This in turn means that sex within romantic relationships also loses its value — it becomes something that now has a market worth and can be valued according to the market, rather than valued for its own good. An analogy might be the buying and selling of children — it is true that we could have a market in children, but the worry is that the commodification of the child–parent relationship undermines the very thing that makes such relationships valuable.

One problem with this line of argument, however, is that it is not clear that a market in sex does undermine what is valuable about non-market sexual relationships. Think of all the things romantic partners do for each other as part of a loving relationship — maybe they care for each other when sick, listen to each other's problems, cook for each other. The existence of nurses, therapists and chefs doesn't appear to undermine the value of romantic relationships which include these activities. It may be true that sex within a loving, romantic relationship is valuable in a way that sex outside of it isn't (in the same way that having a romantic partner with whom you can share your struggles with is valuable in a way that having a therapist or counsellor can't replicate), but it doesn't follow that sexual activity that takes place outside a relationship undermines that value.

IS SEX WORK EXPLOITATIVE OR COERCIVE?

Another moral objection to sex work is the claim that such work is inherently exploitative — for example, that offering sex for money exploits the fact that some people are in vulnerable circumstances.[4] While it may be true in practice that some sex workers engage in such work out of desperation, it is not clear that there is anything about the nature of sex work in particular that means that it is exploitative in a way that other offers of payment for labour are not. Many people engage in dangerous and unpleasant work that they would not choose to do if they were not being paid, but they do it because they need the money. But it does not seem morally wrong to (for example) offer someone a job down a mine or at the freezing works, even if their only other option is the dole.

One worry might be that sexual autonomy — the ability to only engage in sex that you fully and freely consent to — is both morally important and compromised by sex work. But again, there are other kinds of work which involve (temporarily) giving other people control over what we do with our bodies, like modelling or getting paid to be a human test subject, and we don't find these sorts of work morally problematic.

Another objection to prostitution is that sex workers themselves are frequently forced into the industry — trafficked across borders, or coerced by other means. Again, though, we need to be careful to distinguish between problems that may be contingent, and those that are inherent in the work. As an example, in the eighteenth century many people were kidnapped, brought to a different country, and forced to work as slaves on plantations. This was clearly wrong, but it was not wrong because there is anything particularly immoral about the *kind* of work they were doing. There is nothing morally wrong with agriculture. What was wrong about the situation was the fact that they were kidnapped and forced to work.

IS SEX WORK INHERENTLY DANGEROUS?

The danger of sex work is another reason why people have moral objections to this kind of work, but again it is not clear that sex work is particularly dangerous in a way that differs from other kinds of work. It is also dangerous to work in the drug trade — or, at least, in some parts of the drug trade. Some people who sell drugs work in very dangerous situations and are considered dangerous to be around. Others are considered to be well-respected professionals. The difference is that some people sell illegal drugs (people we usually call drug dealers) and some people (pharmacists) sell drugs legally.

As we saw in Chapter 2, one of the main arguments for legalising illegal recreational drugs — particularly 'soft' drugs like cannabis — is that such drug use is only more dangerous than other indulgences (drinking alcohol, eating sugary foods) *because* it is illegal. The same may well be true of prostitution. The New Zealand experience provides a useful test case for this. The purpose of the Prostitution Reform Act 2003 was to move away from a 'moralistic' approach to prostitution in favour of a harm reduction model, focusing on health and safety and human rights. According to the New Zealand Prostitution Law Committee Report on the Act, the decriminalisation of prostitution in New Zealand has not led to an increase in prostitution, but it has led to improvements in employment conditions, and in health and safety.[5] For example, in 2014 a sex worker took a sexual harassment case against a brothel owner to the Human Rights Review Tribunal and won — so it seems that even with regard to sexual harassment there is no reason why a brothel need be any different to other workplaces.

SUMMARY

When discussing the morality of sex work, there are three important questions we need to ask:

- Is there a problem with the work?

- Does this problem have to do with the nature of the work itself, or is it a result of outside factors (such as the legal situation) which could in theory be changed?
- If so, would the changes in practice result in the kind of change which renders the work itself unproblematic?

Answering these questions is not a straightforward matter — there is plenty of disagreement about whether there are any moral problems with sex work, and, if so, what the nature of these problems is. But one important thing to do is to pay attention to the experiences of those who work in and around the sex industry. A lot of the arguments about the morality of sex work depend on claims about what it is like to be a sex worker — that sex workers are frequently coerced, or that they are traumatised by such work. It is important to note that these are empirical claims, and the only way they can be substantiated (or not) is by listening to those who know what it is like to do that kind of work.

Pornography

WHAT IS PORNOGRAPHY?

'Pornography' is a term that is notoriously difficult to define — famously, Justice Potter Stewart in a US Supreme Court decision stated in reference to hard-core pornography that 'I shall not today attempt further to define the kinds of material I understand to be embraced within that shorthand description; and perhaps I could never succeed in intelligibly doing so. But I know it when I see it.'[6]

The term is usually used to describe movies or videos which are sexually explicit, but can also include pictures, writing and even cartoons. The problem is defining what is meant by 'sexually explicit'. Is it any depiction of sex? Does it include sexual images and imagery, such as nude images, even when there are no sexual acts being depicted? When it does include sexual acts, is it pornographic so long as the act is depicted, or do the actors have to actually be having sex as opposed to simulating having sex?

It is very difficult to come up with a good definition of pornography that merely describes what is depicted and doesn't refer to the way in which it is depicted. For example, we can't just say that images of genitalia are pornographic — that would mean that a picture in an anatomy textbook would count as pornography, when it clearly doesn't. It also seems a mistake to say that all depictions of sex are pornographic — many mainstream movies and TV shows include depictions of sex, and we tend not to describe those as pornography. But to some extent, this question is a bit of a red herring.

There are clear cases of things which do count as pornography — a film depicting actual sexual activity between two adults filmed by a company that produces many videos of this type and distributes them to pornographic websites seems like a clear-cut case. Conversely, there are many cases in which it is not so easy to decide whether a given piece of film is pornographic or not. Nevertheless, we can still consider whether there are moral issues with pornography without needing to come up with a definition that covers every potentially tricky borderline case.

THE NEW ZEALAND SITUATION

There is no attempt to define pornography as such in New Zealand law, but there are certainly restrictions on objectionable material. Some of these you will probably be familiar with: all of the films that show in a movie theatre, for example, are given a rating by the Office of Film and Literature Classification, from G (General Audience) through to R18 (Restricted to persons 18 years and over). Some material, however, is classed as 'objectionable' material. Such material is banned, and it is an offence to possess, trade, distribute or display such material.[7]

But when it comes to deciding what kind of material counts as objectionable, there are no strict guidelines. Instead, what matters according to the Act is 'the extent, degree and manner in which the publication describes, depicts, or deals with' things such as sexual violence or coercion, the nudity of children, degrading or dehumanising sexual conduct, and sexual conduct with or by children (as well as other things not of a sexual nature, such as torture and the promotion of terrorism, but these are not relevant for our purposes).[8] But you can see why there could not be a blanket rule that merely described what was depicted: clearly some pictures depicting the nudity of children ought to be banned, but others — like the picture your mum took of you in the bath when you were five — ought not to be.

But why ban pornography at all? What, if anything, is the moral problem with pornography that would justify a legal ban? For the rest of the discussion, we will exclude child pornography, as the issues surrounding child pornography are quite different from the issues surrounding pornography made by and for consenting adults. So our question is this: if all parties involved in both the creation and the consumption of pornography are consenting adults, why should it be banned?

A QUESTION OF CENSORSHIP

Banning pornographic material would of course count as censorship, and there is a very famous philosophical argument against almost all cases of censorship. In Chapter 2 we discussed John Stuart Mill's harm principle, and we examined its application to the issue of recreational drug prohibition. Basically, the principle states that the only justification for restricting what a person who is a competent adult may do is to prevent harm to others.[9] So the State has no justification for restricting what consenting adults choose to do, even if that involves making, distributing or viewing pornography that the vast majority of us would find disgusting and disturbing, unless by doing so they cause harm to others.

THE HARMS OF PORNOGRAPHY

The first and most obvious harm is that pornography might cause people to feel disgusted or offended. But is disgust or offence sufficient reason to ban something? It seems that the mere fact that some people find pornography disgusting or offensive will not suffice to justify a general ban. I think mushrooms are disgusting. I find the smell of fish offensive. But this is certainly no reason for the State to impose a blanket ban on other people eating mushrooms or cooking fish in the privacy of their own homes. But what about in public? I have a slightly stronger claim here — if you cook fish at home, I don't have to smell it, but I do have to walk past the fish counter every time I go to the supermarket. So in a sense I am 'harmed' (in that I have an unpleasant experience) because it is legal to publicly buy and sell fish. Does this justify a ban?

It seems clear that the answer to this should be 'no', and so by analogy the mere fact that some people find pornography offensive is not enough to justify a prohibition on either the private or the public consumption of pornography. Can the harm principle account for this intuition? Joel Feinberg, a contemporary philosopher, argues that being offended does not count as being harmed, although there may be good reason to restrict at least the public display of pornographic material on the grounds that serious offence, even though it is not harm, is itself reason to restrict the actions of others.[10]

I think most of us would agree that there are good reasons to restrict the public display of pornographic material. But note that our law goes beyond this — it makes it an offence for people to merely possess certain kinds of material. So, what, if any, kind of harm might it cause if consenting adults make or consume pornography entirely in private?

FEMINIST ARGUMENTS

First, it is worth noting that there is not a consensus amongst feminists about the issue of pornography: some feminists argue that pornography is, or can be, empowering; others argue that it is harmful, demeaning and exploitative. In this section we will consider the latter argument, focusing in particular on the effects of male consumption of pornography on women.

Second, it is also worth noting that a lot of the objections to sex work that we discussed earlier will also be relevant to the production of pornography. (In both cases people are being paid to engage in sexual activity, so any concerns that apply in the case of prostitution will also apply in the case of pornography.) But pornography raises new concerns: we might be concerned not just with whether pornography harms others because of the way in which it is produced, but also whether it harms because of the way in which it is consumed. Furthermore, it is entirely possible to produce pornography without involving actors — using computer-generated images (CGI), cartoons, or even painting or writing.

So, are there good reasons to think that the consumption of pornography causes harm? There are two main lines of argument for the claim that the consumption of pornography causes harm. The first is that the consumption of pornography can cause those who consume it to engage in sexual violence, so we should ban it for the same reason we might ban a book that encourages people to engage in terrorism. The second is that pornography causes those who consume it to adopt harmful attitudes.

I should note at this point that, while it is of course the case that pornography often depicts both men and women, and that both men and women watch pornography, the arguments we shall be considering are largely concerned with the effects that men's consumption of pornography has on women. So from now on in this section we shall be discussing just the harms that arise in this scenario.

The idea that pornography causes sexual violence is encapsulated in a slogan attributed to feminist activist Robin Morgan: 'Pornography is the theory, and rape is the practice.'[11] But is there reason to think that the consumption of pornography is a cause of sexual violence? There is an analogy here with things like racist hate speech — it is not OK to say things that incite people to go out and commit crimes against racial groups. Similarly, if pornography encourages people to go out and commit crimes against women, we should ban it for the same reason we ban hate speech or other incitements to violence. Whether or not pornography does incite violence against women is an empirical question — that is, we can go out and do scientific studies that compare, for example, whether an increase in the rates of the consumption of pornography in a particular society has led to an increase in the rates of sexual violence. The problem is, though, that there is widespread disagreement among social science researchers about whether or not it is true that pornography causes violent crime. Some studies find that there is a link between pornography and violence.[12] Others suggest there is no causal link between the consumption of pornography and sexual violence.[13] It might even be the case that the consumption of pornography reduces sexual violence — if people who might otherwise be violent have access to a 'safety valve' in the form of pornography, they may be less likely to commit sexual violence.

But is there a reason to think that, even if the consumption of pornography does not cause men to commit sexual violence, it might cause them to adopt harmful attitudes? One common feminist objection to pornography is that large amounts of it involve scenarios in which women are demeaned and degraded, and that the consumption of this kind of pornography causes men to view women in general in a certain way — as objects, or as less than fully human. This type of argument treats pornography as a civil rights issue.

One of the most famous examples of this type of argument against pornography was made by Catherine MacKinnon (a feminist activist and lawyer) and Andrea Dworkin (a feminist activist and writer). In 1983, they drafted a model civil rights ordinance in which they claimed that not only did pornography cause sexual violence, it also had the effects (among others) of promoting bigotry and contempt; demeaning women as a class; lowering the human dignity, worth and civil status of women; damaging mutual respect between the sexes; restricting women from the full exercise of citizenship; and undermining women's equal exercise of rights to free speech and action.[14]

Again, however, whether or not pornography does have all of these effects arising from its impact on men's attitudes towards women is an empirical question, but one on which we don't as yet have good evidence about either way. Even if we did, it is not clear that this kind of harm would be sufficient to justify a legal ban. It might, however, still be an important moral concern — that is, we might think that pornography does cause a shift in men's attitudes towards women, and that this is enough to justify the belief that pornography is morally wrong, even if we don't think it is enough to justify making pornography illegal.

SUMMARY

When discussing the morality of pornography, there are three important questions we need to ask:

- What are the potential moral problems involved with either the production or the consumption of pornography?
- Do we have the empirical evidence we need to back up our claims?
- Are these problems sufficient to justify a ban or other kind of State intervention?

One of the most difficult things about this topic is that the answers to certain empirical questions — does pornography cause harm, and if so, what kind? — are central to the debate, and yet the evidence is not conclusive. But one thing we can do is to consider what our answers would be if a given empirical claim was true. For example, if it is the case that pornography does cause some men to adopt harmful attitudes towards women, is this sufficient to justify State intervention?

Gay marriage

Up until the Homosexual Law Reform Act was passed in 1986, consensual sex between adult men (although not between adult women) was illegal in New Zealand. In 2005 the Civil Union Act was passed, granting legal recognition to same-sex partnerships, but full marriage equality was not achieved until 2013. At the time of writing (June 2017), it is illegal for two people of the same sex to marry in the majority of countries around the world. It has only been four years since same-sex marriage became legal in New Zealand, and it is still not legal in Australia (although there is a strong push for marriage equality in that country).

WHY IS THE LEGALITY OF GAY MARRIAGE OF INTEREST TO ETHICISTS?

In the section on prostitution, we were careful to distinguish between two questions: (1) should prostitution be illegal? and (2) is prostitution immoral? So why should an ethicist — someone primarily concerned with moral questions — be interested in the question of whether or not same-sex marriage should be legal? It is because marriage is a right, and the question of whether a right should or should not be granted to a class of persons is itself an ethical question. So the granting of marriage rights to same-sex couples is a question of justice, and concerns about justice are moral concerns.

A QUESTION OF DISCRIMINATION

One reason why it might seem obvious that justice requires the granting of marriage rights to same-sex couples is that to refuse same-sex couples that right is discriminatory — it means treating people differently depending on what their sexual orientation happens to be. This is illegal (in New Zealand, at least, discrimination on the grounds of sexual orientation is prohibited under the Human Rights Act), and most people think that discrimination on such grounds is also morally wrong. So it seems we have an easy answer to both the moral question and the legal question: it is unjust to deny someone the right to marry because of their sexual orientation, and so same-sex marriage ought to be legal.

This is a bit too quick, however. Although you might think on first hearing the word 'discrimination' that it follows that if you are discriminating against someone you are doing something morally wrong, this is not always the case. 'Discriminating' just means treating people differently. And there are all kinds of instances where it seems there is no moral problem at all with discrimination on the basis of things like gender, race or age. Consider this example: the National Screening Unit in New Zealand offers free breast-cancer screening to women between the ages of 45 and 69. They are discriminating on the grounds of both age and gender, and yet it doesn't seem morally wrong, or somehow unjust, for the National Screening Unit to offer the service only to this group of people. This is because women of that age are most likely to be at risk. So in this case, there is discrimination — people are being treated differently on the basis of age and gender — but there is a good reason for it, so the discrimination is not unjust.

IS DENYING SAME-SEX COUPLES MARRIAGE RIGHTS UNJUST DISCRIMINATION?

So, our question should be this: is there any reason to think that same-sex couples are different from mixed-sex couples in a way which would justify blocking them from marrying?

One argument for blocking same-sex marriage has to do with the definition of marriage — the claim is that 'marriage' is by definition a heterosexual union, just like a 'bachelor' is by definition an unmarried man. The idea is that 'marriage' just means the union of a man and a woman.[15] This argument is, however, unconvincing — while it is true that until recently 'marriage' in most places meant a heterosexual union, there is no reason why we can't extend the use of the term. A good analogy is the term 'citizen'. In some places and times, the term 'citizen' has been used to refer to only men, or only people of a certain race, or only people with a certain level of wealth. But there are rights which go along with citizenship, and the fact that in the past certain kinds of people have not been covered by the term, and have therefore been denied the rights that go along with citizenship, is not a good reason to continue denying them those rights. Similarly, the fact that in the past marriage has been defined in law as a union between two people of different genders is not a good reason why we should not change the definition of marriage in law, thus granting marriage rights to same-sex couples.

Another argument for the claim that denying same-sex marriage rights is discrimination, but not unjust discrimination, has to do with the purpose of marriage. To answer questions about the purpose of marriage, we first need to think about a prior question: why should the State be in the business of granting legal recognition to certain kinds of relationships in the first place?

The legal situation in New Zealand is a little different from that in most places, in that for almost all legal purposes, married couples, civil union partners and de facto couples are treated the same. Yet it is still the case that pairs of people in any one of these three types of relationships are treated differently than pairs of people who are not. For example, the Property (Relationships) Act applies to de facto couples, but not to long-term flatmates, or adult siblings who share a house. What the three types of relationships have in common is that they are romantic relationships. So the question is this: why should the State be in the business of granting legal recognition to romantic relationships, and legal rights to those within such relationships?

One argument is that there are both social and economic benefits to encouraging long-term monogamous romantic relationships, because such relationships lead to more stable communities and families. Children whose parents stay together are likely to do better both economically and psychologically, and adults themselves are likely to benefit economically and socially from being part of a family unit. So the point of the State recognising marriage is to protect and promote the family unit, which is both good for the individuals and good for society as a whole.[16]

But of course there is no reason at all why only heterosexual couples should benefit from this arrangement. First, if marriage is about children, then there are many heterosexual couples who don't (or can't) have children, and many gay couples who can and do. Of course, the difference with a gay couple is that any children are unlikely to be the biological offspring of both partners, but this is true of many heterosexual couples as well. Second, if marriage is about the fact that long-term romantic partnerships help to create stable communities, then there is no reason why these partnerships must be heterosexual in order to create these benefits.

GRANT THE RIGHTS, BUT NOT THE NAME?

One of the reasons that New Zealand first granted gay couples the right to have a legally recognised civil union rather than just amending the Marriage Act right away is that it was seen as a compromise solution — gay couples were essentially granted all of the rights of married couples, but the term 'marriage' could still be reserved for heterosexual unions, mollifying those who believed that gay couples should not be allowed to marry. Given that the Civil Union Act granted gay couples in a civil union almost all of the same rights as a heterosexual married couple, why was there still a need to amend the Marriage Act?

One argument is that 'marriage' is both a social and a legal institution, and granting the rights without the name meant treating gay people as second-class citizens, and denied them the social status of a married couple.[17] Another is that the primary reasons that some people believed that marriage ought to be reserved for heterosexual couples — and therefore the primary reasons for keeping two separate pieces of legislation — were not the right kinds of reasons.

RELIGIOUS ARGUMENTS — THE WRONG KIND OF REASON?

By far the majority of public opposition to both civil unions and amendment to the Marriage Act in New Zealand came from Christian groups. For many of those groups, marriage is a religious institution, and changing the legislation meant changing that religious institution to something that endorsed behaviours and relationships that their religion rejected as morally wrong. Isn't this a good reason for preventing same-sex couples from marrying, then, given that religious freedom is an important value? There are two problems with this argument. First, the right to practise your religion does not extend to the right to make other people live according to the rules of that religion. Second, marriage in New Zealand is (and was) a legal institution, and given that New Zealand is a secular country it seems it would be a mistake to shape a particular piece of legislation according to the religious beliefs of one set of people.

SUMMARY

When discussing gay marriage (or any other instance of apparent discrimination) we can pose three questions which will help frame the discussion:

- Are we discriminating against a group of people?
- What are the reasons offered for why we should treat this group differently?
- Are there good reasons, or is the discrimination unjust?

With regards to same-sex marriage, the answers to these questions are fairly settled — the vast majority of academics, and the majority of the New Zealand public (especially younger New Zealanders), think that there are no moral problems with same-sex marriage and that same-sex marriage should be legal. But this does give rise to a new worry: why is it that only people in relationships that are romantic and sexual in nature get to access the legal and social goods of being recognised as a partnership? And why should only pairs of people be able to have recognised relationships — why not groups of three, or four? In the context of the gay marriage debate, these questions were often presented as a reductio argument against gay marriage; that is, opponents of gay marriage argued that it should not be made legal because it would lead to the legalisation of polygamous marriage. But this argument holds water only if there are in fact principled reasons for prohibiting polygamous marriage, and several philosophers have bitten the bullet on this issue and argued that we should expand the benefits of legality beyond couples, and sometimes even beyond romantic relationships.[18]

Conclusion

In this chapter, we have looked at just three of the topics that are of interest to philosophers who work on the ethics of sex and intimacy. For each of the topics we have looked at, we have considered what (if any) role the law should play in governing the relevant relationship or interaction. But while this is a really important question, it is not the only question worth asking in a discussion about the ethics of a particular issue to do with sex or intimacy. We also need to think about what is valuable to us, and why; about how what we do, even in the context of our personal lives, might affect others; and more generally about how we ought to treat the people we interact with.

For many people, the intimate relationships they have with others (particularly romantic relationships) are one of the most important aspects of their lives, as are their sexual relationships with others, and their sexual identity. Given this, and the fact that both moral and legal norms have governed this aspect of our lives for a very long time and will continue to do so, the ethics of sex and intimacy is not just an interesting topic, but a crucially important one.

---

1 Parliamentary Counsel Office, Prostitution Law Reform Act 2003, Pt 4, accessed June 2, 2017, http://www.legislation.govt.nz/act/public/2003/0028/latest/DLM197815.html.

2 See, for example, Michael Sandel's argument in Chapter 3 of *What Money Can't Buy: How Markets Crowd Out Morals* (New York: Farrar, Straus and Giroux, 2012).

3 See, for example, Chapter 9 in Elizabeth Anderson's *Value in Ethics and Economics* (Cambridge: Harvard University Press, 1993).

4 See, for example, Debra Satz, *Why Some Things Should Not Be for Sale: The Moral Limits of Markets* (New York: Oxford University Press, 2010).

5 Prostitution Law Review Committee, *Report of the Prostitution Law Review Committee on the Operation of the Prostitution Law Reform Act 2003* (Wellington: Ministry of Justice, 2008).

6 *Jacobellis v Ohio* 378 U.S. 184 (1964), accessed June 2, 2017, http://robinmorgan.net/activism.

7 Parliamentary Counsel Office, Films, Videos and Publications Classification Act 1993, accessed June 2, 2017, http://www.legislation.govt.nz/act/public/1993/0094/latest/DLM312895.html.

8 Ibid., Pt 3, s 3.

9 John Stuart Mill, 'On Liberty,' in *Utilitarianism, Liberty and Representative Government* (London: J. M. Dent and Sons, 1947), 75.

10 Joel Feinberg, *Offense to Others: The Moral Limits of the Criminal Law* (Oxford: Oxford University Press, 1985).

11 http://www.robinmorgan.net/activism/.

12 See, for example, a meta-analysis by Gert M. Haid, Neil M. Malamuth, and Carlin Yuen, 'Pornography and Attitudes Supporting Violence Against Women: Revisiting the Relationship in Nonexperimental Studies,' *Aggressive Behavior* 36 (2010): 14–20.

13 Berl Kutchinsky, 'Pornography and Rape: Theory and Practice? Evidence from Crime Data in Four Countries Where Pornography is Easily Available,' *International Journal of Law and Psychiatry* 14, nos 1–2 (1991):47–64.

14 See Appendix A in Andrea Dworkin and Catherine MacKinnon, *Pornography and Civil Rights: A New Day for Women's Equality* (Minneapolis, Minn: Organizing Against Pornography, 1988).

15 Sherif Girgis, Ryan T. Anderson, and Robert P. George, *What Is Marriage? Man and Woman: A Defense* (New York, NY: Encounter Books, 2012).

16 For an example of this type of argument, see Girgis et al., *What is Marriage?*, Chapter 3.

17 See, for example, Cheshire Calhoun, *Feminism, the Family, and the Politics of the Closet: Lesbian and Gay Displacement* (Oxford: Oxford University Press, 2000), Chapter 5.

18 See, for example, Cheshire Calhoun, 'Who's Afraid of Polygamous Marriage? Lessons for Same-Sex Marriage Advocacy from the History of Polygamy,' *San Diego Law Review* 42 (2005): 1023–1042. Also Elizabeth Brake, 'Recognizing Care: The Case for Friendship and Polyamory,' *Syracuse Law and Civic Engagement Journal* 1, 2014, http://slace.syr.edu/issue-1-2013-14-on-equality/recognizing-care-the-case-for-friendship-and-polyamory/.

6

Inequality

STEPHEN CHADWICK

Introduction

In 2017 the charity Oxfam published a study, *An Economy for the 99%*, which showed that the eight richest men in the world have the same combined wealth as the poorest half of all global citizens.[1] In terms of corporations it was found that the world's 10 largest have an aggregate revenue greater than that of the governments of 180 countries combined. These countries are, relatively speaking, extremely poor. It is estimated that over 10 per cent of the global population, over 760 million people, live on less than $20 per week.[2]

There are various causes of this poverty. In some cases history plays an important part, as many of the poorest countries are former colonies which were exploited and plundered by their colonisers. When many of these countries, such as Nigeria and Uganda, gained independence, they were left with weak and corrupt governments, which led to the exploitation of the poor. Weak government can also lead to deficient rule of law, which consequently stifles economic investment. Political violence, caused by international and civil wars as well as general lawlessness, likewise limits economic development. In fact, in this case there can be a vicious circle, for violence can breed poverty and, conversely, poverty can be a major cause of violence.

A third cause of poverty in society arises from tax evasion by the richest citizens and corporations. Overseas tax havens are used to avoid paying high tax bills, and so the State loses revenue that could be used to alleviate poverty. It is estimated that over $1 trillion every year is channelled into tax havens from developing economies, both legally and illegally.[3] Fourthly, national debts play a huge part in global poverty, as money that could be used for internal investment to alleviate domestic poverty is instead used to pay back loans from rich countries. Lastly, vulnerability to natural disasters — such as earthquakes, typhoons and tsunami — can have a huge effect on poverty. For example, after the earthquake and tsunami of 2007, 95 per cent of the Solomon Islands' national budget was wiped out.[4]

New Zealand does not face many of these problems. We do not have any internal war and we are not significantly involved in international conflicts. Although we are a former colony, we are one of the few that was not left poor as a result of independence. Our government is stable and, according to Transparency International, we are the second least corrupt country in the world, although we do have a problem with tax evasion.[5] The most likely thing that could lead to poverty in New Zealand is our vulnerability to natural disasters. For these reasons New Zealand is a relatively rich country. It is also true that the poorest New Zealander is relatively well-off in global terms. Due to New Zealand having a welfare system, the poorest citizen has an income of about $200 per week, compared with the lowest 10 per cent of the global population, which has an income of less than $20 per week.

However, although New Zealand as a whole is a relatively rich country, and poverty is not rife, this does not mean that it is free of inequality. According to Oxfam, one-fifth of New Zealand's wealth is owned by the richest 1 per cent, while 90 per cent of the population own less than half.[6] So, while the poorest person in New Zealand has an income of about $200 per week, the richest has a net worth of over $11 billion.

Many interesting questions arise when we consider these statistics. Why has this inequality arisen? Can such inequality be morally justified? Why should the richest person be so much wealthier than the poorest? Do they deserve this wealth? How should wealth be distributed in a just society? In this chapter we will examine these questions.

Property rights

Most people accept that, for there to be a just society, there needs to be property rights and laws to protect them. If someone does not respect my right to private property, by stealing my car, for example, then we believe that I have been unjustly treated and the criminal justice system needs to deal with the perpetrator accordingly.

However, while we may all agree that a just society requires that my property rights be respected, we actually live in a society in which these rights are not absolute. The government, for example, can force me to give up some of my property, in the form of taxation, and if I refuse to do so then I am branded a criminal and I am punished accordingly. Is there any difference between someone taking my car without my consent and the government taking my money, through taxation, without my consent? Some libertarian philosophers do not think there is any difference, and so consider taxation to be a form of theft. The philosopher Murray N. Rothbard writes, 'just as no one is morally required to answer a robber truthfully when he asks if there are any valuables in one's house, so no one can be morally required to answer truthfully similar questions asked by the State, e.g., when filling out income tax returns'.[7]

Nevertheless, even the most libertarian societies in the world do have systems of taxation, and it is obvious why — without some form of income, society could not function, for at the very least money is required for basic infrastructure, defence and the criminal justice system. Without taxation, who would pay for these things? However, the amount that an individual should pay is a point of major disagreement, and it differs from country to country. The highest income tax rate in New Zealand is 33 per cent, whereas in Belgium it is 64 per cent and in Bulgaria it is 10 per cent, and those inclined towards the libertarian position argue for low income taxation.

Libertarians also tend to believe that fairness requires that tax rates should be identical irrespective of income level. Liberalists on the other hand tend to argue that, whatever tax rates are agreed, they need to be proportional to income level in order to ensure that all people in society have a reasonable standard of living. They therefore argue that there needs to be a range of tax rates, which ensures that the richer pay more. This is the current situation in New Zealand, in which, as of 2017, those on the lowest income pay 10.5 per cent while the richest pay 33 per cent.

So how should wealth and benefits be distributed in a just society — that is, what is required for there to be distributive justice? We will attempt to answer this question by examining the theory of justice proposed by John Rawls.

John Rawls and justice as fairness

When we think of what is required in order to live a good life, many different things come to mind depending on what makes us happy. Some people are wedded to smartphones, others require access to beautiful countryside, while some live for watching or playing sport. But there are some things that we all need to enable us to lead a good life, whatever our individual conception of the good life is. These things Rawls calls 'primary goods', and he divides them into two sorts:

- *Social primary goods*: These are those things that are directly distributed by social institutions, such as civil rights, wealth, income, liberties and so on.

- *Natural primary goods*: These can result from one's genetic makeup and include intelligence, imagination, good health and wellbeing.[8]

As it is only social primary goods that can be directly distributed by society (as we are incapable at present of altering people's genetic makeup), it is these goods that must be considered when we are trying to ensure that there is a just distribution of goods within society.

So how should social primary goods be distributed in order for society to be a just one? An initial response might be to say that a just distribution of social primary goods is a distribution in which everyone gets exactly the same. So a just society is a society in which there is complete equality — everyone has the same income, pays the same level of tax, can access the same health care and has the same standard of housing. But in the real world some people want more out of life than others, due to different ambitions, desires, beliefs, motives and so on. Surely it would be unjust to give those who want to work hard all their lives the same level of social primary goods as people who want to spend all their lives sitting on the sofa doing nothing? It seems, therefore, that for there to be distributive justice, society has to allow for inequalities in the distribution of social primary goods.

However, in many societies in which there is great inequality, this inequality is not simply the result of the rich working harder than the poor. For example, during the apartheid era in South Africa it was true to say that all citizens were free to desire whatever they liked. So both a black person and a white person were equally free to desire to become the manager of a large company, and they may have been equally willing to work hard to achieve this. But in reality, however hard a black person worked they would never have attained that social position, and the consequent larger share of wealth, because the position was reserved for white people. So you cannot simply say that inequalities in a society are acceptable because those who work the hardest get the largest share. For if positions within a society are not open to everyone — regardless of race, religious belief, gender, nationality, ethnicity or sexuality — then the resulting unequal distribution of social primary goods will not be just.

Formal equality of opportunity

In New Zealand we accept that this is the case, and so in our society positions are open to everyone, and we call this equality of opportunity. But does a society in which there is equality of opportunity necessarily lead to a just distribution of social primary goods? This depends on the sense in which there is equality of opportunity. When people say of our society that there is equality of opportunity, they mean that everyone has the same right of access to all social positions regardless of their race, gender, ethnic background and sexuality — there is fair competition in awarding social positions. This sense of equality of opportunity is the legal or formal sense: the law ensures that everyone has a legal right of access to all social positions, so no one is discriminated against. So, for example, anybody can apply for the job of a cleaner, just as anybody can apply for a job as a school principal. If an employer does not allow you to apply for the job, or does not give you the job simply because you are a woman or are Māori, for example, then you have the legal right to sue them.

The reason that formal equality of opportunity seems so necessary in society is because we need it to remove the influence of luck with regard to the share of social primary goods we end up with. It is mere chance which gender you are, because you had no control over it — you were simply born that way. Surely the share of social primary goods that you end up with in society should reflect what you deserve; and what you deserve in life should depend on the free choices you make and not on factors that are beyond your control.

The only thing that might stop someone from applying for the post of school principal is a lack of formal qualifications. A school principal is going to need to be a university graduate, and to have teaching experience, and these requirements will be stipulated in the advertisement for the job. As there is formal equality of opportunity in New Zealand, anyone is free to submit an application form, but it will be an idle ritual if you do not fulfil these criteria, because you know beforehand that you will not even get short-listed. The school does nothing wrong by simply discarding your application form, and you have no recourse to complain when you do not get called for an interview. It is simply a matter of fact that you are not qualified for the job and will therefore not be successful; there seems to be no discrimination occurring in this situation.

In New Zealand there is also formal equality of opportunity with respect to education for school children, and by law all children must be formally educated between the ages of six and 16. Education beyond this age is a matter of personal choice. Returning to the example of the school principal, the successful candidate worked hard enough at school to achieve the required grades to enable her to enter university. She then studied diligently and passed her degree exams, and is now reaping the rewards of this hard work by earning over $100,000 a year. The unsuccessful candidate, on the other hand, did not put in the effort at school, and left without any formal qualifications. He was therefore unable to attend university, and is now only qualified to undertake unskilled labour for the minimum wage with an annual salary of $20,000 a year.

The resulting inequality in the wages is surely fair and just, as it simply reflects the past performances of the two workers. The school principal deserves the higher salary because she worked hard to achieve this position. The unskilled worker deserves the lower salary because he did not work as hard. As Will Kymlicka says 'in a society that has equality of opportunity, unequal income is fair, because success is "merited", it goes to those who "deserve" it'.[9]

The social lottery

However, there is obviously something seriously wrong with this argument. If this is all that equality of opportunity means, then it certainly does not deliver a just society. For surely justice requires that everyone has an equal chance of achieving the positions they desire, and in the above example this is certainly not the case.

Let us take two individuals, Andrea and Stephen, who have the same level of natural ability and motivation. Where they differ is that Andrea is from a poor background and Stephen is from a rich background. Have they got the same chance of becoming a lawyer in a society in which there is formal equality of opportunity? As Stephen was born into a rich family, his parents were wealthy enough to send him to a private school. His parents were highly ambitious and could afford to pay for many extracurricular activities. They were also well connected and could therefore arrange work experience for him in the school holidays in a top law firm. Andrea, on the other hand, was born in a low socioeconomic area and went to a decile one state school. Her parents could not afford expensive extras and in the holidays she worked in Pak 'n Save.

As they live in New Zealand, where there is formal equality of opportunity, both Andrea and Stephen have the same legal right of access to higher education and jobs. However, the chance of Andrea being sufficiently qualified to become a lawyer is significantly lower than for Stephen, even though they both have the same innate ability and worked equally hard at school — and this is because they started at different positions on the social ladder. Rawls calls the social circumstances that affect where you start on the social ladder 'social contingencies', and these include such things as wealth, income and the area in which you were born.[10] But these social contingencies are not under your control and are governed purely by luck: there is a *social lottery* in life, and some people are winners and some are losers. Stephen was a winner in the social lottery, because he came from a rich background with well-connected parents. Unfortunately for Andrea, she was one of the losers. And this outcome had a significant effect on the distribution of wealth they ended up with as adults.

Fair equality of opportunity

As we saw earlier, the reason that formal equality of opportunity seems so necessary in a fair and just society is because it is required in order to remove the influence of luck on the share of social primary goods you end up with. It is pure luck which race, gender or religion you are, and this luck should not affect your share. However, as we have just seen, due to the social lottery, even with formal equality of opportunity the share of social primary goods you end up with as an adult is still the result of luck and hence not something you deserve. The social contingencies that affect your share are 'arbitrary from a moral point of view'.[11]

In order for the distribution of social primary goods in society to be fair and just, it surely has to be the case that social contingencies must not in any way affect the share you end up with. In reality it is probably impossible to completely remove the effects of social contingencies, but the closer we get to the ideal, the closer we will come to a just distribution of social primary goods.

If it were possible to completely remove the influence of the social lottery on the distribution of social primary goods, it would mean that people with similar natural abilities and motivation would have an equal chance of getting a good job irrespective of their social background. Andrea and Stephen would, therefore, be on an equal footing. Rawls calls this sense of equality of opportunity 'fair equality of opportunity'.[12] As Tim Scanlon puts it:

> fair equality of opportunity . . . requires not only that no one be formally excluded from positions to which special benefits attach, but also that persons with similar talents and inclinations should have similar prospects of attaining these benefits regardless of their initial place in the social system, that is, irrespective of the income class into which they are born.[13]

Affirmative action

So how can we arrange society so that we arrive at a position of fair equality of opportunity? How can we minimise the effect that social contingencies — where you start on the social ladder — have on the level of social primary goods you receive as an adult? One way of doing this is to give extra help to those born into deprived areas. In terms of education this can be achieved by channelling extra State grants and funds to low-decile schools in order to help students from disadvantaged backgrounds achieve excellent qualifications. This will not completely resolve the matter, because other social contingencies, such as parental attitudes, also have a great effect, and these cannot easily be dealt with via government regulation.

In some situations it appears that historical social injustice has a great effect on the social positions that certain people attain as adults, and this seems to be borne out by statistics which show that some sections of the population are underrepresented in jobs and education. For example, in 2012 the number of medical doctors was roughly 50–50 by gender, but in terms of ethnicity only 3 per cent were Māori and 52 per cent New Zealand European.[14]

However, it would be wrong to assume that such figures are necessarily the result of historical unfair treatment. For example, in

2016, 73 per cent of school teachers were female, while only 27 per cent were male.[15] Studies show that this is mainly due to the fact that this type of job simply does not appeal to as many men as women. The underrepresentation of men in the teaching profession does not, therefore, seem to be a consequence of unfair treatment and discrimination. In the medical profession, the situation might be different. Are there proportionately fewer Māori doctors because this type of job is less appealing to them than it is to Pākehā? Or does this instance of underrepresentation reflect historical discrimination? If it is the latter, how should it be tackled in a fair and just society?

In 2013 a study showed that the proportion of the population with a Bachelor's degree or higher was 9.1 per cent for Māori and 18.6 per cent for New Zealand European.[16] Given that becoming a doctor requires such a degree it is no surprise that there are proportionately fewer Māori doctors. The reasons for these statistics are far too complex to discuss here, but it is certainly the case that social contingencies play an important role. Of particular importance is the socioeconomic position into which an individual is born, as those from deprived backgrounds are less likely to achieve a higher degree than those from more affluent backgrounds. The chance that you are born into a low socioeconomic area, and attend a low-decile school, is far higher if you are Māori than if you are New Zealand European, and, as we have seen, this is simply a matter of luck — it is not under your control where you were born.[17]

In addition to providing more funds to deprived areas and low-decile schools, another way of addressing underrepresentation in the workplace is to adopt policies of affirmative action. In terms of higher education, this can involve setting aside particular funded places for specific minorities. For example, the University of Otago offers Tū Kahika scholarships in Health Sciences that are open only to Māori.[18] These scholarships provide financial assistance and extra support to the successful applicants, with the aim of ensuring that more Māori enter the medical profession.

A similar initiative is run by Massey University. The Pūhoro STEM Academy is aimed at addressing Māori underrepresentation in the sciences in general. Through government and private funding, some Māori pupils, in Years 11 and 12 at schools mainly in the Manawatū region, are given extra academic support and activities to encourage engagement with the sciences. As these pupils leave school, ongoing educational and social support will be provided to help their transition to university and throughout their degrees.

Underrepresentation can also be addressed at the level of employment, via employers adopting policies of preferential selection. Under such a policy, certain jobs are open only to people from particular backgrounds, such as Māori. These jobs will not, therefore, be given to an New Zealand European if there is an equally well-qualified Māori applicant.

Such affirmative action, or positive discrimination, is commonplace in New Zealand society, and is recognised in both the Human Rights Act and the New Zealand Bill of Rights Act. According to the New Zealand Human Rights Commission, these Acts:

> recognise that to overcome discrimination positive actions may be needed to enable particular groups to achieve equal outcomes with other groups in our society. These positive actions are . . . not discriminatory if they assist people in certain groups to achieve equality. Any special measure must be based on information that shows that the present position is unequal.[19]

But surely these measures are discriminatory, albeit implemented for noble reasons? For such measures mean that someone gets a job not only based on ability but also because of a morally arbitrary factor —

their ethnic background or gender — and this is something that they possess by virtue of luck. As we have seen, fair equality of opportunity requires that positions be open to everyone irrespective of luck, and so, on the face of it, such positive discrimination seems to run contrary to this and is therefore unjust.

So can affirmative action, or positive discrimination, be morally justified? Is it fair to discriminate against people, by virtue of their ethnic background or gender, even if the intentions are good? It can be argued that there are times when factors such as ethnic background and gender are actually relevant qualifications, and in these situations policies of preferential selection are surely acceptable. For example, it does seem fair to shortlist only women for the job of playing a female character in a film. A man may be equally talented, but being a woman is not in this case morally arbitrary as it is a required qualification for the role. However, in a situation where a man or a woman, or a Māori or New Zealand European could do a job equally well, things are morally problematic. It certainly seems grossly unfair to the individual who is deprived of the possibility of a job simply because they are New Zealand European or a man.

However, such positive discrimination, while running contrary to the fair equality of opportunity principle on a local level, may be justified in terms of social utility and by producing greater equality of opportunity for society in general. Society as a whole can benefit in many ways from a diverse workforce. Young people need role models and mentors so that they can see what is possible if they work hard. If Māori-only selection processes can help to bring this about, then, from a societal point of view, this can only be a good thing.

Diversity in the workforce is also needed from the point of view of service users. For example, in situations where familiarity with Māori concepts such as rangatiratanga or kaitiakitanga is advantageous, or where fluency in the language of an immigrant population is essential, then surely preferential selection has to be justified? Likewise, for a service such as the police force to function effectively, it requires the employment of officers from all cultural and ethnic backgrounds in order to win the trust and respect of everyone in the community. Similarly, many people are only comfortable consulting a GP of their own gender, and so having a similar number of male and female doctors in the medical profession is advantageous. (Although this argument could also be used against diversity — for example, in a racist society it could justify not employing doctors from an ethnic minority because few in society are comfortable visiting them.)

So, it seems that, although factors such as ethnicity, gender and sexuality are simply a matter of luck, and are not therefore things you deserve, there is a strong argument for sometimes taking them into account for the sake of social utility and to help accomplish greater fair equality of opportunity. However, once representation in the workplace does reflect the demographics of society as a whole, justice requires that such policies of preferential hiring be dropped.

The natural lottery

So far we have seen that for there to be a just society there has to be fair equality of opportunity. We have also seen that to achieve this might require us, in the short term, to adopt policies of affirmative action in order to address issues of historical social injustice, as well as to ensure that societal demographics are reflected adequately in the workforce. But does this mean that when we have achieved a situation of fair equality of opportunity we will have a just society? Rawls thinks not, and it is easy to see why if we reconsider why fair equality of opportunity was required in addition to formal equality of opportunity.

We saw that a just society does not result from having formal equality of opportunity alone, because the distribution of social primary goods that results from it is decided by the social lottery — i.e. morally arbitrary social contingencies, such as where you start in life, how wealthy your parents are, the town in which you are born. These greatly affect your share, but are the result of luck and not something you deserve. We also saw that fair equality of opportunity, on the other hand, is superior, because it removes the effects of these morally arbitrary social contingencies from influencing the distribution. It means that everyone with similar abilities has an equal chance of achieving positions in society, and the consequential wealth, regardless of their initial place in the social system.

But there is still a problem here, because other factors, over and above social contingencies, hugely affect what job you can achieve. Earlier we saw that, for Rawls, there are two sorts of primary goods that we require in order to lead a good life: social and natural. So far we have only concerned ourselves with the social primary goods, which include civil rights, wealth, income and liberties. We must now turn our attention to the natural primary goods, which are those that result largely from our genetic makeup, and include such human characteristics as intelligence, talents, imagination, physical strength and ability, and propensity to some diseases. Because to a large extent we are born with them, Rawls calls them 'natural endowments'.[20]

Consider this example of two rugby players, Lenny and Dylan. Both Lenny and Dylan were born into middle-income households in the same town, and attended the same school. Both boys were crazy about rugby, and their parents encouraged this interest and financially supported their attendance at after-school rugby practice. Lenny and Dylan were extremely motivated to succeed, trained equally hard and were chosen to play for the school team. Unfortunately for Dylan, however hard he tried he was just not as good at playing the game as Lenny, and when Lenny was chosen to play for his provincial side, Dylan was left to play for a small local team. Ten years later, Lenny now plays for the All Blacks, earning over $1 million a year, while Dylan is a mechanic, earning $40,000 a year, and only plays rugby for an amateur team on a Saturday afternoon.

In this story neither boy was discriminated against on the basis of ethnicity, and they were both subject to the same social contingencies; that is, they were equally lucky in the social lottery. The only difference between them was that Lenny was born with a natural talent for playing rugby whereas Dylan was not. There is therefore a *natural lottery* which we all face at birth, and this lottery determines what natural talents we have. As with the social lottery, what we receive in this natural lottery is beyond our control and is a matter of luck. Lenny was simply lucky that he was born with a level of athletic ability that led to him becoming an All Black. Dylan, on the other hand, was lucky that he was born with technical acumen, and so was able to become an excellent mechanic. It is just unfortunate for Dylan that in New Zealand society All Blacks get paid up to 50 times more than mechanics.

What this shows is that even in a society in which there is both formal and fair equality of opportunity, 'distributive shares are decided by the outcome of the natural lottery; and this outcome is arbitrary from a moral perspective'.[21] Given that natural endowments are just as much a matter of luck as social contingencies, how can the inequalities that arise from them be fair and just? Surely Lenny does not deserve to be born with the ability to play rugby to a high level any more than Dylan deserves to be born with the ability to be a good mechanic? So, surely neither deserves to get paid more than the other, and so any inequality in wealth is unfair and not justifiable? There seems no more reason to permit the distribution of primary social goods (wealth and income) to be settled by the outcome of the natural lottery (skills and intelligence) than by the outcome of the social lottery (historical and social fortune).

So how can we deal with this issue of natural endowments? However hard I train, if I do not have excellent hand–eye coordination, then I will never make a good rugby player, and, unfortunately for me, this is not a property that can be taken from one person and given to another. Given that natural endowments cannot be redistributed, does it mean that distributive justice is impossible and hence it is impossible to have a just society? Rawls does not think so.

The reason we feel that the inequalities in society are unjust is that they arise from morally arbitrary factors — social contingencies and natural endowments. The influence of social contingencies can be removed (theoretically) by fair equality of opportunity. Although the unjust influence of natural endowments cannot be removed directly (because we cannot take them from one person and give them to another), it could be reduced if natural endowments are not only to the advantage of the individual who has them, but are also to the advantage of society as a whole — that is, if natural endowments are treated as common assets. In this case, the fact that Dylan was unlucky in the natural lottery will not matter, because he will benefit from Lenny's luck anyway.

This all seems to lead us back to where we started. If inequalities in wealth unfairly arise because some people are born into better positions in society and with greater natural endowments, then surely the only fair way to distribute wealth is to ensure that everyone gets an equal slice of the pie? We could, for example, ensure that All Blacks players receive the same rate of pay as mechanics. However, if we do this we might find that everyone in society is worse off. For some people might not bother using their natural endowments to their full potential if they know they will earn no more than they would leading a lazy life, and this might be detrimental to society as a whole.

However, Rawls thinks that we do not have to accept a situation of total equality for there to be a just society. For if having a social system in which some people do earn more than others makes everyone in society better off, then surely this is acceptable? In order to show this is the case, he proposes an ingenious thought experiment called the 'original position'.[22]

The original position and the veil of ignorance

Rawls asks us to imagine a hypothetical situation, the 'original position', in which people have to decide what principles of social justice should govern their society. Furthermore, the people in this position are to choose these principles from behind a 'veil of ignorance'.[23] This veil of ignorance conceals from them factors that are arbitrary from a moral point of view. So, first, it prevents them from knowing the social and historical factors that may affect them, such as where they will be born, how rich their parents will be, which school they will attend and so on (social contingencies). Second, it conceals from them any personal characteristics they might have, such as talents, intelligence and level of motivation (natural endowments). Thus, it conceals from everyone how they will fare in the social and natural lotteries. It does not, however, conceal basic truths about what all people want in life, as well as facts about the natural world, science, psychology and economics. Rawls thinks that an original position arranged like this is a fair and impartial point of view from which to choose principles of social justice, and therefore the principles that will be chosen by people in this position will be unbiased, fair and just.

To see why this is the case, let us assume that three of our earlier characters — Lenny, Andrea and Dylan — are in the original position. They are to decide how wealth should be distributed in their society. As they are choosing behind the veil of ignorance, none of them knows who they will be when the veil is raised. They are offered the following three possible distributions of wealth and are asked which distribution they would like in their society.

Distribution	Person A	Person B	Person C
i	60	8	1
ii	3	3	3
iii	7	6	5

Distribution 'i' is tempting because, if they happen to be person A when the veil is raised, they will be, relatively speaking, extremely wealthy. But in this distribution they have just as much chance of being person C, in which case they will be in abject poverty. Surely then the rational thing to do is to choose distribution 'ii'. In this distribution there is total equality, so whoever they turn out to be when the veil is raised they will not be disadvantaged. However, on reflection it is obvious that choosing distribution 'iii' is the most rational. Although there is inequality in this distribution, the worst-off person — person C — has more than they would have had in either of the other situations. Rawls, therefore, argues that Lenny, Andrea and Dylan would choose the distribution that maximises the share of wealth that the poorest in society would end up with, because, from behind the veil of ignorance, they do not know whether it will be them who ends up in that situation.

So, what this shows is that in the original position, in which Lenny does not know he will have the background and ability to become an All Black, Dylan does not know that his forte will be fixing cars, and Andrea does not know she will be born into a poor family, they would all actually agree on how wealth should be distributed in their society. Once all of these factors, which are simply the result of good or bad luck, are hidden from them, they would choose a society which allows for inequality in wealth, so long as it maximises what the person in the worst-off position gets. Rawls calls this the 'difference principle'.[24]

The principles of justice

Rawls actually thinks that two principles of justice would be chosen by people in the original position. He thinks that for a society to be fair and just it should be governed by the following principles:

1. Each person is to have an equal right to the most extensive basic liberty compatible with a similar liberty for others.
2. Social and economic inequalities are to be arranged so that they are both:
   (a) reasonably expected to be to everyone's advantage (the difference principle) and
   (b) attached to positions and offices open to all (fair equality of opportunity).[25]

The second of these principles concerns the distribution of social primary goods. The first part of it is, as we have just seen, known as the 'difference principle'. It ensures that natural endowments are common assets, and are therefore not only to the advantage of the person who has them, but are also to the advantage of everyone in society. The second part of the second principle is the 'fair equality of opportunity' principle. This ensures that social contingencies do not unfairly advantage some members of society. Taken together, Rawls believes they remove the influence of morally arbitrary factors on the distribution of social primary goods. Thus, they minimise the unfair outcomes of the social and natural lotteries.

The liberties he is referring to in the first principle are political and social liberties, such as voting rights, and freedom of speech, conscience and thought. This first principle of justice is, however, lexically prior to the second one, which means it must be fulfilled before the second one is applied. This is to ensure that people do not sacrifice liberty for economic benefit. So, for example, even if the least advantaged would be economically richer if they lost freedom of speech and the right to vote, Rawls thinks this would be unacceptable. For Rawls, a just society requires a fair distribution of social primary goods, but must also enshrine political rights and liberties.

Conclusion

The theory of justice put forward by John Rawls is, of course, just one among many that have been proposed by philosophers, and many objections have been raised against it. But on the whole it does seem to fit well with many of our intuitions. So, if we accept Rawls's theory, does this show that New Zealand is a just society? Certainly Rawls's first principle of justice, regarding political and civil liberties, is well entrenched within our society. We enjoy fair elections, there is freedom of speech, conscience and thought, and the press is relatively free.

With respect to the second principle of justice, things are less clear. It is true that we have a social security system and subsidised health care for those in society who are worse off, and the money that pays for this does partly come from those with higher incomes via taxation. However, is there sufficient redistribution of wealth from the rich to the poor to truly satisfy the difference principle? As we saw earlier, one-fifth of New Zealand's wealth is owned by the richest 1 per cent, while 90 per cent of the population own less than half. Furthermore, the poorest person in New Zealand has an income of about $200 per week, while the richest has a net worth of over $11 billion.

The difference principle states that inequalities are justified so long as they benefit the worse-off members of society, and, given that the richest person is paying tax, some of which goes towards helping the poor, then on the face of it the difference principle is being satisfied in New Zealand. But let us compare three different distributions of wealth that all satisfy the difference principle:

Distribution	Person A	Person B	Person C
i	200	10	3
ii	100	11	7
iii	50	12	10

Although all three of these distributions satisfy the difference principle, it would be rational for someone in the original position to choose distribution 'iii'. This is because this is the one that maximises the share of wealth of the least well-off in society. On Rawls's theory, people in the original position would choose levels of taxation that would maximise the wealth of the poorest in society. Now, taxing the rich too much might mean that those best capable of undertaking a particular job do not do it because the job is too stressful for the level of remuneration. Furthermore, they might move overseas to a country with lower tax rates. Neither of these scenarios is advantageous for society as a whole and, consequently, for its worse-off citizens. But there will be an optimum scenario where society still fully utilises the natural endowments that its citizens possess, and also avoids its citizens from relocating overseas, but where wealth is distributed more fairly in accordance with the difference principle. For example, would rugby players be any less likely to want to play for the All Blacks if they earned half their current salary? Would the person who has a net worth of $11 billion be just as useful for society if his worth was only $6 billion?

To achieve a fairer distribution of social primary goods, strict tax laws and enforcement measures would be required, so long as these did not sacrifice the political liberties enshrined in the first principle of justice. Whatever levels of tax would be needed to achieve a fairer distribution is a matter of debate, but it is highly likely that New Zealand could function just as well as it does at present with more social primary goods — whether it is wealth or health care — being distributed from the rich to the poor. Doing so would further minimise the unfair advantages that result from the chance outcomes of the social and natural lotteries.

One final thought concerns the international domain. At the start of this chapter we were presented with some horrifying statistics about global inequality. We saw that it is estimated that over 10 per cent of the global population, over 760 million people, live on less than $20 per week. In this chapter we have seen that where you are born in New Zealand is a matter of luck, because it is beyond your control. We have seen that it also has a significant effect on the distribution of the social primary goods that you receive as an adult, and for there to be a just society its influence on this needs to be minimised. We have also seen that adopting the difference principle goes some way to addressing this. Now, with respect to the international domain, which country you are born in is also a matter of luck and therefore beyond your control. In global terms, New Zealanders have all been lucky in the social lottery, because even the poorest person has access to social benefits. The citizens of many other countries have been unlucky, and as a result live in abject poverty. Does this mean that there also needs to be a difference principle that applies on a global level? If it does, then this would oblige us, as a society, to share a large proportion of our wealth with the poorest people in the world.

---

1 Oxfam, *An Economy for the 99%*, accessed January 9, 2017, https://www.oxfam.org/sites/www.oxfam.org/files/file_attachments/bp-economy-for-99-percent-160117-en.pdf.

2 The World Bank, *Understanding Poverty*, accessed January 9, 2017, http://www.worldbank.org/en/topic/poverty/overview.

3 Max Bearak, *How Global Tax Evasion Keeps Poor Countries Poor*, accessed June 15, 2017, https://www.washingtonpost.com/news/worldviews/wp/2016/04/08/how-global-tax-evasion-keeps-poor-countries-poor/?utm_term=.63a636154f72.

4 Délice Williams, 'What are the Causes of Poverty?', accessed January 15, 2017, https://borgenproject.org/what-causes-global-poverty.

5 Transparency International, *Corruption Perceptions Index*, accessed January 15, 2017, http://www.transparency.org/news/feature/corruption_perceptions_index_2016#table.

6 Oxfam, *An Economy for the 99%*.

7 For example, Murray N. Rothbard, *The Ethics of Liberty* (New York: New York University Press, 1998), 65.

8 John Rawls, *A Theory of Justice* (New York: Oxford University Press, 1971), 62.

9 Will Kymlicka, *Contemporary Political Theory* (New York: Oxford University Press, 2002). 58.

10 Rawls, *A Theory of Justice*, 12.

11 Ibid., 71.

12 Ibid., 83.

13 T. M. Scanlon, 'Rawls' Theory of Justice,' in *Reading Rawls*, ed. Norman Daniels (Stanford: Stanford University Press, 1989), 192.

14 Medical Council of New Zealand, 'The New Zealand Medical Workforce in 2012,' 22, 29, accessed February 15, 2017, https://www.mcnz.org.nz/assets/News-and-Publications/Workforce-Surveys/2012.pdf.

15 Ministry of Education, 'Education Counts,' accessed March 5, 2017, https://www.educationcounts.govt.nz/statistics/schooling/teaching_staff.

16 Lisa Marriott and Dalice Sim, 'Indicators of Inequality for Māori and Pacific People,' 14, accessed January 20, 2017, http://www.victoria.ac.nz/sacl/centres-and-institutes/cpf/publications/pdfs/2015/WP09_2014_Indicators-of-Inequality.pdf.

17 John Gerritsen, 'Lack of Pākehā in Low-decile Schools Worries Principals,' accessed February 12, 2017, http://www.radionz.co.nz/news/national/326806/lack-of-pakeha-in-low-decile-schools-worries-principals.

18 University of Otago Māori Health Workforce Development Unit, 'Tū Kahika: A Health Sciences Scholarship Programme for Māori,' accessed January 25, 2017, http://www.otago.ac.nz/mhwdu/tukahika.

19 Human Rights Commission, 'Positive Actions to Achieve Equality,' accessed February 12, 2017, https://www.hrc.co.nz/enquiries-and-complaints/faqs/positive-actions-achieve-equality.

20 Rawls, *A Theory of Justice*, 12.

21 Ibid., 74.

22 Ibid., 18.

23 Ibid., 19.

24 Ibid., 75.

25 Ibid., 302.

7

Whānau Ora
Transforming Health and Wellbeing

KRUSHIL WATENE, TIM ROCHFORD AND NATALYA TAMARIKI[1]

Introduction

Te Tiriti o Waitangi (Te Tiriti)[2] is a formal agreement made in the interests of peace and friendship between Māori chiefs and the British Crown.[3] Te Tiriti affirmed, and committed to upholding, the mana, tino rangatiratanga and tikanga of Māori — recognising the system of laws that had existed prior to the arrival of colonial settlers.[4] For representatives of the British Crown, however, the Treaty of Waitangi (the Treaty),[5] detailed the cessation of sovereignty by Māori over Aotearoa New Zealand to Queen Victoria. The assumptions underpinning the Treaty — assumptions regarding State sovereignty, authority, ownership — silenced, oppressed and marginalised the Māori ways of knowing, being and doing that had been affirmed and protected by Te Tiriti.[6] Māori elders, activists and scholars have continued to assert that Māori never ceded sovereignty — that Māori never relinquished their mana, tino rangatiratanga and tikanga.

Central to this scholarship and activism have been movements concerned with transforming (social, political, economic) institutions in ways that nourish and privilege Māori concepts and values.[7] The pursuit and realisation of the self-determination of Māori has been intimately bound up with — among other things — the revitalisation of Māori philosophies. The capabilities of Māori communities to be able to define who they are, and to pursue and realise lives they value, is bound up with the extent to which Māori are able to articulate and appropriately apply and reapply their concepts and values to their lives and futures.

The importance of self-determination is reinforced by the United Nations Declaration on the Rights of Indigenous Peoples.[8] Outlining minimum standards 'for the survival, dignity and well-being of the indigenous peoples of the world',[9] the declaration recognises the need for protections from such things as, for instance, assimilation, discrimination and forced removal from traditionally owned lands. The declaration includes the right to participate in, and consent to, any decisions which affect indigenous peoples, the right to control (and have returned) traditionally owned lands and natural resources, the right to the recognition and enforcement of treaties and agreements made, and the right to revitalise 'histories, languages, oral traditions, philosophies, writing systems and literatures'.[10] Together, these rights enable indigenous peoples to be self-determining — that is, to 'freely determine their political status and freely pursue their economic, social and cultural development'.[11]

The aim of this chapter is to explore one of the ways that Māori have set out to articulate, pursue and realise their self-determination in the area of health. The chapter does this by exploring the Māori health policy Whānau Ora. This chapter begins by tracing the policy journey that has resulted in Whānau Ora, providing the historical context in which Whānau Ora sits. The chapter then explores the philosophical foundations of Whānau Ora, and shows how it resonates with — but also differs from — the capability approach to wellbeing, development and justice pioneered by Nobel Laureate Amartya Sen. The chapter concludes with a discussion of some of the insights that Whānau Ora provides mainstream philosophy.

Whānau Ora: The policy journey

Māori social structure is community-based — focusing on whānau (family), hapū (sub-tribal) and iwi (tribal) affiliations. The fundamental importance of relationships and connections is set out in Māori creation narratives, which place people, non-human animals, environmental landscapes and objects within a genealogical framework.[12] In so doing, the Māori world emphasises the centrality of 'whakapapa' or 'genealogical layering' for understanding our relationships with each other and the natural world.[13] By providing an account of the connections and relationships between people and all things, states of affairs are framed in a relational way. From this starting point, connections and relationships are central to wellbeing. Health is intimately bound up with social, cultural and environmental relationships. Whānau, hapū and iwi are themselves sites of health and wellbeing. Healthy whānau relationships foster good health in whānau members.[14]

A significant component of the colonisation of Māori was the deliberate undermining of the structural importance of whānau.[15] The individualisation of Māori land title made possible the sale and purchase of Māori land, resulting in the widespread breakdown of whānau and hapū.[16] The physical disconnection from lands and natural resources impacted on the life and capabilities of Māori communities. The imposition of the English language and of policies preventing the Māori language from being spoken in schools exacerbated this disconnection.[17] Many Māori were forced to move away from ancestral marae communities in search of the economic stability and opportunities available in urban centres.[18] Today, less than 6 per cent of New Zealand's total land area remains under collective ownership.[19] The majority of tribal descendants live outside of their tribal areas.[20] Around 20 per cent of Māori speak the Māori language.[21] Māori have, on average, the poorest health status of any ethnic group in New Zealand.

The Māori response to colonisation (and the damage of colonisation) has been built around whānau, hapū and iwi. The development of the Māori Women's Health League and Māori Women's Welfare League are examples of an organised response from Māori to the challenges of being on the periphery of the colonial state.[22] Despite these efforts, for nearly 150 years Crown policy remained steadfastly hostile to recognising the structural bones that shaped and defined the Māori world. The Crown began to review its position as part of a reconsideration of the role of the Treaty of Waitangi after 1984.[23] The Treaty of Waitangi was incorporated into legislation in the State Owned Enterprise Act 1986, and in a number of subsequent Acts. A set of principles that summarised the legal place of the Treaty was established by the High Court in 1987. Further consideration was given to the place of the Treaty by the Royal Commission on Social Policy in 1988.[24]

The result of this reconsideration of the Treaty of Waitangi included recognising iwi and hapū as the legitimate representatives of Māori in the resolution of past grievances. As such, iwi and hapū (and their representative entities) were the appropriate bodies to receive and redistribute compensation and establish a partnership.[25] This new sense of partnership required Crown agencies to reconsider their relationship with Māori, and established processes of consultation with Māori to review the effectiveness of government departments in their delivery of services to Māori.

One of the most comprehensive was *Pūao te Ata Tu* for the Department of Social Welfare. Led by John Rangihau, this document identified significant failings in the work of Social Welfare with Māori as a form of institutional racism.[26] The report made a number of recommendations to improve the effectiveness of services for Māori, and included the following objectives:

> To attack all forms of cultural racism in New Zealand that result in the values and lifestyle of the dominant group being regarded as superior to those of other groups, especially Maori, by:
>
> (a) Providing leadership and programmes which help develop a society in which the values of all groups are of central importance to its enhancement; and
>
> (b) Incorporating the values, cultures and beliefs of the Maori people in all policies developed for the future of New Zealand.[27]

Further recommendations included specific references to whānau, including 'the funding of specific family and community welfare projects and initiatives'.[28] The Act was to be reviewed having regard to the following principles:

> (i) . . . in the consideration of the welfare of a Maori child regard must be had to the desirability of maintaining the child within the child's hapu;
>
> (ii) . . . whanau/hapu/iwi must be consulted and may be heard in Court of appropriate jurisdiction on the placement of a Maori child.[29]

The health sector was also challenged over the persistent disparities in health status and unequal access to health services of Māori to non-Māori. Māori-led challenges to the health sector included academic research around disparities and questions of cultural safety to be more effective and culturally appropriate in its response to Māori health needs. Māori developed health models that sought to broaden the bio-medical paradigm that dominates health services and policy. The most widely used was Tā Mason Durie's Whare Tapa Whā, which required health services, when working with Māori, to consider emotional, whānau and spiritual concerns as well as their physical pathologies.[30] The development of cultural safety, where health workers are expected to recognise the cultural needs of patients as part of professional practice, was introduced to nurses' training by Dr Irihapeti Ramsden.[31]

These challenges were based on longstanding concerns Māori communities had with the way health care was delivered to them. These concerns were clearly expressed during the health reforms of the early 1990s, which gave local iwi and Māori communities opportunities to engage with the regional health authorities (RHAs).[32] To provide guidelines for the four RHAs in 1992, the Crown outlined its objectives for Māori health in 'Whāia te Ora Mō te Iwi'.[33] This included an expectation that health funders supported developing Māori health services and ensured that all services were culturally appropriate. To help health services respond, Te Puni Kōkiri (the Ministry for Māori Development) organised 'Te Ara Ahu Whakamua' a gathering of hundreds of participants at Ōhinemutu Marae in Rotorua. The deliberations were summarised by Lorna Dyall, and included the following (among other things):

> What policies should be put in place to achieve healthy Māori?
>
> Delegates advocated policies that are developed by Māori for Māori, [and] that empower whānau, hapū and iwi.
>
> The importance of strengthening the whānau.
>
> Delegates agreed that a greater commitment was needed to ensure the strength of the core institutions of Māoridom — particularly the whānau. It was within the whānau that health status was determined and mana born.[34]

In 1994 the Public Health Commission (PHC), the Crown entity responsible for the development of population health policy at the time, produced 'He Matariki' which was a response to an extensive consultation with Māori communities. The PHC had previously set targets based on age groupings which required an individualised approach.

The Māori response was that this was inappropriate, and suggested targets and programmes around whānau instead.[35] 'He Matariki' expressed this view, and went further by stating that 'the Māori view of public health focuses on empowering whānau to take responsibility for their needs'.[36] 'He Matariki' was expanded to discuss examples of how Māori communities and Māori health services had empowered whānau in *Whāia te Whanaungatanga: Oranga Whānau*.[37] Whānau empowerment was also central to Te Pae Māhutonga, Tā Mason Durie's model for achieving healthy Māori communities in the new millennium.[38]

An integral part of these developments was the importance of autonomy and leadership for Māori, both as individuals and collectives. It was placing the autonomy and leadership of whānau at the centre of health policy that led to the adoption of He Korowai Oranga: The Māori Health Strategy by Associate Minister of Health the Hon Tariana Turia in 2002.

> He Korowai Oranga places whānau at the centre of public policy. It challenges us to create environments that are liberating and enable whānau to shape and direct their own lives, to achieve the quality of life Māori are entitled to as tangata whenua [people of the land] in Aotearoa/New Zealand.
>
> At the heart of He Korowai Oranga is the achievement of whānau ora, or healthy families. This requires an approach that recognises

> and builds on the integral strengths and assets of whānau, encouraging whānau development.
>
> He Korowai Oranga provides a framework for the public sector to take responsibility for the part it plays in supporting the health status of whānau. This includes public policies that actively promote: whānau wellbeing, quality education, employment opportunities, suitable housing, safe working conditions, improvements in income and wealth, and addressing systemic barriers including institutional racism.[39]

Despite the intentions of He Korowai Oranga, the purchasing policies of health and social services were increasingly focused on specific outputs around the provision of individual responses to specific problems. This created difficulties for those services taking a holistic approach to responding to whānau with complex social issues. A number of longstanding whānau-centred Māori providers struggled to meet their contractual requirements in such a reductionist environment.

Without sufficient resource or understanding to deal with the complex real-world problems of whānau, support services focused on isolated problems. For whānau, this meant they could not respond to the unrealistic expectations of services, and became passive in the face of uncomprehending institutions.[40]

In 2008 the incoming National Government reached an agreement with the Māori Party that included the establishment of a Taskforce on Whānau-Centred Initiatives, which was to report on how best to promote such initiatives. The report, released in 2010, became the basis for an approach to policy rather than a specific programme. That policy, Whānau Ora, is an approach to health and wellbeing underpinned by the following principles:

Ngā Kaupapa Tuku Iho: the ways in which Māori values, beliefs, obligations and responsibilities are available to guide whānau in their day-to-day lives.

Whānau Opportunity: all whānau will have chances in life that will enable them to reach new heights, do the best for their people, engage with their communities and foster a strong sense of whanaungatanga — connectedness.

Best Whānau Outcomes: the success of Whānau Ora interventions is measured by increases in whānau capacities to undertake those functions that are necessary for healthy living, and shared contributions to the wellbeing of the whānau as a whole, as well as the wellbeing of whānau members.

Coherent Service Delivery: recognises a unified type of intervention so that distinctions between services provided by health, welfare, education and housing, for example, are not allowed to overshadow wider whānau needs.

Whānau Integrity: acknowledges whānau accountability, whānau innovation and whānau dignity. This principle assumes that a code of responsibility is present in all whānau, though it may sometimes be masked by events or circumstances that propel whānau into survival mode or trigger a defensive reaction.

Effective Resourcing: underlines two important aspects of services to whānau. First, the level of resourcing should match the size of the task — whānau-centred approaches may initially be time intensive. Second, resourcing should be tied to results. Effective resourcing means allocating resources in order to attain the best results and

> an intervention plan should include a set of indicators that can measure successful outcomes.
>
> **Competent and Innovative Provision**: recognises a need for skilled practitioners who are able to go beyond crisis intervention to build skills and strategies that will contribute to whānau empowerment and positive outcomes.[41]

As Amohia Boulton and colleagues point out, Whānau Ora is at once a philosophy, practice and outcome.[42] Whānau Ora is grounded in Māori values, in the importance of capacities and opportunities, and in the value of autonomy and responsibility. Health policy and service delivery ought to be designed to enable these things. In order to achieve this, and thus as a model of practice, Whānau Ora calls for integrated service provision, for relevant and measurable outcomes, and for strengths-based processes and strategies. Services ought to be whānau-centred; that is, they ought to 'focus on the whānau as a whole, build on whānau strengths and increase their capacity'.[43] As an outcome, Whānau Ora is about the support of whānau members (individuals) and whānau units (collectives) to 'undertake those functions that are necessary for healthy living'.[44]

Although the taskforce report recognises that results are likely to vary between whānau because of differing needs and aspirations, they also contend that support services should provide whānau with the best opportunity to be: (1) self-managing, (2) living healthy lifestyles, (3) participating fully in society, (4) confidently participating in te ao Māori (the Māori world), (5) economically secure and successfully involved in wealth creation, and (6) cohesive, resilient and nurturing.[45] Whānau Ora is an inclusive, culturally anchored approach to providing whānau-centred services that highlights at least two broad ways in which services can be better placed to achieve these outcomes. First, by supporting whānau (through services or direct funding) to increase whanaungatanga, they can build resilience, self-reliance and take control of their own destiny. Second, by service and organisational transformation, they can deliver integrated whānau-centred services.

The policy journey that has resulted in Whānau Ora is a journey marked by the revitalisation of Māori ways of framing health and wellbeing. Whānau Ora is centrally about the pursuit and realisation of self-determination for whānau, and of empowering whānau to flourish. Our overview provides insights into the various steps that Māori have taken to rebuild Māori health in ways that benefit Māori, and reflects the ongoing struggle for self-determination.[46]

A great deal has been written about how Whānau Ora has been applied and implemented within whānau and health service design and delivery in Aotearoa New Zealand.[47] Reports focus on whānau outcomes, the insights that Whānau Ora brings to services, and the achievements of the policy for the lives of whānau members. Comparatively little has been written that explores the philosophical foundations of Whānau Ora, and that explores the unique contributions that this policy is able to bring to our ideas about health, wellbeing and justice.

In what follows, we explore the foundations of Whānau Ora within a capability framework — emphasising the way that Whānau Ora resonates with the capability approach in theory and practice. Our discussion highlights two important points. First, that Whānau Ora is an innovative approach that resonates with important movements elsewhere. Whānau Ora resonates with wellbeing and development thinking that is becoming more and more widespread globally. Second, that Whānau Ora nonetheless stands on its own foundation. Whānau Ora is the result of social and political struggle, grounded in the hopes and aspirations of Māori communities.

Theorising Whānau Ora: insights from the capability approach

The capability approach tells us that the extent to which people are able to live the kinds of lives they value and have reason to value ought to be the focus of such things as wellbeing, development and justice.[48] Policies and practitioners should focus on the kinds of lives that people actually live (our functionings), the kinds of lives that people are able to live (our capabilities), and the extent to which people are truly able to live lives they value (our freedom).[49] The capability approach contends that we should think about wellbeing and development in terms of people's lives, recognising the full range of activities and diversities that shape our experiences. In so doing, the capability approach attempts to give us the tools to understand wellbeing within a population in terms of people's capabilities. The theory posits that the freedom to achieve wellbeing is of central normative importance, and that wellbeing ought to be understood in terms of capabilities.[50]

For leading proponents of the capability approach, such as Amartya Sen and Martha Nussbaum, the predominant accounts of wellbeing — those that focus on income, the possession of some bundle of goods, or preference satisfaction — are flawed.[51] What matters is not our level of income or some bundle of goods, but the difference that this income or these goods make to our lives. What matters is not merely having our preferences satisfied, but what we are capable of doing and being, and thus involves the conditions in which our preferences are shaped. The capability approach is put forward as a way of addressing and rectifying our currently accepted wellbeing frameworks, which seem to lack attention to people's actual lives. Within a capability framework, health is not understood just in terms of physical pathologies, but also deals with how people feel, and with what people are able to do and be.[52]

According to a recent New Zealand study on health capabilities in older age, based on interviews with people aged between 63 and 93 years old, we need to move 'towards a more nuanced version of health which includes the role of social structure, unequal incomes, spatial contexts and social provisions'.[53] Our ability to convert goods into valuable capabilities is shaped by a range of factors — social, political, environmental, cultural, individual and collective. By framing health in terms of capabilities to be healthy, the capability approach recognises that many things impact on our ability to live healthy lives.

The capability approach can be found in a range of policy documents in Aotearoa New Zealand. For instance, the New Zealand Treasury paper 'Living Standards, Wellbeing and Public Policy' sets out the landscape in which the Treasury is attempting to incorporate the capability approach explicitly into its policy decisions.[54] In addition, the Ministry of Social Development's Living Standards research works to 'develop a comprehensive description of the living standards of New Zealanders using non-income measures of material well-being and hardship'.[55] The Ministry of Social Development's Community Investment Strategy further contends that:

> [. . .] people have complex lives with a range of families and whānau, cultural health and financial issues that can mean they feel powerless, depressed, and out of control. We learnt that a strengths-based model that is focused on a client's aspirations and goals will assist in building long term independence.[56]

The Māori Potential Approach and Whānau Ora, both of which ground innovations and transformations in Māori health policy in Aotearoa New Zealand, are arguably examples of policies and ideas that resonate most with the capability approach to health in both theory and in practice.[57] Whānau Ora is an approach to health in the vein of people-centred approaches to wellbeing, development and justice that aim to transform people's lives.[58] We glimpse this in the following excerpt from the recent independent report:

> Whānau-centred, strengths-based and aspirational focused initiatives are evident across a range of domains such as education, leadership, enterprise and job creation and provide a range of pathways and opportunities for whānau to build their capability and realise their aspirations.[59]

Additionally, Whānau Ora acknowledges that in order to better understand Māori health needs we must understand Māori ideas about health, including the experiences of Māori within the current health system, and the range of enablers and obstacles there are to the pursuit and realisation of health and wellbeing for Māori. In line with this thinking, and in order to better understand whānau experiences and priorities, extensive consultation with over 5000 whānau and families has taken place. Understanding how these priorities are able to shape policy and service design and delivery is fundamental.[60]

Indeed, there seems to be a great deal that Whānau Ora shares with the capability approach. Whānau Ora is about whānau capabilities, the kinds of lives that whānau members are able to live, and the role that policies and services play in shaping them. Whānau Ora is about what whānau are able to do and be, what whānau aspire to do and be, and what whānau value for themselves. Whānau Ora values the agency and self-determination of whānau units, the capabilities of whānau members to live lives they value, and the function of whānau relationships in enabling agency. Drawing out these connections further, we explore two interdependent parts of Whānau Ora. First, we explore the list of 'whānau capacities' developed by Tā Mason Durie.[61] We then (second) explore the role of 'whānau navigators' for building whanaungatanga and whānau transformation towards the pursuit and realisation of whānau needs and aspirations.

WHĀNAU CAPACITIES

If whānau relationships, self-determination and empowerment are important, then we need to know what features of whānau units should be the focus of policy. One answer to this question is provided by Tā Mason Durie, who remains at the forefront of the development of Māori health frameworks and the application of Māori values to health policy. Durie provides a list of 'whānau capacities' that ought to be nurtured, and that are constitutive of an enabling whānau environment. The capacities on his list express core Māori values, and exist at the collective level. They are about the ways in which whānau units ought to operate to achieve health and wellbeing for their people.

> The capacity to care, **manaakitanga**, is a critical role for whānau especially in respect of children and older members. Care also entails the promotion of lifestyles that are consistent with tikanga Māori, maximum well-being, mobility and independence, full participation in society, and reciprocated care for other whānau members. The best outcome is one where whānau members have a strong sense of identity, feel well cared for, are able to enjoy quality lifestyles with a sense of independence, yet remain concerned about the wellbeing of other whānau members.
>
> The capacity for guardianship, **pupuri taonga**, expects whānau to act as wise trustees for the whānau estate — whenua tūpuna (customary land), heritage sites such as fishing spots, environmental sites of special whānau significance, urupa and wāhi tapu. A desirable outcome is one where whānau assets increase in value and whānau members are actively involved in decision-making.
>
> The capacity to empower, **whakamana**, is a whānau function that facilitates the entry of members of the whānau into the wider

community, as individuals and as Māori. The whānau might be the gateway into the marae, or into sport, or to school, or to work. A good outcome is one where whānau members can participate fully, as Māori, in te ao Māori (the Māori world) and te ao whānaui (wider society), and whānau are well represented in community endeavours.

The capacity to plan ahead, **whakatakato tikanga**, requires a capacity to anticipate the needs of future generations and to manage whānau resources (human and physical) so that those needs may be met. A good outcome will be one where systems are in place to protect the interests of future generations and whānau have agreed-upon broad strategies for further whānau development. The capacity to promote culture, whakapūmau tikanga, is a further whānau function. It depends on the capacity to transmit language, cultural values, narratives, song, music and history. A good outcome is one where whānau members have access to the cultural heritage of the whānau, are both fluent in te reo Māori, knowledgeable about whānau heritage, and actively support the whānau as the major agent of cultural transmission.

The capacity for consensus, **whakawhānaungatanga**, reflects the need for whānau to develop decision-making processes where consensus is possible and collective action strengthened. In order to reach consensus there must be opportunities for contributions to a shared vision and processes that enable whānau to take decisions in a way that is fair and consistent with tikanga. Strong interconnectedness within the whānau and better overall results is a desired outcome of consensual capacity.[62]

The centrality of capabilities is clearly demonstrated by this list. The list paints a picture of the kind of internal operations or capabilities that are constitutive of an enabling whānau environment. That is, the list represents those things that whānau units ought to be able to do and be, in pursuing and realising Whānau Ora. The list reinforces the importance of relationships and of being able to work together, to aspire, to meet needs, to plan for the future, and to navigate te ao Māori and te ao Pākehā. As with Whānau Ora generally, the list is an expression of self-determination. The list of whānau capacities can be framed as capabilities and as starting points for a discussion of relevant local indicators of whānau wellbeing.

This list, however, also highlights at least two important differences between Whānau Ora and the capability approach. First, Whānau Ora is centrally about what whānau as collectives are able to do and be — providing insights into how we ought to think about capabilities. Recent work on the idea of collective capabilities is useful for bringing ideas about whānau to bear on discussions of community wellbeing. For instance, economists Vijayendra Rao and Michael Walton's contention that collectives can 'create an enabling environment to provide members with the tools and the voice to navigate their way out of poverty' help to frame some of the ways that whānau might be thought about.[63] Within the capability literature, however, ideas around collective capabilities remain underdeveloped. Second, Whānau Ora is grounded in Māori concepts and ideas. The foundation of whānau is intimately connected to place. Lands and natural resources provide the context for Māori values. Such a view does not sit well with the capability approach.[64] While the capability approach may be useful for explaining and framing some of the foundations of Whānau Ora, ultimately Whānau Ora stands on its own foundation. Whānau Ora moves us beyond the conceptual terrain of the capability approach.[65]

WHĀNAU NAVIGATORS[66]

Additionally, and in line with the capability approach, transforming the lives of whānau and cultivating these capabilities require a range of knowledge and expertise from within the community. In its initial stages, Whānau Ora provided health and social service collectives with the opportunity to decide how best to improve the lives of communities by providing the opportunity to develop a programme of action (POA). This process required service providers to reflect on their current processes and practices, and to move away from viewing people as passive recipients of programmes, to being actively engaged and involved in improving and creating those services. This led service providers to rethink and to change the way they interacted with people. It led those involved in services to think about services from the experiences and the perspectives of whānau, and to prioritise those experiences in the re-development of services. This enabled the organisation to develop systems for better service provision, simply because it mandated staff to open their minds to collaboration and innovation.

Central to the pursuit and realisation of these POAs are 'navigators', a dedicated workforce whose role it is to (1) build relationships with whānau and support whānau planning, and (2) build collectivism between services by creating communities of support services around whānau needs and aspirations. The navigator role centres on a whānau planning process — a process where whānau meet with a navigator to talk about their needs and aspirations, and where (over time) a pathway is charted towards whānau-defined goals. In their roles, navigators are central to whānau empowerment and transformation. Navigators provide a range of support to whānau by providing entry points to, and guidance through, services. Navigators support whānau to become actively engaged, to build capabilities, and to create pathways forward based on self-defined aspirations.

Additionally, navigators transform services and the provider collective. The navigators utilise existing services, and contribute to the growth of new services within the collective. With their knowledge of whānau needs and aspirations, navigators are able to reinforce the services that the providers offer. Navigator relationship-building within the collective is able to break down barriers to collectivism, create collaborative pathways, and increase the likelihood that a transformation towards interdependence and collectivism is possible. Navigators are able to weave services and (often) unconnected providers much closer together.

The navigator's role is, however, in large part, defined by whānau — by their self-defined needs and aspirations, and by their current situations. The abilities and opportunities that are relevant for whānau depend on the abilities and opportunities that whānau value — and depend on what it is that will enable whānau to achieve or access them. Enabling whānau may require advocacy, confidence-building, planning, opportunities for new experiences, connecting with wider whānau networks, or the creation of broader social networks. Navigators support whānau to develop the autonomy and leadership that is the nexus of Te Pae Māhutonga. When whānau have developed this leadership, they have been able to take control of their own lives and become defined by who they are and their aspirations, and not as some pathology or statistic.

Our discussion of Tā Mason Durie's whānau capacities, and of the role of navigators in the pursuit of Whānau Ora, highlights both the uniqueness of Whānau Ora itself and the various ways in which Whānau Ora can be said to resonate with the theory and practice of the capability approach. Whānau Ora is about nurturing valuable capacities within whānau groups, as well as about creating social services and systems that make the achievement of Whānau Ora possible. Whānau Ora is concerned with nurturing internal collective capabilities (such as the capacity to empower, and the capacity to care), as well as creating the external conditions relevant for the full expression of these capacities (services, agencies, funding systems).

Similarly, Whānau Ora is grounded in Māori concepts and the fundamental importance of the self-determination of whānau. There are many things that contribute to the lives of whānau, many of which may matter in themselves, and there are many ways to formulate and pursue Whānau Ora. The challenge is to develop policies and services that are useful for and relevant to people's lives, and thus to develop policies and services able to capture, and create space for, the diverse ways to achieve Whānau Ora.

Conclusion

Our discussion of Whānau Ora provides us with a number of lessons for philosophy. First, the articulation of Māori philosophy, and the application of that philosophy to the lives of Māori communities, is vital to the pursuit and realisation of self-determination. Whānau Ora is intimately bound up with Māori ideas about health and wellbeing, and with the creation of space in which Māori can be self-determining. There is much we can learn from these ideas, particularly about the importance of relationships, collective wellbeing, the multiple ways in which whānau can flourish, and the centrality of spiritual and environmental wellbeing.

Second, Whānau Ora — in line with the capability approach — teaches us that our theories of wellbeing, development and justice are incomplete. The incompleteness and complexity of Whānau Ora recognises the diverse challenges and opportunities that exist within the human experience. What matters (ultimately) is the application of our theories to people's lives. The challenge, then, is to engage with the voices of the people and communities on the ground, to better understand how our theories can be drawn out from, and transformed by, people's lived experiences, and to learn from practitioners and interdisciplinary engagement. Indeed, Whānau Ora requires a commitment to work across disciplinary and organisational boundaries in order to improve the lives of people and the policies which shape the conditions in which people are able to live.

Philosophers have an important role to play not merely in theorising concepts central to policy, but also in contributing to conversations that provide ways of articulating and applying policy most usefully to people's lives. We can do this, at the very least, simply by creating space for the appropriate articulation of Māori philosophies. More proactively, we can do this by acknowledging the importance of Māori philosophies, and the significant roles that researchers, practitioners, policymakers and communities themselves must play in shaping the ideas that ground social policy. We can go further by acknowledging this diverse range of expertise by proactively seeking out ways to engage with it. We can go further still by committing to engaging in ways that serve to reframe the theories we develop, and by shaping our theories in ways that are more useful and more relevant for people's lives.

The policy journey towards Whānau Ora helps us to see that our ideas, the frameworks that we use and our commitments have a role to play in creating or limiting the space in which Māori philosophies are able to flourish. Whānau Ora helps us to see that our theories of wellbeing, development and justice are at their strongest when they are able to make room for the voices of all of the communities that make up our social landscapes. The continued relevance of our theories of wellbeing, development and justice depends on the extent to which we are willing to acknowledge our diverse philosophical landscapes, and celebrate the role that they play in shaping our nation.

1 Krushil Watene is the lead author, responsible for the chapter overall. Tim Rochford led section 2. Natalya Tamariki co-led with Watene section 3. We wish to acknowledge Brandon Young who was a Massey University research scholar over the summer of 2016/17. The project explored the use of the capability approach in New Zealand policy. The authors draw on this important research in section 3.

2 Written in te reo Māori.

3 Waitangi Tribunal, *Ko Aotearoa Tēnei: Te Taumata Tuatahi (Wai 262)* (Wellington: Legislation Direct, 2011); Waitangi Tribunal, *Ko Aotearoa Tēnei: Te Taumata Tuarua (Wai 262), volume 2* (Wellington: Legislation Direct, 2011); Margaret Mutu, 'Te Tiriti o Waitangi in a Future Constitution: Removing the Shackles of Colonisation,' 2013 Robson Lecture, 22 April 2013, accessed May 29, 2017, http://www.converge.org.nz/pma/shackles-of-colonisation.pdf; Ranginui Walker, *Ka Whawhai Tonu Matou / Struggle Without End* (Auckland: Penguin, 2004); I. H. Kawharu, 'Mana and the Crown: A Marae at Orakei,' in *Waitangi: Maori and Pakeha Perspectives of the Treaty of Waitangi*, ed. I. H. Kawharu (Auckland: Oxford University Press, 1989), 211–233.

4 Mutu, 'Te Tiriti o Waitangi'.

5 Written in the English language.

6 McCully Matiu and Margaret Mutu, *Te Whānau Moana: Ngā Kaupapa me Ngā Tikanga: Customs and Protocols* (Auckland: Reed, 2003); Mutu, 'Te Tiriti o Waitangi'; M. S. Mutu, 'Custom Law and the Advent of New Pākehā Settlers: Tuku Whenua Allocation of Resource Use Rights,' in *Huia Histories of Māori: Ngā Tāhuhu Kōrero*, ed. D. Keenan (Wellington: Huia Publishers, 212), 93–108; Moana Jackson, 'The Colonisation of Māori Philosophy,' in *Justice, Ethics, and New Zealand Society*, ed. Graham Oddie and Roy Perrett (Auckland: Oxford University Press, 1992), 1–10.

7 Matike Mai Aotearoa, 'He Whakaaro Here Whakaumu Mō Aotearoa: The Report of Matike Mai Aotearoa — The Independent Working Group on Constitutional Transformation,' accessed May 29, 2017, http://www.converge.org.nz/pma/MatikeMaiAotearoaReport.pdf; Linda T. Smith, *Decolonizing Methodologies: Research and Indigenous Peoples* (London: Zed Books, 1999); Taskforce on Whānau Centred Initiatives, *Whānau Ora: Report of the Taskforce on Whānau-Centred Initiatives*. Report produced for Hon Tariana Turia, Minister for the Community and Voluntary Sector (Wellington: Ministry of Social Development, 2010); Mason Durie, *Ngā Kāhui Pou: Launching Māori Futures* (Wellington: Huia Publishers, 2003).

8 United Nations Permanent Forum for Indigenous Issues 2007 (UNPFII), 'United Nations Declaration on the Rights of Indigenous Peoples' (UNDRIP), 2007, accessed May 29, 2017, http://www.un.org/esa/socdev/unpfii/en/drip.html.

9 Ibid.

10 Ibid., art 13.

11 Ibid., art 3.

12 Rev. Māori Marsden and Te Aroha Henare, 'Kaitiakitanga: A Definitive Introduction to the Holistic Worldview of the Maori,' unpublished paper, 1992; Rev. Māori Marsden, *The Woven Universe: Selected Writings of Rev. Māori Marsden* (Ōtaki: Estate of Rev. Māori Marsden, 2003).

13 Merata Kawharu, 'Kaitiakitanga: A Maori Anthropological Perspective of the Maori Socioenvironmental Ethic of Resource Management,' *Journal of the Polynesian Society* 110(4) (2000): 349–370; Marsden, 'Kaitiakitanga'; Marsden, *The Woven Universe*; Matiu and Mutu, *Te Whānau Moana*; Hone Sadler, 'Mātauranga Māori (Māori Epistemology),' *International Journal of the Humanities* 4 (2007): 1–16.

14 Krushil Watene, 'Indigenous Peoples and Justice,' in *Theorizing Justice: Critical Insights and Future Directions*, Krushil Watene and Jay Drydyk (London: Rowman and Littlefield International, 2016), 133–152; Krushil Watene, 'Valuing Nature: Māori Values and the Capability Approach,' in *Oxford Development Studies* (Special issue: Indigenous Peoples and Human Development), published online January 5, 2016, accessed May 29, 2017, http://www.tandfonline.com/doi/full/10.1080/13600818.2015.1124077.

15 Taskforce, *Whānau Ora*; Smith, *Decolonizing Methodologies*; Waitangi Tribunal, *Ko Aotearoa Tēnei: Te Taumata Tuatahi* ; Waitangi Tribunal, *Ko Aotearoa Tēnei: Te Taumata Tuarua*; Donna Awatere, *Maori Sovereignty* (Auckland: Broadsheet, 1984); Walker, *Ka Whawhai Tonu Matou*; Mason Durie, *Te Mana, Te Kāwanatanga: The Politics of Māori Self-determination* (Auckland: Oxford University Press, 1998).

16 Kawharu, 'Mana and the Crown'; Ian Hugh Kawharu, *Maori Land Tenure: Studies of a Changing Institution* (Oxford: Clarendon Press, 1997); D. V. Williams, 'Māori Social Identification and Colonial Extinguishments of Customary Rights in New Zealand,' *Social Identities: Journal for the Study of Race, Nation and Culture* 13(6) (2007), 735–749; Mutu, 'Custom Law'.

17 Margie Hohepa, 'Te Reo Māori and Schooling,' in *Maranga Mai! Te Reo and Marae in Crisis?* ed. Merata Kawharu (Auckland: Auckland University Press, 2014), 103–127.

18 Paul Tapsell, 'Tribal Marae: Crisis? What Crisis?' in *Maranga Mai! Te Reo and Marae in Crisis?* ed. Merata Kawharu (Auckland: Auckland University Press, 2014), 35–64.

19 Tanira Kingi, 'Maori Land Ownership and Land Management in New Zealand,' in *AusAID, Making Land Work Volume two — Case Studies on Customary Land and Development in the Pacific* (Canberra: AusAID, 2008), 129–152.

20 Statistics New Zealand, 'Te Kupenga 2013 (English) — Corrected,' accessed May 29, 2017, http://www.stats.govt.nz/browse_for_stats/people_and_communities/Maori/TeKupenga_HOTP13.aspx.

21 Ibid.

22 Erihāpeti Rehu Murchie, *Rapuora: Health and Māori Women* (Wellington: Māori Women's Welfare League, 1984).

23 Awatere, *Maori Sovereignty*; T. O'Regan, 'The Evolution of a Tribe: Issues for an Old Culture in a New Century (address to a Conference of the Consortium of the Humanities, Canberra, Australian National University, 2001); Walker, *Ka Whawhai Tonu Matou*; D. O'Sullivan, 'Needs, Rights, Nationhood and the Politics of Indigeneity,' *MAI Review* 1 (2006), Target Article 1, accessed May 29, 2017, http://review.mai.ac.nz/index.php/MR/article/viewFile/1/1.

24 M. Henare, *Ngā Tikanga me Ngā Ritenga o Te Ao Māori: Standards and Foundations of Māori Society. The April Report: Report of the Royal Commission on Social Policy*. (Wellington: New Zealand Royal Commission on Social Policy, 1988); Mason Durie, *Whaiora: Māori Health Development* (Auckland: Oxford University Press, 1998).

25 Durie, *Whaiora.*

26 The Ministerial Advisory Committee, *Pūao te Ata Tu: The Report of the Ministerial Advisory Committee on a Māori Perspective for the Department of Social Welfare* (Wellington: The Department of Social Welfare), accessed May 29, 2017, https://www.msd.govt.nz/documents/about-msd-and-our-work/publications-resources/archive/1988-puaoteatatu.pdf.

27 Ibid., 9.

28 Ibid., 28.

29 Ibid., 10–11.

30 Durie, *Whaiora.*

31 Irihapeti Ramsden, 'Cultural Safety and Nursing Education in Aotearoa and Te Wai Pounamu.' (PhD thesis, Victoria University of Wellington, 2002).

32 L. Dyall, 'Te Ara Ahu Whakamua: The Pathway Forward — Views of the Hui, Wellington,' *Social Policy Journal of New Zealand* 2 (1994): 3–5.

33 Department of Health, 'Whāia te Ora Mō te Iwi: The Government's Response to Māori Health Issues in the Health Sector' (Wellington: Department of Health, 1992) http://www.moh.govt.nz/notebook/nbbooks.nsf/0/7019FDE27D0901464C2565D700185EC7/$file/WHAIA-TE-ORA-MO-TE-IWI.pdf (accessed May 29, 2017).

34 Dyall, 1994.

35 Public Health Commission, *He Matariki: A Strategic Plan for Māori Health* (Wellington: Public Health Commission, 1994), accessed May 29, 2017, http://www.moh.govt.nz/notebook/nbbooks.nsf/0/2A79228F8756131DCC256ABC0081B7E2/$file/He%20Matariki.pdf.

36 Ibid., 4.

37 Ministry of Health, *Whāia te Whanaungatanga: Oranga Whānau / The Wellbeing of Whānau* (Wellington: Ministry of Health, 1998), accessed May 29, 2017, http://www.moh.govt.nz/notebook/nbbooks.nsf/0/9EC55EFB4D00F4F34C25664000094F71/$file/WHAIA-TE-WHANAUNGATANGA.pdf.

38 Mason Durie, *Te Pae Mahutonga: A Model for Maori Health Promotion.*

(Palmerston North: Massey University, 2000).

39 Ministry of Health, *He Korowai Oranga: The Māori Health Strategy* (Wellington: Ministry of Health, 2002), accessed May 29, 2017, https://www.health.govt.nz/system/files/documents/publications/mhs-english.pdf, iii.

40 H. Waititi, 'Toitū Te Mana Rangatahi: Marae-Based Youth Courts: Negotiating Pathways for Rangatahi Offending' (MSc thesis, Victoria University of Wellington, 2012).

41 Taskforce, *Whānau Ora*, 22, accessed May 29, 2017, https://www.msd.govt.nz/documents/about-msd-and-our-work/publications-resources/planning-strategy/whanau-ora/whanau-ora-taskforce-report.pdf.

42 Amohia Boulton, Tula Brannelly, and Jennifer Tameha, 'Whānau-Centred Health and Social Service Delivery in New Zealand: The Challenges To, and Opportunities For, Innovation,' *MAI Journal* 2, no. 1 (2013): 18–31.

43 Taskforce, *Whānau Ora*, 7.

44 Ibid., 19.

45 Ibid., 38.

46 Ibid.; Durie, *Ngā Kāhui Pou*; Durie, *Te Pae Mahutonga* 2003, 2000.

47 See, for instance: J. Kidd, V. Gibbons, E. Kara, R. Blundell, and K. Berryman, 'A Whānau Ora Journey of Māori Men with Chronic Illness: A Te Korowai Analysis,' *AlterNative: An International Journal of Indigenous Peoples* 9(2) (2013), accessed May 29, 2017, http://journals.sagepub.com/doi/pdf/10.1177/117718011300900202; S. Akroyd, T. Lanumata, N. Wehipeihana, and L. Were, *Formative Evaluation of the Whānau Ora Commissioning Agency Model: An Independent Evaluation Report* (Wellington: Te Puni Kōkiri, 2016).

48 A. Sen, *The Idea of Justice* (London: Penguin Books, 2009); M. Nussbaum, *Women and Human Development: The Capabilities Approach* (Cambridge: Cambridge University Press, 2000); Martha Nussbaum, *Frontiers of Justice: Disability, Nationality, Species Membership* (Cambridge, Mass: The Belknap Press, 2006).

49 S. Alkire, *Valuing Freedoms: Sen's Capability Approach and Poverty Reduction* (Oxford: Oxford University Press, 2002); Ingrid Robeyns, 'Capabilitarianism,' *Journal of Human Development and Capabilities* 17(3) (2016): 397–414; Nussbaum, *Frontiers of Justice*; M. Qizilbash, 'The Capability Approach: Its Interpretation and Limitations,' in *The Capability Approach: Practice and Public Policy in the Asia-Pacific Region* ed. F. Panzironi and K. Gelber (New York, NY: Routledge, 2012), 9–22.

50 Robeyns, 'Capabilitarianism'.

51 Sen, *The Idea of Justice*; Nussbaum, *Women and Human Development;* Nussbaum, *Frontiers of Justice.*

52 S. Venkatapuram, *Health Justice: An Argument from the Capabilities Approach* (Cambridge: Polity, 2011).

53 C. Stephens, M. Breheny, and J. Mansvelt, 'Healthy Ageing from the Perspective of Older People: A Capability Approach to Resilience,' *Psychology and Health*

30(6) (2015): 715–731 at 728–729. doi:10.1080/08870446.2014.904862.

54 U. Mukherjee and D. Weijers, *Living Standards, Wellbeing, and Public Policy* (Wellington: New Zealand Treasury, 2016), http://www.treasury.govt.nz/government/longterm/fiscalposition/2016/ltfs-16-bg-lswpp.pdf.

55 Ministry of Social Development, 'Living Standards Research' (Wellington: Ministry of Social Development), https://www.msd.govt.nz/about-msd-and-our-work/publications-resources/monitoring/living-standards/index.html; B. Perry, *The Material Wellbeing of New Zealand Households: Trends and Relativities Using Non-income Measures, With International Comparisons* (Wellington: Ministry of Social Development, 2016), 1, https://www.msd.govt.nz/documents/about-msd-and-our-work/publications-resources/monitoring/household-income-report/2016/2016-non-incomes-report.docx.

56 Ministry of Social Development, *Community Investment Strategy Update* (Wellington: Ministry of Social Development), 10, http://www.msd.govt.nz/documents/about-msd-and-our-work/work-programmes/community-investment-strategy/community-investment-strategy-update-2016.pdf.

57 Barcham, 'Thinking About Māori Development in Terms of the Capability Approach: The Shift Towards the Adoption of the Māori Potential Approach,' in *The Capability Approach: Development Practice and Public Policy in the Asia-Pacific Region* ed. F. Panzironi and K. Gelber (Oxford: Routledge, 2014), 55–67; Taskforce, *Whānau Ora*; Durie, *Ngā Kāhui Pou.*

58 Boulton et al., 'Whānau-Centred Health'.

59 Akroyd et al., *Formative Evaluation*, p. 33.

60 Te Puni Kōkiri, *Whānau Ora Annual Summary Report* (Wellington: Te Puni Kōkiri, 2016).

61 Durie, *Ngā Kāhui Pou.*

62 Mason Durie, 'Measuring Māori Well-being,' New Zealand Treasury Guest Lecture Series 2006, August 1, 2006, accessed May 29, 2017, http://www.treasury.govt.nz/publications/media-speeches/guestlectures/pdfs/tgls-durie.pdf, 4–5.

63 Vijayendra Rao and Michael Walton (eds), *Culture and Public Action* (Stanford, CA: Stanford University Press, 2004), 361.

64 Watene, 'Valuing Nature'.

65 A. Sen, 'How Does Culture Matter?', in *Culture and Public Action*, ed. V. Rao and M. Walton (Stanford, CA: Stanford University Press, 2004), 37–58; Nussbaum, *Frontiers of Justice.*

66 This discussion is based on the first-hand experiences of Mai Whānau (the Whānau Ora programme undertaken by Ngāti Whātua Ōrākei) by Tamariki and Watene. Tamariki was the Mai Whānau team leader, and Watene led the Mai Whānau research project.

8

The Environment

STEPHEN DUFFIN

Introduction

Environmental ethics attempts to study the value, moral status and relationship between humans and the environment of which they are a part. The challenge has been to overcome the anthropocentric attitude that appears to be embedded within Western thought. This chapter will look at the history of a recent development in New Zealand where a tract of land was granted the rights of a person. The discussion will include both the progress made by philosophers to overcome the Western anthropocentric attitude towards Nature and the Māori views regarding the environment, and show how these two views have influenced this important decision.

Anthropocentrism

The Te Urewera Act of 2014 saw the New Zealand government give up formal ownership of an 821-square-mile section of land in the North Island. Known for its lakes, forests and natural beauty, Te Urewera had been a national park from 1954 until the Act took effect in 2014. From then on the land became a legal entity with all 'the rights, powers, duties and liabilities of a legal person'.[1] Personhood, among other things, means that lawsuits to protect the land can be brought on behalf of the land itself: something similar to the legal status that companies enjoy.

This result is central in the quest to recognise the value and attribution of rights to the natural world. This outcome is all the more surprising given that traditionally, Western ethics has denied any direct moral obligation to the natural environment. Its approach has been human-centred or, as we say, anthropocentric. The words of ancient Greek philosopher Aristotle are typical of this view:

> Plants exist for the sake of animals . . . all other animals exist for the sake of man, tame animals for the use he can make of them as well as for the food they provide; and as for wild animals, most though not all of these can be used for food and are useful in other ways; clothing and instruments can be made out of them. If then we are right in believing that nature makes nothing without some end in view, nothing to no purpose, it must be that nature has made all things specifically for the sake of man.[2]

In the thirteenth century, Thomas Aquinas, a medieval philosopher and theologian, put the issue into a more theological perspective when he said:

> We refute the error of those who claim that it is a sin for a man to kill brute animals. For animals are ordered to man's use in the natural course of things, according to divine providence. Consequently, man uses them without any injustice, either by killing them or employing them in any other way. For this reason, God said to Noah: 'As the green herbs, I have delivered all flesh to you.'[3]

The influential French philosopher René Descartes (1596–1650) also reinforced the view that mankind and Nature are separate and distinct when he argued that all reality is composed of two substances: 'minds' and 'bodies'. The mind, or soul, is non-material and includes all thinking, consciousness and sensations, whereas the body has material qualities and works like a machine. Humans are the only ones that have consciousness, minds or souls. Non-human animals, however, while living and organic, are automatons. This attitude contributed to the notion of a division between humans and the rest of Nature. Descartes' views were persuasive and are still held by many today. It would appear, then, that the Western philosophical tradition has been unfriendly to the idea of moral responsibility towards the environment. But it isn't only the Western philosophical traditions that may have contributed to this anthropocentrism; some also point the finger of blame at Western religious traditions.

In 1967, medieval historian Lynn White Jnr published his influential paper, 'The Historical Roots of Our Ecological Crisis'.[4] White contended that our current ecological crisis is due to the 'orthodox Christian arrogance to nature', which, he argued, is rooted in an anthropocentric attitude traced back to the book of Genesis in the Bible. God tells Adam and Eve to multiply and replenish the earth and subdue it — and have dominion over it (Genesis 1:28). White contrasted the anthropocentric Christian attitude to that of pagan panpsychicism where spirits are believed to be in all things, including inanimate objects. In the pagan worldview, animals, trees and rivers are viewed as sacred, so it is wrong to harm them without good reason and without performing the necessary rituals. Not surprisingly, White's paper caused a bit of a stir. The following two passages from Genesis indicate the attitude that White was concerned with:

> And God said, let us make man in our image, after our likeness: and let them have dominion over the fish of the sea, and over the fowl of the air, and over the cattle, and over all the earth, and over every creeping thing that creepeth upon the earth.[5]

> Be fruitful, and multiply, and replenish the earth, and subdue it: and have dominion over the fish of the sea, and over the fowl of the air, and over every living thing that moveth upon the earth.[6]

From these passages of the Bible it appears as if God has created a moral hierarchy in which humans are superior to Nature.[7]

But White's claim was not that this anti-ecological reading is the only or even the most reasonable interpretation of Christian theology, but that it is the one that had been adopted. His focus, though, was not on how one ought to interpret biblical texts, but rather on how biblical texts have been interpreted in the past.

A year later, Lewis Moncrief, an assistant professor in the department of recreation resources administration of the School of Forest Resources, published his article 'The Cultural Basis of Our Environmental Crisis',[8] which replied to White and suggested that, rather than religion, the nature of capitalism and technology had caused the demise of the environment. While agreeing with White that human ecology is conditioned by our beliefs, he disagreed that religion is the primary conditioner of human behaviour. Rather, he placed the blame on technology, democracy, urbanisation, an increasing individual wealth and an aggressive attitude towards Nature.

In addition to this attitude towards Nature, whether it is caused by religion or culture, we might also consider the labour theory of property. This theory of natural law has been used to justify the acquisition of land whereby a person may gain permanent ownership of an unowned resource by performing an act of original appropriation, such as working the land. In his *Second Treatise on Government*, the English philosopher and physician John Locke (1632–1704) outlines how this can be achieved.

John Locke and property rights

According to Locke, prior to cultivation, land is 'waste' provided by God for use. 'Tis very clear,' he says, 'that God, . . . *has given the Earth to the Children of Men*, given it to Mankind in common.'[9] However, the main concern is how private property arises prior to, and without permission of, all of the commoners. Locke's problem, then, is how the concept of private property can emerge from that which is held in common. Locke justifies his position by saying that:

> God who hath given the World to men in common, hath also given them reason to make use of it to the best advantage of Life and convenience . . . yet being given for the use of Men, there must of necessity be a means to appropriate them some way or other before they can be of any use, or at all beneficial to any particular Man.[10]

God gave the world to men in common; but since it was given to them for their benefit it cannot be supposed that it was meant to remain in common and uncultivated. He gave it to be used by the industrious and rational, and labour was to be their title to it. Locke believes that he can establish a connection between external possessions and the human self by claiming that every man has a property in his own person.

From this it follows that the labour of his body is his, and as a consequence the fruits of his labour also. 'Whatsoever then he removes out of the State that Nature hath provided, and left it in, he hath mixed his *Labour* with, and joined to it something that is his own, and thereby makes it his *Property*.'[11] Thus, by mixing their labours with the earth, persons come to have property: cultivated, and thus improved, pieces of land. The earth remains the property of God, but the labourer has a property in his improvement of it.

It could also be asked why Locke uses labour as the means to appropriation and not something else. Why should it be the case that, just because a farmer in the Waikato cultivates a piece of land, it becomes his? Locke explains it like this: labour is a command from God, for 'God, when he gave the World in common to all Mankind, commanded Man also to labour, and the penury of his condition required it of him.'[12] It may appear that this only gives mankind a duty to labour, not a right to the fruits of its labour. However, God also commands us to preserve our lives, and such preservation can only be achieved by appropriation. Therefore, the right to what we appropriate is necessary to doing our duty, and hence is also the will of God.

His argument looks something like this:

- God gave the world to humanity in common and for its benefit and support.
- Land in common and uncultivated is not of benefit to individuals.
- Therefore, there must be some way of acquiring property, or we would be unable to support ourselves.
- We have property in ourselves (our labour).
- If we mix what is ours (our labour) with land that is held in common, then that land becomes our property.
- Thus, by mixing our labour with the earth we come to have a property: cultivated and thus improved pieces of land.
- Earth remains the property of God, but the labourer has a property in their improvement of it.

There are some difficulties with Locke's account of private property. As the American philosopher Robert Nozick points out:

> This gives rise to many questions. What are the boundaries of what labour is mixed with? If a private astronaut clears a place on Mars, has he mixed his labour with (so that he comes to own) the whole

planet, the whole uninhabited universe, or just a particular plot? Which plot does an act bring under ownership?[13]

Furthermore, why should the mixing of labour with something make one the owner of it? Presumably because one comes to own a previously unowned thing by mixing what is yours (your labour) with it. But as Nozick states: 'why isn't mixing what I own a way of losing what I own rather than gaining what I don't? If I own a can of tomato juice and spill it into the sea so that its molecules mingle evenly throughout the sea, do I come to own the sea, or have I just lost my can of tomato juice?'[14]

Additionally, there is only a limited amount of land, so once some people have acquired land there may not be enough left for others. Locke, however, places some limits on how much property we may take. We must, he says, leave enough and as good for everyone else, and we mustn't take more perishable goods than we can ourselves consume. Locke also believed that there was ample land in the Americas, and in fairness he probably never envisaged the growth in world population. This does highlight another problem, though, for Locke recognised only some uses of land as being legitimate. He would not have thought, for example, that the American Natives were using the land productively, and hence their use of it would not have entitled them to a legitimate claim.

Locke's assertion that land should be used productively is in part due to his abhorrence of anything wasteful. The English theological writer Lady Masham (1659–1708) tells us that Locke's personal attitudes matched his philosophical convictions about waste: 'Waste of any kind he could not bear to see . . . nor would he, if he could help it, let anything be destroyed which could serve for the nourishment, maintenance, or allowable pleasure of any creature.' We know from the same source that Locke abhorred idleness. The idle holding (or destruction) of what could be used by others, then, whether the goods spoil or not, will be morally objectionable. Land, of course, doesn't 'spoil' in any literal sense when it lies unused; the grass may or may not rot on the ground (depending on the climate and the kind of grass). But land can be wasted (for example, by the idle rich) by lying unused.[15]

Historically, uncultivated areas have been viewed as wild and untamed and a threat to human survival. Often cited is the wilderness found within the religious traditions of Judaism and Christianity. Adam and Eve were banished from the Garden to a wilderness with thorns and thistles; Moses, with the Israelites, wandered in the wilderness for 40 years; and Jesus was tempted by Satan in the wilderness. This symbolism implies that the wilderness is not only a dangerous place, but is also home to the Devil.

When the *Mayflower* arrived in the New World in 1620, the settlers are quoted as having found a 'hideous and desolate wilderness'.[16] The wilderness was an area to be avoided: a place that was forsaken by God and home to the Devil. Yet this was a place where they could escape persecution, and so the wilderness now becomes an area to be overcome, cultivated and in a sense returned to its paradisiacal glory. The Lockean model supports this attitude, as wilderness is viewed as a commodity to be exploited for human gain.

One way to help us understand Locke's argument in favour of private property is to consider what he was trying to achieve by it. The rest of the *Second Treatise* deals with limiting the powers of government. Under the medieval view of kingship, all estates of the realm were held by the king, who then gave some to his lords, who in turn passed it on down a chain of feudal loyalties. In theory, land grants could be revoked at the will of the king. Although this was unlikely, Locke removes even the possibility of it happening by reducing the king's power and setting aside property which is privately held and thus unable to be interfered with.

Whether the criticisms of Locke's theory hold or not, there seems little doubt that it has been influential in how we think about land. It is just a commodity, it has no rights of its own, and the owner, so long as they act within the bounds of local and governmental laws, can do whatever they wish with it. Given these sorts of attitudes to the non-human environment, it will be worth looking at how we have managed to move towards a more non-anthropocentric approach that has led ultimately to the granting of personhood to a piece of land in New Zealand.

Moving from anthropocentrism

The idea that the members of other species, and even the land itself, should be treated well only because of the benefit that we, as humans, can derive from them is a familiar one. The New Zealand farmer who fattens lambs has an interest in the lambs being healthy, but it is generally because the farmer wants the best price for the lamb. It is lucky for the lambs that their interests happen to coincide with the farmer's, at least for a while. Briefly put, we can say that according to the farmer the lambs are of instrumental value, but do not have intrinsic value.

Some things are valued purely because they enable us to obtain other things that are valued. Thus we say they are instruments in obtaining items of value. For example, I value money because it enables me to do things that give me pleasure. Thus money possesses instrumental value for me. This is because it is instrumental in the obtaining of something else that I value. For example, I value money as it enables me to buy a bar of chocolate. This seems to be the start of a chain of items of instrumental value. But it seems that this chain must terminate.

Somewhere down the chain we must come to something that is valuable in and of itself. I value the bar of chocolate for the sake of the pleasant experiences that accompany it when I eat it. So the chocolate is also of instrumental value, but the pleasant experience that accompanies it is valued for itself. This pleasurable experience is not valued because of what it leads to. We might say, then, that this experience is valuable in and of itself, and thus is what we call intrinsically valuable, whereas things that are valuable because they lead to something else of value are instrumentally valuable.

So how do these terms apply to the environment? Probably the most fundamental question we can ask with regards to Nature and the environment is this: what should be our attitude towards Nature? People value things in different ways. For example, we may consider the forests as valuable because they are pleasant to look at or because we like to go walking in them. We consider them valuable because they are useful as a means to further ends. They are valuable as instruments rather than being valuable in their own right. In the past we have not generally treated other species and land as intrinsically valuable, but on the whole have viewed them as if they had instrumental value only. We treated them as instruments for the production of other things which we value (food and clothing, for example).

But attitudes are beginning to change. In general, people in New Zealand now believe that other sentient creatures (creatures capable of experiencing pain and pleasure, frustration and satisfaction) have a moral claim on us by virtue of their sentience. For example, most in New Zealand now recognise that it is wrong to inflict wanton and gratuitous pain on at least some sentient beings. Extending our consideration beyond just the human species is an indication that our circle of moral concern is expanding.

Expanding the circle of moral concern

Imagine if we start with the self — it seems natural to think of the self as the most valuable thing in the world, and everything else to be of merely instrumental value. But then we realise the value of other human beings who are close to us — family and friends. Next we extend our moral concern to other human beings. And then, it might be argued, eventually to the members of other species and even to Nature itself.

So what's happening here? What enables us to extend our moral concern in this way? Well, we might reason that the types of things that make *me* valuable are also the same types of things that make my family and friends valuable, and what makes them valuable also makes other beings which are similar to them, in relevant respects, just as valuable. But what is it about us, as human beings, that makes us valuable in the first place?

One answer is simply that we are human beings, members of the species *Homo sapiens*, and it is this membership that makes us valuable. But this answer seems to be lacking. Imagine another species from a different planet that are like us in all relevant respects but with the one exception that they are not members of our species. That is, they are not members of the species *Homo sapiens*. Would it mean that they do not have intrinsic value? It appears that they would have everything it takes to be as equally valuable as us. This suggests that what makes humans valuable isn't just that they are human and thus members of a certain species, but rather it is because they enjoy certain mental states such as rationality, self-consciousness, autonomy, etc. We are now in a position to see that the kinds of states which we recognise to have value and disvalue in human beings (rational, self-conscious, autonomous, etc.) are also shared by other sentient creatures. And so we may feel compelled to include such creatures in the circle of our moral concern.

Beyond sentient creatures, though, there is also non-sentient biological life. Although we might not be able to determine where sentience starts or ends, we can presume that it ends somewhere.

So whether we are prepared to extend our moral concern further is dependent on whether we think that non-sentient biological life has intrinsic value or merely instrumental value. We cannot use the above argument, based on the possession of mental states, to extend our moral concern to non-sentient beings such as plants, forests and ecosystems, so another approach may be required.

Such an approach was given at a conference in 1973. Australian environmentalist and philosopher Richard Sylvan (then Richard Routley) (1935–1996) suggested a thought experiment that helped launch environmental ethics as a branch of philosophy. Sylvan's thought experiment came to be known as the 'Last Man' argument.

His argument, or thought experiment, goes something like this: the last man (or person) alive sets about to destroy and eliminate, so far as he can, every living thing, animal or plant (painlessly if you like). He does this, supposedly, for no other reason than that he can. Sylvan then asks if the Last Man acts wrongly.

Most people intuitively think that the Last Man's behaviour is wrong, yet what he does, according to basic Western anthropocentrism, is quite permissible.

Sylvan argues that the tradition of Western ethics is human-centred (anthropocentric), and thus cannot condemn the Last Man's actions. Nevertheless, on environmental grounds, and according to commonly held intuitions, it is nevertheless wrong.

Here is the argument:

Premise 1. A human action is only wrong if it harms some human being.

Premise 2. The Last Man does no harm to human beings.

Therefore

Conclusion. The Last Man does nothing wrong.

This argument is valid; that is, if its premises are true, then its conclusion must also be true. However, that's not enough; we need an argument that is sound. So in addition to it being valid, its premises must also be true. In this case, if we believe that the conclusion is false, which most people seem to — the Last Man does act wrongly — we must contest at least one of the premises. Sylvan believes that premise 2 is true, and this seems reasonable, for in this thought experiment there are no other humans to harm. So it must be premise 1 that is false. Thus, it is not the case that a human action is only wrong if it harms some human being. Therefore, there are some wrongs that do not harm human beings. Sylvan is now in a position to claim that a new ethic is needed: one that takes into account the non-human element of the environment, and one that recognises that it isn't only human life that has intrinsic value. Sylvan is attempting to move us from a traditional anthropocentric (human-centred) ethic to a non-anthropocentric one.

In 1972, professor of law Christopher Stone argued in his paper 'Should Trees Have Legal Standing?'[17] that we should assign rights to natural objects such as trees and rivers and mountains. Stone's article came about because of a dispute between the Disney Corporation and the American environmental organisation Sierra Club. Disney wanted to build a ski resort in the Mineral King Valley, but the Sierra Club opposed the development and tried to sue the Disney Corporation on behalf of the trees. Stone showed how, over time, the law had moved to a point where rights were now confirmed upon entities and persons that were previously deemed unworthy or incapable of possessing such rights. Women, children, slaves, fetuses, racial minorities and endangered species were all beneficiaries of the drive to give legal rights.

Stone agrees that the idea of granting rights to trees, etc., will be unthinkable to many, but reminds us that at one time the idea of granting equal rights to women, children and black people was also thought, by some, to be unthinkable. The question might also be asked how trees or other natural objects could possibly be represented in law. After all, they are not like people in that they cannot speak for themselves when they feel their rights have been violated. Stone believes that natural objects could be represented in the same way that companies, persons with intellectual disabilities or those in comas are. A legal guardian or representative would be appointed to speak on behalf of the interests of the natural objects. Furthermore, we can know the interests of natural entities with as much certainty as we do in corporate cases. He claims:

> The guardian-attorney for a smog-endangered stand of pine could venture with more confidence that his client wants the smog stopped, than the directors of a corporation can assert that 'the corporation' wants dividends declared.[18]

Despite the efforts in recent years to widen this circle of moral concern, many will argue that, globally at least, we appear to have made little progress in our relationship with Nature. And yet, as previously stated, a piece of land in New Zealand has been afforded personhood. What is it that is different about New Zealand that has enabled this to happen? Here, I believe, we must turn to the beliefs of the indigenous people of New Zealand, the Māori, and their attitude and ethics regarding the land and its ownership.

The Māori view of land

We have seen how the writings of John Locke have influenced the concept of private property and the notion that we can come to own land by working on it and mixing our labour with it. Furthermore, under this Lockean model, once we own land then we are free to do almost anything with it that we wish. It is ours and, apart from our responsibility to other humans, we have no moral responsibility to the land itself.

The Māori people of New Zealand have a different attitude towards the land. They describe themselves as 'tangata whenua' — people (tangata) of the land (whenua). Central to this is that Māori narratives speak of Earth-Mother as their ancestor. This image is reinforced when we discover that whenua refers to the placenta as well as to the land. The Earth is their mother who cares for them and they care for her. This attitude in turn fosters a personal relationship with the Earth.

Although Māori don't have the same concept of land ownership as the West, they do speak of having mana over the land. The English understanding of 'mana' is authority, prestige, power or influence. However, it should be remembered that, as with any translation, there may not be any English words that adequately describe such a thing as 'mana'. It appears, though, that mana over the land (whenua) represents some form of power or authority over the land. This notion is different to ownership as conceived of by Europeans. Indeed, Māori experts declare that ownership of land is not a Māori concept. Thus, Judge Eddie Durie: 'One did not own the land. One belonged *to* the land.' Mana whenua, however, has some of the connotations of land ownership, central to which is the idea of some special status or standing in some specific land.[19]

RESPECT FOR ALL THINGS

According to the New Zealand philosopher John Patterson, within the Māori worldview the people of the land, the tangata whenua, afford respect for all creatures within their lands. Patterson claims that 'part of the authority and power of mana whenua is the ability to see to the well-being of all creatures'.[20] However, it is applicable only in the lands in which one has mana whenua. In this respect, tangata whenua may not have any responsibility outside of the people's own lands. Nevertheless, even though lacking in universality, it seems at least an adequate starting point for an environmental ethic.

Furthermore, aside from this special link that Māori share with the creatures in their particular lands, according to Māori thought we are related to all creatures and are thus responsible for their welfare. 'This means that all of us are responsible for the wellbeing of all creatures, in precisely the ways that kin are responsible for one another, independently of any mana whenua we may have in any particular place.'[21] Such a linking of all creatures through kinship forms a good basis for Māori environmental philosophy.

The roots of this belief in kinship may be attributed to the ancient whakapapa or genealogical tables going back to Ranginui and Papatūānuku, Sky and Earth. After Tāne-Mahuta, one of the sons of Rangi and Papa, had separated Ranginui and Papatūānuku, another son, Tāwhiri, representing winds and storms, turned on Tāne, Tangaroa (the sea god), and Rongo and Haumia (the gods of cultivated and uncultivated food). Only Tū, the war god, was able to pacify Tāwhiri, but in his anger at the other four, who had left him to withstand Tāwhiri on his own, he felt a wish to injure Tāne. Next, Tū took revenge on Tangaroa and similarly on Rongo and Haumia. Having defeated his four brothers of the earth and sea, their offspring were now his food. Unable to defeat Tāwhiri, he remains an enemy of Tū today. Tū, as the god of war, is man, but only the spirit and not the body, for man was not yet made, there being no woman. It was Tāne who was to put this right, not Tū.[22] Although there are different stories as to how Tāne finally acquired a human woman, the most common is that he made one for himself from the soil and breathed into her mouth, thus giving her life.[23]

Even though these myths give a grounding for kinship, it may seem that, rather than giving a feeling of love and care (manaaki) for our kin, these stories could be interpreted to portray an alternative view, one that fosters competition rather than cooperation. It appears that the spirit of man, at least, is in a constant battle with his other brothers who represent Nature and its elements. Furthermore, the only creation of Tāne's that has life breathed into it is that of a human, which suggests a distinct separation between human life and the rest of Nature.

Another, different interpretation may, however, do greater justice to these myths. As is common in many of the creation myths throughout the world, order is seen to arise out of apparent chaos. If these Māori myths are viewed in this way, we may develop a different appreciation. Out of the chaos and warring between the brothers, a balance and harmony arises between them and a respect for each other. This interpretation is similar to that of the Māori writer and academic the late Ranginui Walker: 'Although Tū emerged superior, he was a god made in man's image and likeness, he was neither vanquished nor victorious over Tāwhiri. The elements wage continuous war against man, who in turn has to maintain constant vigilance.'[24] Thus, too, should all things enjoy a mutual respect: the elements, Nature, forests and plant life, and the sea.

Other narratives suggest that kin should protect and care for each other. For example, the motive behind Tāne's action of separating his parents, Earth and Sky, is so that he and his brothers can flourish. Furthermore, he does not leave his parents like this; he covers his mother with trees, and his father he decorates with stars. From this story Patterson concludes that:

> Here is a graphic example of the idea that we should protect our kin, even when great harm has been done. It involves more than protection: the action of decorating the sky with stars illustrates a creative, supportive and caring relation between kin, which is part of what is meant by whanaungatanga. So even when we are forced

to do harm to our kin, if there is scope for recompense and for enhancing their lives we are expected to do this.[25]

If we accept that this idea of kinship is prevalent in Māori thought, it would indeed be a fundamental factor for an environmental ethic that was non-anthropocentric. This point seems to be crucial, because the criticism of the traditional Western viewpoint is that it is centred only on humankind, where other things are valued only for their use to humans, and are thereby considered to have little if any intrinsic value. In Māori thought, all things have a natural sacredness or 'tapu' because they are descended from the gods or 'atua'. By accounting for the tapu of the natural world in terms of mana, Māori find another way to afford respect and intrinsic value to all creatures:

> the tactic is to make use of a link between tapu on one side and mana plus atua on the other, and then come to see the atua as being so intimately linked with the natural world that the mana of the atua can be seen as the mana of the natural world itself. That way, respect for the natural world is seen in terms of respect for the mana of the creatures themselves. To say that a creature has mana in the natural world is very like saying that it has standing, that it is entitled to a place in the world in its own right.[26]

All creatures and even plants and inanimate objects can, according to Māori thought, trace their descent from one or other of the atua. For example, a tree has as its ancestor Tāne-Mahuta so that tree carries with it the mana of Tāne. Furthermore, the relationship between a creature and its atua is not seen as two distinct entities, thus the tree is seen not only as a descendent of Tāne, but simply as Tāne.[27] Regarding all of Nature with tapu, and seeing the creatures as personifications of atua, gives Nature an intrinsic value. Hence, when any act that may be considered harmful needs to be undertaken (such as felling a tree), it must be done with great care and with the use of the appropriate rituals.

THE INTERDEPENDENCE OF ALL THINGS

Another reason why Māori say we should respect the natural world is because each creature has a 'mauri' or life force, and this life force joins all beings — humans, gods, plants and animals, mountains, rivers and seas — into one interdependent whole, each part depending for its wellbeing on the health of each other part and of the whole itself. The Danish historian of religion J. Prytz Johansen describes mauri as a concentration of life, a centre from where it acts and wells out. This life may be either mana concentrated in an object, or it may be life experienced as concentrated in a point in humans.[28]

Patterson notes that mauri is still an important and real part of a traditional Māori world, and cites an example of how a Māori leader, commenting on a proposal to cease discharging sewage into the Manawatū River, states that this discharge has brought about an imbalance of the mauri of the river.[29] If we accept the view that all things, regardless of their value to humans, contain mauri, then this would join all things into one interdependent whole. There is a similarity here to the point made earlier by Lynn White Jnr regarding pagan panpsychicism. In that view, spirits are believed to be in all things, including inanimate objects. Thus, in this pagan worldview, animals, trees and rivers are viewed as sacred, so it is wrong to harm them without good reason and without performing the necessary rituals.

The Māori belief in mauri delivers a similar conclusion. Respect for the forest is reflected in the story of Rātā as he tries to fell a tree for carving into a canoe. After felling the tree he returns the next day only to find that the tree is standing in its original position. He fells the tree again, but the same thing happens the next day, and the next. Eventually, Rātā hides and sees the hakuturi (forest guardians in the form of birds, insects and other life) replanting the tree. When Rātā confronts them, they tell him that he has failed to perform the appropriate rites. After doing so, the hakuturi release the tree.[30] So even though it is recognised that humans must take from Nature to provide for their needs, it is not done without due care and respect for other life.

How Western ethics deals with future generations

Much of the discussion about how we should treat the environment focuses on the effects it will have on those of us that inhabit the planet now. For example, there is concern that rising sea levels will cause severe problems for the low-lying islands in the Pacific region. And while this is important and relevant, we should also ask questions about how our behaviour regarding the environment will affect those who are yet to come. However, traditional Western thought has some difficulty coming to terms with attributing rights to what we call 'future generations'. Take the following by Robert Solow, Nobel Laureate in economics: 'future people . . . we don't know what they will do, what they will like, what they will want. And to be honest, it is none of our business.'[31]

Also the advice from the Bible not to concern ourselves with the things of the future reinforces a view that the future is out of our control so we shouldn't worry about it: 'take therefore no thought for the morrow: for the morrow shall take thought for the things of itself'.[32] For Western philosophers, the problem of obligations to future generations is puzzling; future people do not exist, so how can we have responsibilities to them? Attributing rights to things that don't yet exist is problematic. Generally, when we think of a person as having 'rights' we say certain conditions must apply:

- The rights holder must exist.
- The thing they have a right to must also exist.

It doesn't make much sense to say that Fred has rights when there isn't such a being as Fred. Similarly, if I claim to have a right to something, we assume that that something exists. Properties such as being green, wealthy or having rights can only be predicated on something if it exists. X is Y, or X has Z, or X prefers A only make sense if there is an 'X'. If there is no X, then the proposition is meaningless. If I say that Fred has an excellent stamp collection, it only makes sense if Fred exists.

In the same way that it doesn't make sense to say X has Y when X doesn't exist, it also doesn't make much sense to say X has a right to Y, if Y isn't available or doesn't exist. For example, do you and I have a right to see or touch a dodo? We exist but dodos don't, and before dodos became extinct we didn't exist. Insofar as it is implausible that we have the right to the preservation of live dodos, it is implausible to say that non-existent unborn future generations have any right now to inherit any asset. Even if we argue that the unborn will have rights once they exist, they don't have any now and thus have no claim on us.

Some might argue that reference to the human family has a temporal dimension. But future generations are not members of the human family. They are not members of anything, because they don't exist. We may feel that they are a special class of people waiting in the wings to come onto the stage of life, but the fact is, they are not already out there.

How Māori ethics deals with future generations

Māori hold strong views regarding the notion of kinship, which extends beyond our own species to all things. Patterson says, 'In a society that takes kinship seriously, what an individual is free to do is bound up with the needs and activities of a range of kinship groups.'[33] Even so, as he points out: 'The picture is further complicated, from a European point of view because the kin-group includes ancestors and future generations.'[34] When a formal speech (whaikōrero) is given, Māori always remember their dead. To them the dead are still living in the spirit realm. Accordingly, there is an unbroken link from the gods to past, present and future generations.[35] This linking to future generations through kinship extends not just to humans, but to all things, and has implications environmentally.

The question of whether we should be concerned about future generations is solved within this framework. If kinship extends to the future, then it is assumed that the unborn have a similar standing to those who are living. If this is the case, then all decisions regarding the environment must take into account those generations yet to be born. When we apply this sort of principle to all of our interactions with the natural environment, the results are radical. The idea of respect for mauri fleshes out as the idea that we should respect the essence or character of each creature and of each habitat.

Another Māori concept that benefits future generations and ensures that resources are preserved is the form of tapu or restriction known as 'rāhui'. A particular area might be set aside for a special purpose, such as trees for carving. Access may be restricted to food sources such as fishing grounds, pigeon reserves, wild berries, etc., in order to conserve them for special occasions. Alternatively, an area could be left to lie fallow so that the life and vitality of the land can be replenished and thus provide resources for the future.[36] So while traditional Western moral theory has had some difficulty accommodating the attribution of rights for future generations, Māori, within their framework of extended kinship and rāhui, seem to be more fruitful.

Conclusion

The granting of legal status to a piece of land in New Zealand is a landmark decision. It appears to have come about as the result of a gradual change as philosophers started to think about how we analyse issues relating to the natural world and the need to respond to issues such as global warming. Furthermore, it has become evident that the decisions we make now will have an effect on those future generations that will follow us. This more sympathetic and caring approach to non-human life, coupled with the views held by Māori, has enabled discussion that culminated in the radical decision to grant Te Urewera all 'the rights, powers, duties and liabilities of a legal person'. In 2017, the Whanganui River was also granted legal status similar to that of Te Urewera; it will be interesting to see whether other entities in New Zealand will follow.

---

1 New Zealand Government, Te Urewera Act 2014, Subpt 3, s 11.

2 Aristotle, *Politics,* trans. T. A. Sinclair (Harmondsworth: Penguin Books, 1962), 40.

3 Thomas Aquinas, *Summa Contra Gentiles,* ed. English Dominion Friars (London: Burns and Oates, 1924), Book 3, Pt 2.

4 Lynn White Jnr, 'The Historical Roots of Our Ecological Crisis,' *Science* 155 (1967): 1203–1207.

5 The Bible, King James Version, Book of Genesis, 1:26.

6 Ibid., 1:28.

7 This notion of a hierarchy was a view that dominated Western thought from Plato's time. The Great Chain of Being included everything from God, along with the angels, at the top, to rocks and minerals at the bottom. Those beings of spirit are at the top, and those comprising of matter are at the bottom of the chain. Humans sit somewhere in the middle, being mostly made of matter but with a soul or spirit, and as a result are the highest of earthly creations.

8 Lewis W. Moncrief, 'The Cultural Basis of Our Environmental Crisis,' *Science* 170 (1970): 508–512.

9 John Locke, *The Second Treatise of Government: An Essay Concerning the True Original Extent and End of Civil Government,* ed. Peter Laslett (Cambridge: Cambridge University Press, 1960), chap. V, 25.

10 Ibid., chap. V, 26.

11 Ibid., chap. V, 27.

12 Ibid., chap. V, 32.

13 Robert Nozick, *Anarchy, State and Utopia* (Oxford: Basil Blackwell, 1974), 174.

14 Ibid., 175.

15 A. John Simmons, *A Lockean Theory of Rights* (Princeton: Princeton University Press, 1992), 286–287.

16 William Bradford, 'Of Plymouth Plantation,' in *Excerpts from William Bradford's*

Journal: Of Plymouth Plantation, accessed March 21, 2017, https://www.quia.com/files/quia/users/terri%20delebo/ALLHONORS10/William_Bradford-OF_PLYMOUTH_PLANTATIONL.pdf.

17 Christopher Store, 'Should Trees Have Legal Standing? Toward Legal Rights for Natural Objects,' *Southern California Law Review* 45 (1972): 450–501.

18 Ibid., 471.

19 John Patterson, *People of the Land* (Wellington: Dunmore Press, 2000), 17.

20 Ibid., 25.

21 Ibid.

22 Anthony Alpers, *Māori Myths and Legends* (Auckland: Longman Paul, 1964), 22–23.

23 Some traditions state that he first made a human male, named Tiki, but more often we are told that he first looked for a female.

24 Ranginui Walker, 'The Relevance of Māori Myth and Tradition,' in *Te Ao Hurihuri: Aspects of Māori Tanga,* ed. Michael King (Auckland: Reed, 1992), 172.

25 Patterson, *People of the Land,* 25.

26 Ibid., 54.

27 Ibid., 55.

28 J. Prytz Johansen, *The Māori and His Religion: In its Non-Ritualistic Aspects* (Kobenhavn: Ejnar Munksgaard, 1954), 237.

29 Patterson, *People of the Land,* 64.

30 'Te Ngahere — forest lore,' *Te Ara: The Encyclopedia of New Zealand,* accessed March 22, 2017, http://www.teara.govt.nz/en/te-ngahere-forest-lore/page-1.

31 Robert Solow, 'Sustainability: An Economist's Perspective,' in *Economics of the Environment: Selected Reading,* ed. R. Dorfman and N. Dorfman (New York: W. W. Norton and Company, 1999), 182.

32 The Bible, King James version, Matthew, 6:34.

33 Patterson, *People of the Land,* 41.

34 Ibid., 42.

35 Cleve Barlow, *Tikanga Whakaaro: Key Concepts in Māori Culture* (Auckland: Oxford University Press, 1996), 167.

36 Ibid., 105.

9

War and Peace

MARCEL ZENTVELD-WALE

Introduction

Matters of war and peace are among the most important and enduring problems facing humanity. They are also among the most ethically fraught. The question of when and how to wage war is literally a matter of life and death, the answer to which can determine the fate of entire nations, not to mention the lives of the individual men and women involved or caught up in the conflict. There are no easy answers to this question, which remains a major source of academic and public debate.[1]

While New Zealand may seem far removed from the realities of war, the country has been involved in wars, and debates about war, since its inception. Those wars have left their marks on the country, and have shaped the nation's history and identity. In today's globalised world, the insulating effects of geographical distance have diminished. The communications revolution has brought the horrors of war into our living rooms. Nor are we now mere witnesses to distant wars; in an increasingly interconnected world, wars fought in far-off places can have real consequences for those at home, as the rise of 'home-grown' terrorism graphically illustrates. This chapter explores a number of perspectives on the ethics of war and peace and their relevance to historical and contemporary New Zealand. But before doing so, however, a definition of 'war' and of 'peace' is in order.

DEFINING 'WAR' AND 'PEACE'

The definition of, and distinction between, war and peace is less straightforward than it might initially appear. Strictly speaking, 'war' refers to an acknowledged state of violent conflict between two or more states.[2] But there are exceptions to each of these conditions. There are secret wars, which are unacknowledged; cold wars, in which the antagonists do not engage in violent conflict; and civil wars, which are fought within a single state. 'Peace', which normally refers to the absence or cessation of war, suffers, by extension, from the same ambiguities.[3] Thus, for instance, the Cold War of the twentieth century has been described as 'The Long Peace'.[4]

To add to the confusion, the term 'war' has been used by governments to describe their efforts to combat various perceived evils, including the 'war on poverty', the 'war on crime', the 'war on drugs' and, most recently, the 'war on terrorism', efforts which sometimes include, but are not limited to, military action. It has also been used to describe private forms of violent conflict, such as 'gang wars', and has even been extended to the business world to describe forms of non-violent economic competition, such as 'price wars'.

While the latter cases may be excluded, a more pressing difficulty for defining war and differentiating between war and peace is the ambiguous nature of contemporary conflict, which eludes easy classification. The wars of today (if they can properly be called wars) tend to be low-level, long-duration conflicts, with extended lulls punctuated by often-unexpected bouts of intense fighting. They may lack a clear starting-point, such as a declaration of war, or a definite end-point, such as a peace treaty.[5]

They tend to be fought, not between states, with clear divisions between allies and enemies, but rather between states and non-state actors, comprising a complex, changeable and sometimes contradictory web of allegiance and opposition, with various levels and types of involvement. Parties to the conflict are often vastly different in terms of military capacity and capability, operate under completely different sets of rules and principles, and employ very different strategies and tactics.

The distinction between combatants and non-combatants in such conflicts is often unclear, and parties to the conflict are often unable or unwilling to make the distinction. Combatants may hide among and even disguise themselves as non-combatants, who (willingly or otherwise) provide them material and moral support. Non-combatants may be deliberately targeted or suffer the effects of collateral damage. Great power rivalry, with its arms races, propaganda and proxy wars, is played out in local conflicts between rival ethnic and religious groups. The ongoing conflicts in Syria and Iraq exemplify a number of these features. Such ambiguous states of affairs have been described, in the context of another such conflict, as 'not war, not peace',[6] a description that highlights the problems of definition and differentiation.

In order to circumvent some of these problems, it may be best to avoid adopting an overly restrictive definition of war, and to discuss the ethics of war and peace in terms of armed conflict more generally. While military scholars might understandably disapprove of such a loose use of terms, ethicists working in this area typically do not limit their discussions to war in a narrow sense. Most take the same approach adopted here, in continuing to refer to the field of study as the 'ethics of war and peace', while broadening their analysis to armed conflict more generally.[7]

Others have opted to break with tradition by adopting the more precise designation 'ethics of armed conflict'.[8] Despite these different classifications, both groups approach the subject matter in more or less the same way. Such an approach is not without problems of its own, insofar as different types of armed conflict may be ethically distinct, but these distinctions can be addressed as they arise.

PERSPECTIVES ON THE ETHICS OF WAR AND PEACE

The ethics of war and peace is concerned with several related, but distinct, types of action; namely, acts of war and acts of peace. Acts of war include the act of initiating a war or actions tantamount to war, as well as actions taken in war. Acts of peace include the act of ending a war, as well as actions taken to avoid or prevent war. The main focus here will be on acts of war.

The ethical status of acts of war can range from prohibited, to permitted, to required. The status of specific acts of war depends on the criteria by which they are assessed and the perspective one adopts. Acts of war can be assessed on a number of different grounds, including strategic, legal and moral criteria, with different perspectives emphasising different criteria. Strategic value is assessed in terms of efficacy in advancing the aims of the actor. Legal value is assessed in relation to relevant laws. Moral value is assessed in terms of abstract normative principles.

One of the key underlying debates in the ethics of war and peace is the degree of ethical separation between the military and the civilian spheres of activity, and whether acts of war ought to be governed by a different set of ethical principles than other sorts of action. Civilian life is subject to various legal and moral constraints, the most fundamental of which is a prohibition on violence, and homicide in particular. War is inherently violent, and requires its participants to involve themselves, directly or indirectly, in the killing of other human beings. To what extent and by what means these normally prohibited behaviours may be justified in the context of war is one of the fundamental questions of the ethics of war and peace, and one of the main ways in which different ethical perspectives on war and peace may be distinguished.[9]

In addition, ethical perspectives on war and peace differ in the extent to which they permit or prohibit war, and may be placed on a spectrum ranging from unqualified acceptance of war, to qualified acceptance, to unqualified rejection. Perspectives on the ethics of war and peace can therefore be distinguished on three different bases: the ethical criteria by which acts of war are assessed, the degree of ethical exceptionalism accorded to acts of war, and the extent to which war is deemed to be ethically acceptable.

Three main perspectives are normally identified. They are realism, pacifism and just war theory. Realism sits near the permissive end of the spectrum, assesses acts of war in purely strategic terms, and regards civilian and military activity as ethically distinct. Pacifism occupies the prohibitive end of the spectrum, tends towards moralism in its outlook, and typically makes no distinction between the ethics of war and the ethics of ordinary life. Just war theory sits somewhere in the middle, is largely legalistic in its outlook, and maintains that war ethics and ordinary ethics are analogous but not identical.[10]

Other perspectives that are sometimes considered in addition to these include militarism and pacificism.[11] Militarism is even more permissive with respect to war than realism, while pacificism is somewhat less prohibitive with respect to war than (stricter forms of) pacifism. However, due to the conceptual proximity of militarism to realism, and pacificism to pacifism, they may be considered alongside them.[12] At the same time, different variants of each of these perspectives sit at different points along the permissive–prohibitive spectrum, which leads to a certain degree of overlap between them.

I will examine each of the three main perspectives in turn, beginning with a brief account of their respective histories and sources, followed by an overview of their main features, and key issues and areas of debate, particularly as they apply to the case of New Zealand. I conclude each section by highlighting the ongoing ethical challenges and controversies that the issues raised therein present for contemporary New Zealanders.

Realism

Realism lays claim to being the oldest and historically most popular perspective on the ethics of war and peace.[13] Realist thinking is embodied in some of the earliest surviving military treatises from a range of unconnected ancient cultures. Its ultimate origins are lost to us, but its basic tenets no doubt predate the written word and may be as old and ubiquitous as war itself. In the West, the realist tradition is usually traced to Thucydides' *History of the Peloponnesian War* (431BCE). Since that time, realist thinking has been restated and refined, including by such famous figures as Niccolò Machiavelli, Thomas Hobbes and Carl von Clausewitz. The modern revival of realism can be traced to the work of E. H. Carr and Hans Morgenthau, writing around the time of World War II.[14] Since then, the tradition has undergone further refinement, by the likes of Kenneth Waltz, Robert Gilpin, Stephen Walt and John Mearsheimer, and has spawned a number of branches, separated by various intramural debates. Realism peaked in popularity during the Cold War of the twentieth century and remains influential today.

Realism is characterised by its amoral stance on war and warfare. Realists draw a sharp distinction between the civilian and military domains, denying that the same sort of legal and moral principles that govern the former play any real role in the latter.[15] The distinction is based on the Hobbesian view that law and justice prevail only where there is an overarching authority to uphold them, and so apply to the inhabitants of (functioning) states in their relations with one another, but not to states themselves or to interactions that take place outside the bounds of State authority. As Hobbes himself puts it, 'Where there is no common Power, there is no Law; where no Law, no Injustice.'[16] Realists place little stock in international law or international institutions to uphold international norms, since none of these command force, beyond what states — and powerful states in particular — are willing to commit to them (which tends to be very little and only when it serves their strategic interests).

Given the absence of legal and moral constraints in such conditions, acts of war are to be assessed entirely on strategic grounds. Strategy, as the philosopher Michael Walzer puts it, is the 'language' of realism.[17] It is no accident that many realist thinkers are also strategists, generals and statesmen. War is to be pursued wherever it is strategically advantageous (for instance, to acquire territory or resources, or to eliminate an actual or potential rival), and by whatever means are most conducive to victory. War is to be avoided or abandoned where its initiation or continuation would be strategically disadvantageous (for instance, where victory is unlikely or uncertain, or where the objective is of little or no strategic value). Realists therefore oppose wars fought for moral rather than strategic reasons, as in cases of (genuine) humanitarian intervention (see below).[18] Strategically useful but legally or morally sanctioned forms of warfare (for instance, the use of banned munitions or attacks on civilian populations) are to be abstained from only insofar as their use would be detrimental to the war effort (for instance, where they would provoke retaliation, embolden opponents or alienate allies).

How strategic interests are to be defined, and by what means they are to be pursued, is a source of debate among realists. Classical realism equates strategic interest with State power,[19] whereas neo-realism identifies strategic interest with national security.[20] The latter is further divided on the question of whether the pursuit of State security dictates a more defensive or aggressive foreign policy. So-called 'offensive realists' maintain the view that offence is the most effective form of defence, and therefore that security is best pursued through military expansion.[21] In contrast, 'defensive realists' hold that expansionism exposes the State to increased threat, and that a purely defensive policy is a more effective means of achieving security.[22]

Realism is sometimes identified with militarism, but this is not entirely accurate, and most scholars in this field now recognise a distinction between them.[23] Where realists tend to see war as a necessary and useful means of achieving strategic aims, but not something to be pursued for its own sake, militarists regard war as an end in itself, to be pursued for reasons other than, or in addition to, any relevant strategic aims. In particular, militarists see war as an exercise in character-building and nation-building that promotes the development of martial virtues in soldiers and inspires feelings of patriotism in the wider public. So where realists see war as essentially amoral, militarists regard it as morally desirable.[24] Militarists are therefore typically more inclined towards war than realists. Militarist views are often associated with fascism, and with the twentieth-century Italian dictator Mussolini in particular, where they find their strongest and clearest expression.[25]

Few today publicly promote such views. But less extreme and more benign manifestations of this sort of thinking still find expression.[26] The belief that military life is morally edifying can be seen as a mild form of militarism, which often goes hand-in-hand with support for compulsory military training or service, but not necessarily with support for war itself. Compulsory military training has been in force in New Zealand during various periods in its history. Introduced under the Defence Act of 1909 and championed by the New Zealand National Defence League, it provoked the formation of anti-militarists groups, including the New Zealand Peace Council and the Passive Resisters' Union.[27] Compulsory military training was reintroduced by the Fraser Labour Government in 1950, following a 1949 public referendum in which it received popular support, and was ultimately abolished in 1972, at the height of the Peace Movement and in fulfilment of a campaign promise by the incoming Third Labour Government.[28]

Although permissive with respect to war, realism can be quite peaceable in application, as its proponents are quick to point out, simply because war is often regarded as excessively risky or costly on strategic grounds. These risks have increased over time with advances in military technology, and especially since the development and dissemination of nuclear weapons technology.[29]

Nor is realism devoid of moral foundation, in spite of its amoral stance on war and warfare. If the State is regarded as the sole source of justice in a lawless world, then the protection and advancement of the State by any means necessary, however immoral by the standards of civilised life, is not only a moral right but a moral duty.[30] Conversely, realists are inclined to see appeals to morality in the context of war as an extension of power politics, as simply a different, and ultimately inferior, form of power play used by the weak to further their strategic aims in the face of the strong. If the positions were reversed, the thinking goes, their respective ethical positions would also be reversed. Realism therefore denies that there is anything genuinely moral about a moralistic position on war.

Thucydides' 'Melian Dialogue' provides an early and colourful illustration of this line of thinking.[31] It is an idealised account of an ultimatum issued by imperial Athens to independent Melos. The Athenians offer a choice: unconditional surrender or total destruction. They will hear no word of justice, which they say applies only to equals; where there is no equality, justice dictates that 'the strong do as they wish and the weak suffer what they must'. If the Melians were in their position, the Athenians say, they would be saying the same thing. The point the Athenians are trying to make is that there is nothing inherently just about Melians' appeal to justice, which is as devoid of moral content as the Athenians' own brand of justice. For smaller, weaker states, it makes strategic sense to adopt a moral stance, in an attempt to level the playing-field with their more powerful peers.

Realist thinking highlights the ways that states, either alone or in concert, can work to preserve peace by shaping the strategic landscape to their advantage. Large and powerful states can do this by maintaining a large and powerful military, and through militaristic posturing and rhetoric, in order to deter potential aggressors.[32] Nuclear-armed states can do so through nuclear deterrence, which can deter a conventionally much more powerful foe.[33] Unfortunately, as realists also highlight, efforts to discourage attack can often be perceived as preparations for an attack, resulting in increased tensions between potential adversaries. In this way, the pursuit of peace can, ironically, lead to war, a conundrum known as the 'security dilemma'.[34]

A related phenomenon is the arms race, whereby attempts by adversaries to gain a strategic edge through enhanced weaponry result in spiralling military costs and risks, with little or no benefit to either side. The tensions that characterised the relationship between the Cold War powers, and the resulting nuclear arms race, exemplify these issues. Nonetheless, realists remain convinced that preparing for war remains the most effective way of preserving peace. The fact that the Cold War remained 'cold' is often cited in support of this view.[35] Smaller, weaker and non-nuclear states are unable to influence the strategic landscape on their own, and may be vulnerable to attack from aggressive neighbours. The usual solution for states in such circumstances is to align themselves with more powerful protectors.

ANZUS AND THE 'FIVE EYES'

New Zealand is one such state. From 1951 until 1986 the country was part of the Australia, New Zealand and United States (ANZUS) military alliance, which aimed to check the expansion of communism in the Asia-Pacific region, and saw New Zealand become involved in the Vietnam War. After the suspension of New Zealand from ANZUS, due to the anti-nuclear policy adopted by the Lange Labour Government in 1984, relations with the United States cooled. However, the relationship has thawed in recent years, with New Zealand committing forces to a number of US-led military engagements, including the 2001 invasion of Afghanistan, and a resumption of military cooperation between the two countries in 2007.[36]

The military relationship with the United States remains a source of ongoing public debate in New Zealand, a debate which has returned to the fore recently with New Zealand's commitment of troops to serve in a training capacity in Iraq in 2016. Supporters argue that a military relationship with the United States is essential to this country's national security, and that maintaining that relationship necessitates involvement in US military endeavours ('the price of the club', as then Prime Minister John Key once put it).[37] Opponents argue that such thinking has involved New Zealand in 'other people's wars', wars of questionable legality that have cost the lives of New Zealand soldiers and have not been in New Zealand's national interest.[38]

New Zealand is also a member of the 'Five Eyes' intelligence partnership, under the UKUSA Agreement of 1948 (the details of which remain classified), along with Australia, the United States, the United Kingdom and Canada. Like ANZUS, the Five Eyes was originally a product of the Cold War, tasked with intercepting the radio communications of communist states. Technological and political developments since the end of the Cold War, most notably the advent of the internet and rise of international terrorism, have led to a dramatic expansion of its function and powers.

New Zealand's involvement in the partnership has long been debated. This debate has returned to the fore recently following the disclosures of whistle-blower Edward Snowden, which revealed that the New Zealand Government Communications Security Bureau (GCSB) was collecting vast amounts of communications information on the country's Pacific neighbours on behalf of the US National Security Agency.[39] The government has claimed that membership of

Five Eyes is essential to New Zealand's national security, particularly in helping to protect the country from the threat of terrorism.[40] Critics allege that the Snowden disclosures reveal that most of the information collected by the GCSB and its counterparts abroad has little if anything to do with terrorism, or any other genuine security threat, and primarily targets friendly nations, which could jeopardise New Zealand's reputation and relationships.[41]

Pacifism

Like realism, pacifism existed long before there was a word to describe it, and while the word itself is relatively new, dating to the nineteenth century,[42] what the word encapsulates is much older. As with realist thinking, pacifist ideas have probably existed, in one form or another, for as long as there have been wars. But the history of pacifism is rather more fragmented than that of the other perspectives examined here. It is an intellectual tradition only in the loosest sense of the term, as a set of similar ideas, and not in the sense of a school of thought. Pacifism lacks the theoretical rigour of realism or the scholarly attention garnered by the just war tradition.

Historically, its main proponents have been prophets, poets, novelists and activists rather than scholars. Pacifist strands of thought can be found within the work of many eminent philosophers, but few can be counted as consistent advocates of pacifism. Like most other lines of philosophical thought, pacifist thinking in the Western tradition may be traced to the Ancient Greek philosopher Plato.[43] Modern philosophers who propounded pacifist ideas include Henry David Thoreau[44] and Bertrand Russell.[45] Robert L. Holmes's recent book *Pacifism: A Philosophy of Nonviolence* represents one of the most interesting developments in pacifist philosophy in recent years. Pacifism has been less influential, in certain respects, than the other traditions examined here, but famous examples are widely celebrated.

Millions of people today profess to be followers of Buddha or Jesus, and express admiration for Mahatma Gandhi and Martin Luther King, but far fewer are consistent adherents to the doctrine of non-violence that these figures espoused.

Pacifism is defined by its ardent opposition to war, and is equivalent to 'anti-warism'.[46] It holds that war is rarely, if ever, justified. It is closely linked to the more general doctrine of non-violence, and most (although not all) pacifists oppose violence generally, as well as organised political violence more specifically.[47] Pacifists usually deny that the military sphere is exempt from moral prohibitions on violence that apply to civilian life, and maintain that homicide is morally wrong regardless of the circumstances.[48] Since war inevitably entails violence and killing, they hold that 'war is incompatible with morality'.[49]

However, not all pacifists reject war on moral grounds; some do so on strategic grounds, reasoning that war is simply an inefficient way of achieving strategic goals.[50] These more practically minded pacifists are similar, in certain respects, to more peace-oriented realists, so that at a certain point the realist–pacifist spectrum circles back in on itself. In either case, pacifists hold that war is to be avoided wherever possible, and all reasonable efforts be made to bring specific wars, and the institution of war, to an end.

In its most extreme form, pacifism involves a total rejection of war, even in self-defence or in defence of innocents, and supports the abolition of the military and even the State as a whole. Such a view has few serious adherents, and is often regarded as self-defeating.[51] More moderate forms of pacifism allow that war may be justified in certain extreme cases and endorse more modest forms of demilitarisation, such as disarmament and the abolition of conscription.[52]

Whether any actual wars meet pacifist standard of justification is unclear. The Allied response to German military expansion in World War II is often held up as an exemplar of justified military action,[53] although some pacifists would, and did, beg to differ. The philosopher G. E. M. Anscombe opposed British entry into the war on the grounds that involvement would necessitate the killing of innocents, which she considered morally unacceptable.[54] Although not a pacifist herself, her argument would no doubt resonate with pacifist opponents of the war. In any case, most pacifists will allow that there may be circumstances in which war is justified in principle but would be sceptical as to whether these circumstances ever arise in practice.[55]

One such moderate form of pacifism is pacificism, which holds that war is only acceptable in order to advance the cause of peace. It would allow, for instance, entering into a war against an aggressor if such action could reasonably be expected to bring the war to a speedier conclusion or improve the prospects for lasting peace after its conclusion.

Another variation is defencism, which allows for purely defensive military action. This can include defensive wars along with defensive activity short of war, such as deterrence. Defencism is normally regarded as the more moderate of the two, in that it is considered to be further from extreme pacifism and closer to the centre of the pacifist–militarist spectrum. This is because pacificism would only endorse defensive military action to promote the cause of peace and not for defensive reasons alone; if inaction was more conducive to peace than defensive action, pacificists would argue that military action is unacceptable.[56]

However, things are not quite that simple, as there are situations in which a pacificist might advocate military action where a defencist would not. For instance, pacificists would be more inclined to support military action to bring a war to an end in cases where the intervening state is not directly threatened. In the case of German aggression in the lead-up to World War II, for example, a pacificist might argue in favour of intervention by the likes of Britain and the United States, whereas a defencist likely would not. However, this would depend on whether the defencist is willing to tolerate war in defence of others, or only in self-defence.

Pacifist views are commonly rooted in religious belief, often having their origins in sacred texts. While most such texts contain passages that could be interpreted as an endorsement of pacifism, many of those same texts include contradictory passages, a situation that has, somewhat ironically, been a source of violent sectarian conflict. Virtually all of the major religions include sects that embrace some form of pacifism, many of which are or were at one time regarded as heresies by the religious orthodoxy, and some of which faced persecution as a result.

Some political ideologies, including certain forms of socialism and anarchism, also embrace pacifism. For 'socialist anti-militarists', opposition to war is tied up in notions of worker solidarity and an unwillingness on the part of its adherents to engage in, or support, the killing of workers on the other side.[57] However, many of these are not opposed to war as such; some support ideologically specific forms of war, such as class warfare. Rather, they are opposed to those forms of war, prevalent in modern times, where the majority of combatants on both sides are, as they see it, members of the same economically and militarily exploited class. For anarcho-pacifists, opposition to the State goes hand-in-hand with opposition to war, as they regard the State as an inherently militaristic institution. Here the pacifist rejection of war is coupled with the belief, shared by realists, that war is the State's raison d'être.[58]

Most pacifists naturally opt for non-violent forms of resistance to further their anti-war agenda, but some adopt the paradoxical position that violence is justified in the pursuit of pacifist political aims. For example, the American militant group, Weather Underground, carried out a series of bombings in the United States in the 1970s to protest against the Vietnam War, although their intention does not seem to have been to kill or injure anyone, and the only people hurt in the attacks were its own members.[59]

Somewhat less paradoxically, most pacifists take the view that suffering violence is acceptable while inflicting it is not, which goes hand-in-hand with the belief that 'it is morally wrong to use force to resist, punish or prevent violence'.[60] This view has analogues in Socratic philosophy,[61] in the teachings and example of Jesus according to the Gospels,[62] and in the ideas and practice of martyrdom that prevailed among early Christians after the example of Jesus.[63] Some anti-war protestors have taken this a step further, actively harming themselves in the pursuit of pacifist causes. The most extreme manifestations of this approach are the use of suicide as a form of anti-war protest. Self-immolation has become the preferred method, popularised during the Vietnam War and employed by Christian anti-war protestors in the United States after the famous example of South Vietnamese Buddhist monks.

Few pacifists adopt such extreme measures. But virtually all avoid involvement in war or attempt to limit their involvement to non-combat roles. Historically, conscientious objectors (those who resist military service on principled grounds) who have refused to yield to the military service demands of states have faced incarceration and even death. It is worth noting, then, that while pacifists — and conscientious objectors in particular — are sometimes labelled as cowards by more militaristically minded sections of society, many have bravely suffered and died for their principles, just as many who fought bravely suffered and died for theirs.

CONSCIENTIOUS OBJECTION AND COLLECTIVE REMEMBRANCE

Most modern states make some allowance for what they regard as genuine conscientious objection, but historically the criteria for exemption from service on principled grounds were very restrictive. Traditionally, states have been prepared to make exceptions only for a small number of avowedly pacifist religious movements.[64] Quakers, Christadelphians and Seventh-day Adventists were the only groups in New Zealand exempted from military service on principled grounds during World War I and World War II.[65]

In World War I, around 600 conscientious objectors were denied exemptions. Of those, 286 refused to serve and were imprisoned for disobeying orders. Around half cited religious objections, while around a quarter were socialists. Most were sentenced to hard labour. Infamously, 14 were shipped to the Western Front. Some opted at that point to fight. Others agreed to serve in a non-combat capacity. The rest were subjected to various forms of severe punishment and returned to New Zealand only when death or injury rendered them unfit for service.[66] One, Archibald Baxter — who had refused to serve on the grounds that 'all war is wrong, futile, and destructive alike to victor and vanquished' — went on to publish a well-known memoir titled *We Will Not Cease*, which was later adapted into the film *Field Punishment No. 1*.[67]

In World War II, 3000 appealed conscription on principled grounds, but only 600 were granted exemptions. Of the remainder, 800 refused to comply and were imprisoned; 200 of them remained in prison until the end of the war; some were not released until 1946.[68] World War II was the last time that conscription was invoked in New Zealand. In contrast to the United States, it was not reintroduced in New Zealand during either the Korean or the Vietnam wars.

In recent years, some allowance has been made for principled objection to overseas service on the part of active military personnel. Members of the New Zealand Defence Force (NZDF) called up to serve in a training capacity in Iraq in 2016 reportedly received the option of opting out, including those who objected to New Zealand's involvement in the conflict on grounds of principle.[69] Whether any took up this option (and whether any offered it felt as though they had any real choice in the matter) is unknown. But the fact that the option was even presented highlights the vast shift in public perceptions of the moral validity of conscientious objection that has occurred over the past century. The focus of conscientious objection campaigners is now on the 'right not to kill' or the 'right to refuse to kill', which they have sought to have recognised as a civil and human right under constitutional and international law.[70]

As well as advocating for the rights of conscientious objectors, anti-war campaigners have protested against what they see as efforts to promote militarism in society, including, most controversially, public collective remembrance occasions. Pacifists are inclined to regard such occasions as celebrating or romanticising war, and as a support and recruitment drive for current and future military campaigns. Such opposition is expressed in various ways, from passive refusal to publicly acknowledge such occasions, to active attempts to disrupt ceremonies. Such expressions are often criticised as disrespectful to those being remembered. More extreme manifestations are criticised by supporters of collective remembrance as well as by more moderate critics who consider it counterproductive.

Some anti-war groups have attempted to establish alternative symbols and ceremonies. Perhaps the most well-known example in the Commonwealth countries is the 'White Poppies for Peace' movement, an initiative by the Peace Pledge Union (PPU), which it presents as an alternative to official collective remembrance and its red poppy symbol. The PPU claims that the movement is not about disregarding those who fought and died for the country, but rather about remembering all victims of war, including enemy soldiers and civilians.[71] In New Zealand, the White Poppy movement has been criticised for being timed to coincide with Anzac Day, and is seen as an attempt to divert funding from the Red Poppy Appeal, which is used to help fund the Returned Services Association.[72] The timing is, of course, not accidental. But those who support the movement would claim to be concerned with challenging the official and popular narratives surrounding war that are expressed around Anzac Day, rather than competing economically with the country's veterans.

Just war theory

Like the other approaches presented here, the 'just war' tradition has a long and complex history, with multiple points of origin. The Western branch runs from Antiquity, through the Middle Ages and the Renaissance (where it was closely tied up in Christian theology), the Enlightenment (where it was secularised), and down to the present era. Its sources include such philosophical luminaries as Plato, St Augustine of Hippo, St Thomas Aquinas, Francisco de Vitoria, Hugo Grotius and Immanuel Kant.[73] Other cultural traditions also embody elements of just war thinking, some of which claim historical priority over the Western variant that predominates today.

Some elements are universally accepted in principle, if not always adhered to in practice.[74] Virtually every group that engages in armed conflict claims to be fighting a just war, and attempts to justify its aims and conduct in some way, although ideas about what justice demands in this context differ considerably. Michael Walzer is widely regarded as the leading contemporary just war theorist. His 1977 book *Just and Unjust Wars* has come to represent the orthodoxy in contemporary just war theory, and is the source of much current scholarly discussion on the subject.[75]

Just war theory maintains that war is justified under certain conditions, and that certain forms of warfare are acceptable. It holds that the relationship between individuals in a state, and the relationship between states, is analogous but not identical. Contrary to realists, who argue that the international system is characterised by anarchy, just war theorists take the liberal view that there is an international community, regulated by international institutions and laws. However, they recognise that it is an imperfect system, given that there is (as realists are quick to point out) no common authority to enforce law and order.[76]

This means that the same sort of moral and legal constraints that apply to individuals also apply to states. Both individuals and states are said to possess certain basic rights, with the rights of states deriving, ultimately, from the rights of their citizens. Most fundamentally, individuals are attributed a right to life and liberty, and therefore a right not to be attacked or interfered with, provided they do nothing to forfeit those rights.

The right to life and liberty entails a right of self-defence and a right of resistance against unwarranted interference. It also entails a right to defend the lives and freedoms of innocent others. Those who infringe on the rights of others forfeit certain rights of their own. A person who attacks another person loses the right not to be attacked in self-defence or by an intervening third party.

States that uphold the rights of their citizens possess equivalent rights with respect to other states. They have a right not to be attacked or interfered with by any other state, provided they do not attack or interfere with any other state. They also have an equivalent right to defend themselves and others against aggression.[77]

The rights of states and individuals correspond to two levels of justification, traditionally referred to as *jus ad bellum* (right to war) and *jus in bello* (right in war) — what the philosopher John Lango calls 'resort principles' and 'conduct principles'.[78] The former refers to the conditions under which recourse to war is justified, whereas the latter refers to the methods by which war may be justly carried out. A more recent addition, *jus post bellum* (right after war), relates to the decision to end a war and the actions taken in the aftermath of war.[79]

There is much debate regarding the specific criteria of *jus ad bellum* and *jus in bello*, but the general tenets are reasonably clear and uncontroversial. Recourse to war is justified if the reason for, and aims of, the war are just, the expected consequences of war are positive on balance, there is no feasible alternative to war, and the war is initiated by a legitimate authority. A war is justly carried out where attacks are carried out in the pursuit of genuine strategic aims, only morally acceptable types of attack are carried out, only legitimate targets are targeted, and the effects of collateral damage are weighed against the strategic value of the intended objective.[80]

Of these various conditions, the most fundamental are usually taken to be the 'just cause' and 'legitimate targets' clauses, where the former is typically understood in terms of self-defence or the defence of others, while the latter is typically identified with 'non-combatant immunity'.[81] The legitimate targets clause, then, prohibits attacking those not involved in fighting, which includes not only civilians, but also enemy soldiers who have surrendered or been captured, or who are injured or shipwrecked. These conditions stem from the respective right of states and individuals not to be attacked and to defend themselves against attack. Only states and individuals that have forfeited their right not to be attacked by participating in the conflict are legitimate targets.[82]

The conditions of *jus post bellum* have received less attention historically, but have been much discussed in recent times. There is little consensus on what those conditions should be. The philosopher Brian Orend, widely considered one of the main authorities on *jus post bellum*,[83] argues that its conditions are analogous to certain *jus ad bellum* and *jus in bello* principles. First, war can only be justly brought to an end by a legitimate authority whose reasons and intentions are good. Second, punishment for war crimes should be imposed only upon guilty parties, and should be commensurate with the crimes committed.[84]

Just war theory is by far the most prevalent and influential perspective on the ethics of war and peace, in part because its principles are easily codified and because it allows for clear guidance for action. Such is the popularity of just war theory that it is sometimes equated with the ethics of war and peace itself.[85] Just war theory has, however, been attacked from both ends of the realist–pacifist spectrum.

Realists argue that restricting the war-making powers of governments — for instance, by prohibiting preventative war — is inherently dangerous, since it allows an adversary to grow stronger and reduces the likelihood of victory when war does break out (since for realists it is always only ever a matter of time). They also argue that limiting the means of warfare prolongs war and increases the number of casualties, and is therefore contrary to humanitarian principles. The latter argument has been invoked to suggest that the US nuclear attacks on Japan in World War II were an act of mercy.[86] At the same time, realists argue that acting according to conscience, rather than cold calculation, can lead states into dangerous and costly military entanglements.[87]

Strict pacifists, on the other hand, argue that war is inherently unjustifiable. For them, a just war theory is as absurd and perverse as a 'just murder theory' or a 'just rape theory' would be.[88] Aside from the belief that just war theory defends the indefensible, pacifists worry that, by normalising war, it increases the propensity for war. To support these criticisms, pacifists point to cases in which just war principles have been invoked in an attempt to legitimate self-evidently illegitimate wars, such as Argentina's so-called 'Dirty War', in which security forces and paramilitaries engaged in a campaign of systematic violence against communists and other 'subversives' during the 1970s and 1980s.[89]

Just war theorists, for their part, often ignore realism and pacifism entirely, or dismiss them out of hand. But some have engaged seriously with them, offering responses to their criticisms and criticising them in turn.[90] Walzer challenges realism on the grounds that people intuitively recognise that there are moral and legal constraints on war and warfare, even if they do not always adhere to them. Those charged with making decisions about when and how to engage in war, he argues, are keenly aware of the moral ramifications of those decisions, and experience pride or shame according to the rightness or wrongness of those decisions.[91]

Walzer's response to pacifism is that it ignores the fact of war. As much as most of us would all prefer to see the end of war, that end is nowhere in sight. In a world in which war is very much a reality, we should work to minimise the excesses of war, a task that focusing on the unrealistic goal of abolishing war detracts from. In other words, pacifism, in this view, allows the perfect to become the enemy of the good. In addition, Walzer argues that refusing to respond militarily to acts of aggression encourages aggression, so that adopting pacifist principles would actually increase the amount of violence and injustice in the world.[92]

Despite these differences between just war theory and the other perspectives surveyed here, there are also some similarities, which highlight that these different perspectives are not completely separate from one another but exist on a spectrum. Some variants of realism and pacifism overlap with some areas of just war theory. While just war theory is normally contrasted with realism,[93] some just war theorists identify a realist strand of the theory. This strand focuses heavily on 'prudential' principles of just war theory, including lesser evil, proportionality and reasonable chance of success.[94]

Likewise, while pacifism is widely regarded as opposed to just war theory,[95] there are points on which just war theorists and at least some pacifists agree. Both pacificism and defencism embrace some version of the just cause principle. Pacificists equate just cause with the pursuit of peace, a view that has a long history in the just war tradition,[96] while defencists equate just cause with self-defence, a view prevalent, as we have seen, among contemporary just war theorists. By the same token, a very stringent just war theory, whose restrictions are so strong that they effectively prohibit war as we know it, would be virtually indistinguishable from pacifism.[97] Some pacifists 'have even arrived at pacifism via a just war route'.[98]

There are also a number of debates among just war theorists. One such debate relates to the status of the main *jus ad bellum* and *jus in bello* principles. Some regard certain principles as more central than others. John Lango, for instance, argues that 'the just cause, last resort, proportionality and noncombatant immunity principles are the core just war principles', while the legitimate authority, right intention and reasonable hope principles are peripheral.[99]

Another debate concerns the relationship between *jus ad bellum* and *jus in bello* principles. Walzer represents the orthodox view that these are 'logically distinct. It is perfectly possible for a just war to be fought unjustly, and for an unjust war to be fought in strict accordance with the rules.' An important consequence of this distinction is that participants in just and unjust wars are taken to be 'morally equal'.[100] Others reject this separation and the moral equality it entails.

The philosopher Jeff McMahan is regarded as one of the leading critics of the orthodox view.[101] He argues that the soldiers of a state that is the victim of a surprise attack for which there is no just cause (contrary to *jus ad bellum*) are not legitimate targets (contrary to *jus in bello*). Invoking the domestic analogy, he argues that such soldiers stand in the same relationship to the enemy as an ordinary person who is the victim of a violent home invasion does to their attacker. The victim has a right to defend themselves, but the attacker has no right to attack in the first place or to continue the attack once the victim has fought back. Just as victim and attacker are not morally equal, combatants on either side of such a conflict are not morally equal. If the analogy holds, then *jus in bello* would seem to depend in an important way, at least in certain cases, on *jus ad bellum*.[102]

McMahan has also taken issue with certain cherished *jus in bello* principles, including the principle of non-combatant immunity. He argues that attacks on civilians who bear direct moral responsibility for an unjust war are justified. Civilian leaders who launch a war of aggression, for instance, are legitimate targets on this account. In this case, *jus ad bellum* culpability gives way to *jus in bello* liability.

One worry with this argument is that it could be used to justify indiscriminate attacks on citizens of democratic states, who elect and are therefore ultimately responsible for the actions of their governments; it could, for instance, be used in defence of mass terrorist attacks against civilian targets. But McMahan denies that this level of culpability is sufficient to meet the 'responsibility criterion', although he accepts that it does make allowance for certain limited forms of terrorism in such cases, such as political assassinations. In addition, he argues that the responsibility criterion should not be embodied in international law, as it is open to abuse in the ways just described.[103]

JUST WAR PRINCIPLES AND INTERNATIONAL LAW

There is a close relationship between the traditional just war principles and international law. Both are derived from principles of natural justice and customary law, and each has influenced the other. War is one of the chief concerns of international law, and war crimes are among the most serious international crimes. Many just war scholars are also international jurists, and many tenets of just war theory are embodied in international law.[104] Walzer sees international law as forming an important part of the 'war convention', the written and unwritten rules of war.[105] Peace and conflict scholar Alex Bellamy considers it part of a greater 'just war tradition'.[106]

The United Nations Charter embodies a number of key *jus ad bellum* principles.[107] Principles of non-intervention and non-interference are set out in Article 2. Article 51 establishes the right to self-defence, while Article 39 allows the United Nations Security Council (UNSC) to authorise military action in response to acts of aggression.[108] The main *jus in bello* principles are embodied in the Law of Armed Conflict (LOAC), of which the Hague and Geneva conventions are the chief sources.[109] The principle of non-combatant immunity is set out in all four Geneva Conventions. The first and second relate to the treatment of wounded, sick and shipwrecked forces, the third relates to the treatment of prisoners of war, while the fourth relates to the treatment of civilians.[110]

The largely legalistic nature of contemporary just war theory is noted by Walzer, who seems to regard adherence to the LOAC as a necessary, but not sufficient, condition of a just war.[111] Some other just war theorists challenge the view that adherence to the LOAC is a necessary condition of a just war. Such arguments are typically based on inductive appeals to particular counter-examples; in particular, to specific acts of war that are contrary to the laws of war but are widely regarded as justified in the context, such as those carried out by the French Resistance.[112] Such arguments do not undermine the moral validity of the LOAC in general, although they might point to extenuating circumstances.

Partly as a consequence of the close relationship between just war theory and the LOAC, the former has been incorporated into the ethical doctrine of professional militaries, and is widely taught in courses on ethics in military academies around the world. Just war theory is therefore the basis of much professional military ethics.

The Advanced Command and Staff Course programme delivered at the NZDF Command and Staff College at Trentham, which is taught in partnership with Massey University's Centre for Defence and Security Studies, includes a component on ethics, the main focus of which is just war theory. All members of the NZDF are required to attend a basic four-hour presentation on the LOAC. Those members whose duties require a more in-depth knowledge receive additional, specialised training. Those deployed on operations are given refresher courses, and carry with them a 'Code of Conduct' card, listing key rights and obligations under the LOAC.[113] The first four rules listed on the card embody the principles of non-combatant immunity, proportionality, discrimination, and using no means that are *mala in se* (wrong or evil in itself):

- Fight only opposing forces or persons taking a direct part in the hostilities.
- Attack only military objectives and destroy no more than the mission requires.
- When attacking military objectives take care to minimise incidental civilian casualties and property damage.
- Do not use prohibited weapons. Do not alter your weapons or ammunition.

However, concerns about the conduct of some NZDF members were raised in 2017, following allegations that the New Zealand Special Air Services (NZSAS) forces committed war crimes, as reported by Nicky Hager and Jon Stephenson in the book *Hit and Run*. The book alleges that members of the NZSAS, in cooperation with US forces, carried out a raid that saw six civilians killed, a further 15 injured, several homes destroyed and a prisoner mistreated, in contravention of the LOAC and the NZDF Code of Conduct. It claims that the raid was a response to the killing of Lieutenant Tim O'Donnell of the New Zealand Army, after reports were received indicating that the insurgents responsible for Lieutenant O'Donnell's death could be located at the site that the SAS subsequently raided, only to find no insurgents there. It further alleges that the NZDF attempted to conceal the facts of the raid from the public.

The NZDF has denied the allegations, and questioned some of the facts reported. In particular, it maintains that the NZSAS has never operated at the location in which the raid was said to have taken place. It acknowledges that an NZSAS raid, Operation Burnham, did take place, some 2 kilometres south of the location reported in the book, but maintains that those involved in the mission acted appropriately, that no civilians were killed, and that there was no cover-up. The authors have admitted that they were mistaken about the location of the raid, but stand by their other allegations. They have called for an independent investigation, but the government has said that it has no plans to launch one.[114]

Much of the current work on just war theory attempts to update the theory in light of new developments, including, most recently, the rise of international terrorism and the global war on terrorism.[115] Such attempts face many challenges due to the complexities and ambiguities of contemporary warfare mentioned above. The issues involved are the source of much ethical and legal debate. Two major *jus ad bellum* issues have come to the fore in recent years; namely, pre-emptive military action and humanitarian intervention.[116]

PRE-EMPTIVE SELF-DEFENCE

The concept of pre-emptive self-defence has a long history within the just war tradition, and has also long been a source of contention. The broad consensus is that states have a strictly limited right to pre-emptive self-defence. In light of the September 11 2001 attacks on the United States, it was generally accepted that those limits would need to be relaxed, but to what extent remained controversial.[117] After a

UNSC resolution authorising military action against Iraq failed to pass, the United States attempted to justify its subsequent 2003 invasion of Iraq as pre-emptive self-defence, on the grounds that Iraq possessed weapons of mass destruction (WMDs) and had links to Al Qaeda. The action was criticised after no WMDs or links to terrorist organisations were uncovered.

According to Bellamy, justified pre-emptive military action must satisfy three conditions. First, the threat must be imminent, although not necessarily immediate. Second, military action must be necessary to mitigate that threat. Third, the response must be proportionate to the threat. He argues that the invasion of Iraq failed to meet any of these conditions.[118]

The New Zealand government did not support the initial invasion of Iraq, but 61 NZDF personnel were deployed to support the United Nations' post-war reconstruction and humanitarian mission in late 2003. New Zealand's recent contribution to the Building Partner Capacity mission has already been mentioned.[119]

HUMANITARIAN INTERVENTION

The other main *jus ad bellum* issue that has come to prominence in recent years — and which has challenged traditional moral and legal constraints on the use of military force — relates to the issue of humanitarian intervention. Humanitarian intervention refers to the use of military force to protect civilian populations in states where their governments are unwilling or unable to provide such protections and which are often opposed to intervention.

The issue raises a raft of legal and moral conundrums. On the one hand, the right to non-intervention is regarded as a fundamental right of states and is enshrined in international law, including the UN Charter, as we have seen. On the other hand, upholding human rights is regarded as a moral and legal obligation of states and the international community as a whole. How, then, are the rights of states and individuals to be balanced?[120] For Walzer, the solution goes back to the idea that the rights of states derive from the rights of their citizens (see above). Where states violate or fail to uphold human rights, they lose their right to non-intervention, and other states acquire a corresponding right to intervene.[121] This right is not absolute, however. Intervention remains subject to just war criteria, including just cause, legitimate authority and proportionality.[122]

In cases of humanitarian intervention, principles of *jus post bellum* were traditionally ignored, but have come to be regarded as critically important.[123] On this rights-based approach, states are granted the right to intervene, but they do not accrue an obligation to intervene: 'Somebody ought to intervene, but no specific state . . . is morally bound to do so.'[124] Others have found this solution unsatisfactory, particularly in light of the failures of humanitarian intervention arising from its non-obligatory status. Due to the high economic and political cost of military action, states are often unwilling to engage in or fully commit to intervention that does not advance their strategic aims, as was the case in Rwanda in 1994 and Darfur in 2003–4. (On the other hand, states often make dubious appeals to the principles of humanitarian intervention to justify military action that serves their strategic aims, including, most recently, the US invasion of Iraq in 2003 and the Russian intervention in Georgia in 2008.)[125]

Critics of the rights-based approach to humanitarian intervention have opted instead for a responsibility-based approach. According to this approach, it is the responsibility of each state to protect its citizens, and it is the responsibility of the international community to respond in situations where states are unwilling or unable to do so.[126] The Responsibility to Protect (R2P) has been incorporated into the UN framework, under UNSC Resolution 1674 on the Protection of Civilians.[127]

New Zealand has been involved in a number of humanitarian interventions. One of its most significant contributions was to the UN-sanctioned, Australian-led peacekeeping mission in East Timor, in response to a civil conflict in which around 1400 civilians are believed to have lost their lives. The mission brought an end to the conflict, and saw control of the country transferred to a transitional government. More than 6000 NZDF personnel were deployed to East Timor between 1999 and 2012;[128] five lost their lives.[129]

THE WAR ON TERRORISM

A number of *jus in bello* issues have also come to the fore in recent years, particularly in the context of the global war on terrorism. A number of these issues pertain to the use of airstrikes, including by Unmanned Aerial Vehicles (UAVs, colloquially known as 'drones'), to target suspected terrorists. Questions have been raised regarding the proportionality and discrimination of such attacks, following reports of high civilian casualty rates. Others have questioned whether some of those targeted in airstrikes represent legitimate targets of attack.[130]

The US Administration maintains that those targeted are involved in attacks on US forces or US allies, and that strikes are 'surgical', minimising collateral damage. These claims are difficult to assess. The information used to determine targets of strikes is classified, although leaked reports give some insight into the process.[131] The United States does not report on the number of civilians killed in airstrikes, and counts any military-aged males killed as militants in its official statistics. However, reports by humanitarian organisations call into question the claims of surgical precision, as well as calling into question the legality of the US drone-strike programme.[132]

The debate about the legitimacy of the US drone campaign came to the fore in New Zealand in 2014 when it was reported that New Zealander Daryl Jones had been killed in a drone strike in Yemen.

Official reports state that Jones was not the intended target of the attack, but was a suspected Al Qaeda associate and was in the company of suspected Al Qaeda militants when he was killed. Both then Prime Minister John Key and opposition leader David Shearer accepted that the strike was justified, while co-leader of the Green Party Russel Norman called it 'extra-judicial assassination', and argued that drone strikes undermine human rights and the rule of law.[133]

Conclusion

The ethics of war and peace is a source of historical and contemporary scholarly and public debate in New Zealand and around the world. This debate has evolved, and will continue to evolve, in response to new political, strategic and technological developments. Three main theoretical perspectives on the ethics of war and peace — and many different variations of these — can be identified, only a few of which could be considered in any detail here. These can be represented on a continuum ranging from militarism to pacifism; however, this continuum is not completely linear, positions on the spectrum are not clearly delineated, and even the relative position of some perspectives is not entirely clear.

Just war theory remains the leading general theoretical perspective on the ethics of war and peace, and has had the greatest scholarly and practical impact of the perspectives examined here. However, it is far from the only perspective and is not without its critics. There is also a great deal of debate among just war theorists, debates which have intensified as the theory struggles to grapple with the complexities of contemporary warfare.

The debates between and among the different perspectives on the ethics of war and peace, and the issues at stake in those debates, while intellectually interesting, are not only matters of scholarly concern. They have real and important practical implications, not just for our political representatives or those who fight on our behalf, but also for each of us. It is our duty as ethicists, and as citizens, to grapple with these issues and participate in this discussion.

---

1 I would like to acknowledge Negar Partow's contributions to, and comments on, an earlier version of this paper. I would also like to thank Matthew Russell and Terence Johanson for their feedback on a later draft.

2 Nigel Dower, *The Ethics of War and Peace: Cosmopolitan and Other Perspectives* (Cambridge: Polity, 2009), 4–5.

3 This traditional 'negative' conception of peace as 'not-war' has been challenged in recent times by advocates of a 'positive' conception of peace as something like 'harmony' (see Dower, *The Ethics of War and Peace*, 6–7, 137–144).

4 John Lewis Gaddis, *The Long Peace: Inquiries Into the History of the Cold War* (Oxford: Oxford University Press, 1989).

5 There has not been a formal declaration of war since World War II, and the Korean War, which ended with an armistice rather than a peace treaty, is technically still ongoing.

6 George Perkovich and Toby Dalton, *Not War, Not Peace? Motivating Pakistan to Prevent Cross-border Terrorism* (Oxford: Oxford University Press, 2016).

7 Dower, *The Ethics of War and Peace*; Helen Frowe, *The Ethics of War and Peace: An Introduction* (London: Routledge, 2010); Paul Christopher, *The Ethics of War and Peace: An Introduction to Legal and Moral Issues* (Upper Saddle River, NJ: Prentice Hall, 2004).

8 John W. Lango, *The Ethics of Armed Conflict: A Cosmopolitan Just War Theory* (Edinburgh: Edinburgh University Press, 2014).

9 Frowe, *The Ethics of War and Peace*, 1–4; Richard Norman, *Ethics, Killing and War* (Cambridge: Cambridge University Press, 1995), 1–3.

10 Michael Walzer distinguishes between the three perspectives in the following way: '[Just war theory maintains] that war is sometimes justifiable and that the conduct of war is always subject to moral criticism. The first of these propositions is denied by pacifists . . . and the second is denied by realists . . .' (*Arguing About War* (New Haven, CT: Yale University Press, 2004), ix). Richard Werner makes the same distinction with respect to three irreconcilable propositions: '[1.] It is strongly presumptively wrong to kill children intentionally. [2.] Modern war involves killing children intentionally. [3.] Most modern wars are morally justified. . . . Realism denies 1. Just War Theory denies 2. . . . Pacifism denies 3.' ('Pragmatism for Pacifists,' *Contemporary Pragmatism* 4, no. 2 (2007), 93–94).

11 Dower, *The Ethics of War and Peace*, 9; A. J. Coates, *The Ethics of War* (second edition) (Manchester: Manchester University Press, 2016), 3–5; Martin Ceadel, *Thinking about Peace and War* (Oxford: Oxford University Press, 1987), 4–5.

12 This is the approach taken by Dower, *The Ethics of War and Peace*, 9, 34–36, 144–146.

13 Realism in the context of the ethics of war and peace is sometimes referred to as 'war realism' to distinguish it from political realism more generally (Robert L. Holmes, *Pacifism: A Philosophy of Nonviolence* (London: Bloomsbury, 2017), 60).

14 See E. H. Carr, *The Twenty Years' Crisis 1919–1939: An Introduction to the Study of International Relations* (New York: Macmillan, 1939) and Hans J. Morgenthau, *Politics Among Nations: The Struggle for Power and Peace* (New York: Alfred A. Knopf, 1948).

15 Frowe, *The Ethics of War and Peace*, 95.

16 Thomas Hobbes, *Leviathan*, ed. Richard Tuck (Cambridge: Cambridge University Press, 1996), 1.13.13.

17 Michael Walzer, *Just and Unjust Wars: A Moral Argument with Historical Illustrations* (second edition) (New York: Basic Books, 1992), 13–14.

18 Coates, *The Ethics of War*, 24–25.

19 Hans J. Morgenthau, *Politics Among Nations: The Struggle for Power and Peace* (fifth edition) (New York: Alfred A. Knopf, 1978), 5–6.

20 Kenneth Waltz, *A Theory of International Politics* (New York: McGraw-Hill, 2010), 91–93.

21 See John Mearsheimer, *The Tragedy of Great Power Politics* (New York: Norton, 2001).

22 See Stephen Walt, *The Origin of Alliances* (Ithaca, NY: Cornell University Press, 1987).

23 Dower, *The Ethics of War and Peace*, 9; Coates, *The Ethics of War*, 3–5; Ceadel, *Thinking about Peace and War*, 4–5.

24 Coates, *The Ethics of War*, 41.

25 Dower, *The Ethics of War and Peace*, 35; Ceadel, *Thinking about Peace and War*, 21.

26 Coates, *The Ethics of War*, 40–41.

27 A. H. McLintock, 'The Defence Act of 1909,' *Te Ara: The Encyclopedia of New Zealand* (2009), accessed May 15, 2017, http://www.TeAra.govt.nz/en/1966/compulsory-military-training/.

28 Ian McGibbon, 'The Cold War,' *Te Ara: The Encyclopedia of New Zealand*, accessed May 15, 2017, http://www.TeAra.govt.nz/en/video/34512/compulsory-military-training-1950.

29 Thus Marc Trachtenburg argues that realism is, in fact, 'a theory of peace' ('The Question of Realism,' *Security Studies* 13, no. 1 (2003): 194).

30 See Michael C. Desch, 'It Is Kind to Be Cruel: The Humanity of American Realism,' *Review of International Studies* 29, no. 3 (2003): 415–426.

31 *History of the Peloponnesian War*, trans. M. I. Finley (Harmondsworth: Penguin, 1972), 84–116.

32 Paul K. Huth, 'Deterrence and International Conflict: Empirical Findings and Theoretical Debates,' *Review of Political Science* 2 (1999), 25–48.

33 Bernard Brodie, *Strategy in the Missile Age* (Princeton, NJ: Princeton University Press, 1959), 147–150.

34 John H. Herz, 'Idealist Internationalism and the Security Dilemma,' *World Politics* 2, no. 2 (1950): 157.

35 Kenneth Waltz, 'Structural Realism After the Cold War,' *International Security* 25, no. 1 (2000): 27–29.

36 William Hoverd, Christopher Paul, and Nicholas Nelson, 'A Promising Thaw,' *Proceedings Magazine* 1 (2014), 60–65.

37 'Price of the Club: Being a Part of Five Eyes Could See NZ Join ISIS Fight,' *One News* (21 January 2015), accessed May 15, 2017, https://www.tvnz.co.nz/one-news/new-zealand/price-of-the-club-being-a-part-five-eyes-could-see-nz-join-isis-fight-6221601.

38 See Nicky Hager, *Other People's Wars: New Zealand in Afghanistan, Iraq and the War on Terror* (Nelson: Craig Potton Publishing, 2011).

39 Nicky Hager and Ryan Gallagher, 'The Price of the Five Eyes Club: Mass Spying on Friendly Nations,' *New Zealand Herald*, March 5, 2015, accessed May 15, 2017, http://www.nzherald.co.nz/nz/news/article.cfm?c_id=1&objectid=11411759.

40 Audrey Young, 'Five Eyes Gives NZ an Advantage in Fighting Terrorism, Says Key,' *New Zealand Herald*, November 15, 2015, accessed May 15, 2017, http://www.nzherald.co.nz/nz/news/article.cfm?c_id=1&objectid=11545844.

41 Hager and Gallagher, 'The Price of the Five Eyes Club.'

42 Martin Ceadel, *The Origins of War Prevention: The British Peace Movement and International Relations 1730–1854* (Oxford: Clarendon Press, 1996), 28–29.

43 For example, *Plato, Laws*, trans. Thomas L. Pangle (New York: Basic Books, 1980), 803.

44 See Henry David Thoreau, 'Civil Disobedience,' in *Civil Disobedience and Other Essays* (New York: Dover Publications, 1993).

45 See Bertrand Russell, 'The Ethics of War,' *International Journal of Ethics* 25, no. 2 (1915): 127–142.

46 Jenny Teichman, *Pacifism and the Just War* (Oxford: Basil Blackwell, 1986), 1; Brian Orend, 'Evaluating Pacifism,' *Dialogue* 40 (2001): 3–24. Some pacifists prefer to portray pacifism in 'positive' terms, as support for peace rather than opposition to war. (See Andrew Alexandra, 'Political Pacifism,' *Social and Political Practice* 29, no. 4 (2003): 596.) A positive conception of pacifism goes hand-in-hand with a positive conception of peace (see note 3). If peace is defined in negative terms, then pacifism is best defined in the same way.

47 Pacifism part and parcel of non-violence: Jan Narveson, 'Pacifism: A Philosophical Analysis,' *Ethics* 75 (1965): 63. Pacifism as opposed to war specifically: Alexander, 'Political Pacifism,' 596–597.

48 Holmes, *Pacifism*, 236–237.

49 Michael Fox, *Understanding Peace: A Comprehensive Introduction* (New York: Routledge, 2014), 121.

50 Werner, 'Pragmatism for Pacifists,' 93–94.

51 Narveson, 'Pacifism,' 259–271.

52 Coates, *The Ethics of War*, 78–79.

53 See, for example, Michael Walzer, 'World War II: Why Was This War Different?' *Philosophy and Public Affairs* 1, no. 1 (1971): 3–21.

54 G. E. M. Anscombe and Norman Daniel, *The Justice of the Present War Examined: A Criticism Based on Traditional Catholic Principles and on Natural Reason* (London: John S. Burns, 1941).

55 Coates, *The Ethics of War*, 79. This seems to be the view of Russell ('The Ethics of War,' 127–142).

56 Norman, *Ethics, Killing and War*, 238.

57 Peter Brock and Nigel Young, *Pacifism in the Twentieth Century* (Syracuse, NY: Syracuse University Press, 1999), 13–15.

58 See Geoffrey Ostergaard, *Resisting the Nation-State: The Pacifist and Anarchist Tradition* (London: Peace Pledge Union, 1982).

59 Ron Jacobs, *The Way the Wind Blew: A History of the Weather Underground* (London: Verso, 1997).

60 Narveson, 'Pacifism,' 63.

61 For example, *Plato, Crito, in Four Texts on Socrates: Plato's Euthyphro, Apology and Crito, and Aristophanes' Clouds*, trans. Thomas G. West and Grace Starry West (Ithaca, NY: Cornell University Press, 1984).

62 For example, Matthew, 5:39.

63 *Eusebius, Church History*, trans. G.A. Williamson (Minneapolis, MN: Augsburg. 1975), 192–203.

64 Brock and Young, *Pacifism in the Twentieth Century*, 301–302.

65 Mark Derby, 'Conscription, Conscientious Objection and Pacifism,' *Te Ara: The Encyclopedia of New Zealand* (2012), accessed May 15, 2017, http://www.TeAra.govt.nz/en/conscription-conscientious-objection-and-pacifism/.

66 Tim Shoebridge, 'Conscientious Objection and Dissent in the First World War,' *New Zealand History*, accessed May 15, 2017, https://nzhistory.govt.nz/war/first-world-war/conscientious-objection.

67 Bridget Jones, 'Forced to the Front,' *New Zealand Herald*, April 19, 2014, accessed May 15, 2017, http://www.nzherald.co.nz/entertainment/news/article.cfm?c_id=1501119&objectid=11240574.

68 Derby, 'Conscription, Conscientious Objection and Pacifism.'

69 Matthew Theunissen, 'Fight Against ISIS: NZ Troops Can Opt Out of Iraq,' *New Zealand Herald*, March 1, 2015, accessed May 15, 2017, http://www.nzherald.co.nz/nz/news/article.cfm?c_id=1&objectid=11409756 .

70 Mark Rienzi, 'The Constitutional Right Not to Kill,' *Emory Law Journal* 121 (2012):

121–178. *War Resisters International*, 'The Right to Refuse to Kill Programme,' accessed May 15, 2017, http://www.wri-irg.org/co/rrk-en.htm.

71 Peace Pledge Union, 'White Poppy for a Culture of Peace,' accessed May 15, 2017, http://www.ppu.org.uk/whitepoppy.

72 Kay Blundell, 'Timing of White Poppy Appeal "contemptible",' *Dominion Post*, March 4, 2014, accessed May 15, 2017, http://www.stuff.co.nz/dominion-post/news/9951019/Timing-of-white-poppy-appeal-contemptible.

73 Frowe, *The Ethics of War and Peace*, 3; For the history of the just war tradition, see Alex J. Bellamy, *Just Wars: From Cicero to Iraq* (Cambridge: Polity, 2006).

74 See Sohail H. Hashmi and Stephen Lee (eds.), *Ethics and Weapons of Mass Destruction* (Cambridge: Cambridge University Press, 2004).

75 Frowe, *The Ethics of War and Peace*, 3; Bellamy, *Just Wars*, 2; Lango, *The Ethics of Armed Conflict*, 4; Caron E. Gentry and Amy E. Eckert (eds.), *The Future of Just War: New Critical Essays* (Athens, GA: University of Georgia Press, 2014), 4; Jeff McMahan, 'The Ethics of Killing in War,' *Ethics* 114 (2004): 693–733.

76 Walzer, *Just and Unjust Wars*, 61–62.

77 Ibid., 53–54.

78 John Lango, *The Ethics of Armed Conflict*, 3.

79 Brian Orend, 'Justice After War,' *Ethics and International Affairs* 16, no. 2 (2002): 43–56.

80 Bellamy, *Just Wars*, 122–126; Frowe, *The Ethics of War and Peace*, 101–116.

81 Bellamy, *Just Wars*, 122, 159; Lango, *The Ethics of Armed Conflict*, 2–3.

82 Walzer, *Just and Unjust Wars*, 135–137.

83 Lango, *The Ethics of Armed Conflict*, 3; Bellamy, *Just Wars*, 214.

84 Orend, 'Justice After War,' 55–56.

85 Frowe, *The Ethics of War and Peace*, Christopher, *The Ethics of War and Peace* and Lango, *The Ethics of Armed Conflict* are all preoccupied with just war theory. Orend's *The Morality of War* is chiefly concerned with just war theory, but includes a section on realism and pacifism. Dower, *The Ethics of War and Peace* and Coates, *The Ethics of War* consider all three perspectives, as well as militarism and pacificism.

86 Frowe, *The Ethics of War and Peace*, 95–99.

87 Bellamy, *Just Wars*, 119.

88 Walzer responds that the moral difference between war, on the one hand, and rape or murder, on the other, is that war is a rule-governed activity, whereas rape and murder are not (*Just and Unjust Wars*, 128).

89 Manfred B. Steger, *Judging Non-Violence: The Dispute Between Realists and Idealists* (New York: Routledge, 2003), 91–94.

90 For a summary of the arguments, see Brian Orend, 'A Just-War Critique of Realism and Pacifism,' *Journal of Philosophical Research* 26 (2001): 435–477.

91 Walzer, *Just and Unjust Wars*, 3–20.

92 Ibid., 329–335. For a fuller discussion of these issues, see Brian Orend's 'A Just-War Critique of Realism and Pacifism' and Michael Waltzer on *War and Justice* (Cardiff: University of Wales Press, 2000).

93 Frowe, *The Ethics of War and Peace*, 4; Walzer, *Just and Unjust Wars*, 3–4.

94 Bellamy, *Just Wars*, 7–8, 117–119; Orend, *The Morality of War*, 269–270.

95 Frowe, *The Ethics of War and Peace*, 4; Michael Walzer, *Arguing about War* (New Haven, CT: Yale University Press, 2004), ix; Werner, 'Pragmatism for Pacifists,' 93–94.

96 Holmes, *Pacifism*, 26.

97 Walzer, *Arguing about War*, 86.

98 Coates, *The Ethics of War*, 77.

99 Lango, *The Ethics of Armed Conflict*, 2–3.

100 Walzer, *Just and Unjust Wars*, 21, 34.

101 Frowe, *The Ethics of War and Peace*, 124–125.

102 Jeff McMahan, *Killing in War* (Oxford: Oxford University Press, 2009), 175–188.

103 Ibid., 203–231.

104 Bellamy, *Just Wars*, 119–121.

105 Walzer, *Just and Unjust Wars*, 44–45.

106 Bellamy, *Just Wars*, 8.

107 Davis Brown, 'The Just War Tradition and the Continuing Challenges to World Public Order' in *The Just War Tradition: Applying Old Ethics to New Problems*, ed. Davis Brown and Henrik Syse (New York: Routledge, 2014), 1.

108 United Nations, 'The Charter of the United Nations and Statute of the International Criminal Court,' accessed May 15, 2017, http://www.un.org/en/charter-united-nations/.

109 Frowe, *The Ethics of War and Peace*, 101; Bellamy, *Just Wars*, 120.

110 International Committee of the Red Cross, 'Geneva Conventions and Commentaries,' accessed May 15, 2017, https://www.icrc.org/en/war-and-law/treaties-customary-law/geneva-conventions.

111 Walzer, *Just and Unjust Wars*, 41–44.

112 Marcus Agnafors, 'The Right to Resist, Deceptive Tactics and the Primacy of the Right to First Identity' (paper presented at the 51st Societas Ethica Annual Conference, Maribor, Slovenia, August 21–24, 2014). See also, Anthony Lamb, *Ethics and the Laws of War: The Moral Justification of Legal Norms* (London: Routledge, 2013), 48–51.

113 Treasa Dunworth, 'New Zealand' in *Yearbook of International Humanitarian Law, Volume Four*, ed. H. Fischer (Cambridge: Cambridge University Press, 2001), 598–599.

114 Colin Peacock, '*Hit and Run*: Claims and Counterclaims,' Radio New Zealand, April 9, 2017, accessed May 15, 2017, http://www.radionz.co.nz/national/programmes/mediawatch/audio/201839481/hit-and-run-claims-and-counterclaims.

115 Nicholas Fotion, *War and Ethics: A New Just War Theory* (New York: Continuum, 2007); Walzer, *Arguing About War*, 55–66, 130–142; Bellamy, *Just Wars*, 135–157; Brown and Syse (eds.), *The Just War Tradition*; Lango, *The Ethics of Armed Conflict*; Frowe, *The Ethics of War and Peace*; Gentry and Eckert (eds.), *The Future of Just War*, 17–29.

116 Brown, 'The Just War Tradition,' 1.

117 Bellamy, *Just Wars*, 158–163; Frowe, *The Ethics of War and Peace*, 74–80.

118 Bellamy, *Just Wars*, 168–170, 175–178.

119 New Zealand Army, 'Iraq: 2003–2013,' accessed May 15, 2017, http://www.army.mil.nz/about-us/what-we-do/deployments/previous-deployments/iraq/default.htm.

120 Bellamy, *Just Wars*, 199, 205–207.

121 Walzer, *Arguing about War*, 68–69.

122 Bellamy, *Just Wars*, 207–214.

123 Orend, 'Justice After War,' 43–56; Walzer, *Arguing about War*, 70–73.

124 Walzer, quoted in Frowe, *The Ethics of War and Peace*, 213–214; see, also, Bellamy, *Just Wars*, 206–207.

125 Alex Bellamy, 'Humanitarian Intervention,' in *Contemporary Security Studies*, ed. Alan Collins (Oxford: Oxford University Press, 2016), 327–335.

126 Luke Glanville, 'Is Just Intervention Morally Obligatory?' in *The Future of Just War*, ed. Gentry and Eckert, 48–61.

127 Bellamy, 'Humanitarian Intervention,' 335–341.

128 New Zealand Army, 'Deployments: Timor Leste 1999–2012,' accessed May 15, 2017, http://www.army.mil.nz/about-us/what-we-do/deployments/previous-deployments/timor+leste/default.htm.

129 Cathy Aronson, 'Fifth NZ Soldier Dies in East Timor,' *New Zealand Herald*, July 28, 2002, accessed May 15, 2017, http://www.nzherald.co.nz/indonesia-and-east-timor/news/article.cfm?c_id=589&objectid=2197691.

130 Bellamy, *Just Wars*, 180–198; Brent J. Steele and Eric A. Heinze, 'From Smart to Autonomous Weapons,' in *The Future of Just War*, ed. Gentry and Eckert, 98–114.

131 The Intercept, 'The Drone Papers', October 15, 2015, accessed May 15, 2017, https://theintercept.com/drone-papers/.

132 Amnesty International, 'Will I Be Next? US Drone Strikes in Pakistan' (2013), accessed May 15, 2017, https://www.amnestyusa.org/sites/default/files/asa330132013en.pdf.

133 Michael Fox, 'Kiwi Believed Killed in US Drone Strike,' *Stuff*, April 16, 2014, accessed May 15, 2017, http://www.stuff.co.nz/world/middle-east/9948795/Kiwi-believed-killed-in-US-drone-strike.

10

Abortion

GERALD K. HARRISON

Introduction

It comes as a great surprise to many — including myself and all of those I have spoken to who have had abortions — that apart from under very exceptional circumstances, abortion is actually illegal in New Zealand.

According to section 187A(1) of the 1961 Crimes Act, abortions under 20 weeks' gestation are criminal unless two consultants sincerely believe that one of the following conditions applies:

> (a) that the continuance of the pregnancy would result in serious danger (not being danger normally attendant upon childbirth) to the life, or to the physical or mental health, of the woman or girl; or
>
> (aa) that there is a substantial risk that the child, if born, would be so physically or mentally abnormal as to be seriously handicapped; or
>
> (b) that the pregnancy is the result of sexual intercourse between —
> a parent and child; or
> a brother and sister, whether of the whole blood or of the half blood; or
> a grandparent and grandchild; or

(c) that the pregnancy is the result of sexual intercourse [with a guardian] or

(d) that the woman or girl is severely subnormal . . .

Yet despite this, New Zealand has a rate of abortion comparable to that found in countries in which there is a right to an abortion, such as the United States and Canada. This is because in the vast majority of cases (98 per cent) consultants deem that condition (a) is met, because they believe — or say they believe — that continuing the pregnancy would pose a serious danger to the mental health of the pregnant person of a kind that would normally not be attendant upon childbirth. So, note, risks to the mental (and physical) health of the woman — even very serious ones — that normally attend childbirth do not count. New Zealand law (rather astonishingly) insists that a pregnant woman *must* run those risks, no matter how great they may be or become.

It would seem, then, that where abortion is concerned there is a significant mismatch in New Zealand between the law and practice. This was certainly the view of His Honour Miller J, who said in 2008 that 'there is reason to doubt the lawfulness of many abortions authorised by certifying consultants'.[1] That is, the spirit of the abortion law seems not to be being upheld. Why might this be?

Normally when this happens it is because the moral values and norms to which the law in question is attempting to give expression are not, in fact, endorsed by those charged with upholding the law (in this case, the certifying consultants). The purpose of the law was, as Dixon puts it, 'to respect the rights of the unborn child'.[2] The law, then, gives expression to the idea that fetuses have a significant moral status, and that as a result their destruction is morally bad, and thus its occurrence requires justification. And the law expresses, as well, the idea that no such justification will exist unless the woman's situation satisfies one of the elements set out in section 187A(1). By contrast, it would seem most certifying consultants believe either that the fetus does not have a significant moral status (and thus the demand for justification is misguided), or else that, despite its significant moral status, a women does not, in fact, have to satisfy conditions set out in section 187A(1) in order to be justified in aborting.

Who is right? Does the fetus have a significant moral status such that its destruction is morally bad? And even if it does have a significant moral status, does its destruction require the kind of weighty justification the law in New Zealand supposes it to? This chapter will explore these philosophical issues.

We will see that there is good reason to believe that the fetus probably does acquire a significant moral status at some point, although there seems no way of establishing beyond any reasonable doubt exactly where this point may be. There is a case for believing it begins at conception, but there is also a case for believing it begins at some other point prior to birth. We will also see that even if the fetus does have a significant moral status — indeed, if it has a moral status equivalent to our own and from conception — it is highly unlikely that its destruction requires satisfying the conditions laid down in New Zealand law.

Method

When it comes to an emotionally charged and very personal issue such as abortion, there is a risk that an analytic philosopher's armchair-based approach will come across as almost offensively detached. It 'rips it out of the context of women's lives' as American philosopher Kathryn Addelson has put it.[3] To some extent this is unavoidable. But I would want to stress before I begin that I believe there is a limit to how far the kinds of reflection I am about to engage in can take us. In most ethical matters there is, I think, a role for intuition and judgement that will normally trump the deliverances of our best theorising.

For an analogy: my house needs painting, and I am wondering what colour to have it painted. In trying to reach an informed judgement, I engage in thought experiments — I do my best to imagine it painted different colours and see how it looks in my mind's eye, so to speak. When I imagine it painted black, it seems to look horrible. That, I think, is good evidence that it will probably look horrible (and it is why I am not going to have it painted that colour). However, if someone were secretly to paint my house black and I found that, much to my surprise, it looked very nice, this would be trumping evidence that it doesn't look horrible after all. It would — I think quite obviously — be misguided for me to defer to my earlier theory that it would look horrible, in defiance of how it is actually looking. Reality, we might say, always beats theory.

Applying this to the ethics of abortion: the reflections that follow can be compared to my thought experiments about the colour of my house. I will be imagining a variety of cases — and inviting you to imagine them as well — and forming judgements about them. But reality is always going to win. And in this case it is those who actually find themselves pregnant and confronting the issue of abortion who constitute reality. As such, I believe the intuitions and judgements of people so situated have the power to trump the deliverances of any and all of the reflections that follow.

A quick word about terminology: *conception* marks the point at which the spermatozoon combines with the ovum to produce a single cell *zygote*. This zygote contains the full genetic code. After the cell begins its process of division, it officially becomes known as an *embryo*. After eight weeks, the embryo is designated a *fetus*. However, for ease it has become commonplace in discussions of the morality of abortion for the term 'fetus' to be used as the general term for the developing entity throughout all its stages up to birth. I will follow that convention in this chapter.

What makes us morally valuable?

When it comes to any debate over a controversial issue, it is useful to find some common ground from where to begin. In respect of the debate over abortion, disputants on all sides are going to agree that we — fully grown adult humans, that is — possess moral value, and that destroying one of us would be a bad thing. If we can get clearer about why we have moral value, this will give us some insight into whether and why a fetus does.

USEFULNESS

Most of us are useful to others and to our communities. Is our usefulness to others the source of our moral value? It does not seem to be, for I can easily imagine discovering that I am useless yet my reason assures me that I would still be morally valuable under those circumstances. Similarly, I can imagine encountering someone who has no useful skills, and once more my reason tells me that I still owe this person respect and a degree of goodwill, and that it would be bad, other things being equal, to destroy them.

If your reason concurs, then it would seem we are morally valuable *irrespective* of our usefulness to others, rather than because of it. This is not to deny the moral importance of being useful to others and one's community — these are obviously morally important in their own right — it is just to deny that our moral value is grounded in such matters. This is significant where fetuses are concerned, for they cannot put up shelves, tarmac drives, write entertaining books or educate anyone. They are, in relevant respects, useless. Yet it would seem we cannot on this basis conclude that they lack moral value.

RELATIONSHIPS

We are embedded in a network of relationships of one sort or another. We are liked and valued. Are these relationships the source of our moral value? Again, it does not seem to be so, for I can easily imagine not being liked or valued by anyone yet my reason assures me that I would still be morally valuable. Similarly, when I imagine encountering someone who is not liked or valued by anyone — a hermit, say — my reason tells me that I still owe this person a degree of goodwill and respect, and that destroying them would be bad.

If your reason concurs, then it would seem we are morally valuable *irrespective* of the relationships we stand in to others, rather than because of them. Once more, this is not to deny the moral importance of the relationships we stand in; far from it — they can dramatically alter what we are morally entitled to do to someone, as we shall see later. It is just to note that the moral value of *us* does not seem to be grounded in these relationships. Again, applied to the fetus this means that the fact a fetus may be valued by no one — indeed, may even be positively disvalued — does not, in and of itself, entail that the fetus lacks moral value.

SHAPE, SIZE AND APPEARANCE

What about our physical features? Are any of these responsible for our possession of moral value? It does not seem so. I can easily conceive of having radically different physical features, and it seems to make no difference to my moral value. With apologies to Kafka, I can imagine waking one morning from uneasy dreams to find myself transformed into a giant insect. And when I do, my reason assures me that I would still be owed respect and goodwill, and it would still be bad — other things being equal — to destroy me, despite my radically altered physical form. In fact, I can go one step further and imagine that I have no physical features whatsoever — that I am a disembodied immaterial entity — and my reason assures me that, even under these circumstances, I would be morally valuable and my destruction would be bad. (Yes, it is hard to see *how* I could be destroyed if I am an immaterial entity, but that's beside the point, for it remains clear that my destruction — however it might be achieved — would be bad.)

If your reason concurs, then it would seem that we are morally valuable *irrespective* of any and all of our physical features. Indeed, we seem to be morally valuable irrespective of whether we even have any. Applied to a fetus, this means that the many ways in which it is radically physically dissimilar to one of us does nothing, in and of itself, to imply that it lacks the same moral value as one of us.

BEING HUMAN

What about our status as humans? Is that, perhaps, why we are morally valuable? Once more, it does not seem so. I currently believe I am genetically human, although I have never had this officially verified. But I can imagine finding out that I am actually genetically something else — an alien species maybe, or a curious kind of giraffe. My reason assures me that this, too, would make no difference to my moral value. I am sure yours does, too. (Just imagine that genetic tests reveal that *you* are not a human — is it now okay to destroy you?) Similarly, I can imagine encountering someone who, it turns out, is genetically not human — a real Dr Spock, say — yet my reason assures me that this person is owed respect and goodwill, and that it would be bad, other things being equal, to destroy him.

If your reason concurs, then it would seem that we are morally valuable irrespective of our human status, rather than because of it. Applied to the fetus, all too often it is thought that all one needs to do to establish the moral value of a fetus is to demonstrate that it qualifies as a human. The above reflections imply that this is a mistake (one noted by many of those who write on this topic, for instance see Marquis[4] and Tooley[5]). We are morally valuable, it would seem, *irrespective* of whether we are genetically human, rather than because we are genetically human.

HISTORY

What about our histories? As Annette Baier puts it, 'a person has a life *history*, and that a people collectively have a history depends upon the humbler fact that each person has a childhood in which a cultural heritage is transmitted'.[6] This is true, yet I can imagine it not being: I can imagine I popped into existence a few moments ago and all my memories to the contrary are false. As Bertrand Russell famously noted, 'there is no logical impossibility in the hypothesis that the world sprang into being five minutes ago, exactly as it then was, with a population that "remembered" a wholly unreal past'.[7] And when I imagine this possibility, my reason once more assures me that I would still matter morally under such circumstances. It would still be bad to destroy me, despite my lack of a history. Similarly, when I imagine encountering someone who has popped into existence, fully formed, a moment or two ago, my reason tells me that I owe this person a degree of respect and goodwill, and that destroying them would be bad.

If your reason concurs, then it seems that our histories are not the source of our moral value. Applied to the fetus, this means that its history is not going to affect its moral value either. For instance, a fetus that came into being as a result of an act of rape is going to be no more or less valuable than one that did not.

LOCATION

What about our location? I am located in Palmerston North, in New Zealand, on the planet Earth. Does this have anything to do with my possession of moral value? Am I morally valuable *because* I am in New Zealand? I think the answer is clear enough: no. It is morally bad for me to be destroyed in Palmerston North, and it is just as morally bad for me to be destroyed in Port Moresby, or on the Moon.

If your reason concurs, then it would seem we are morally valuable *irrespective* of our geographical location, rather than because of it.

Applied to the fetus, this means that the fact it is located inside a person does not, in and of itself, have any bearing on its moral worth.

REASON

What about our capacity to reason? Might this be responsible for our moral value? Virtually all of us possess reason. If you are reading this book, you certainly do. We can also note that our reason confers on us an important kind of free will. For our reason allows us to recognise and weigh reasons for action and make decisions on this basis. That is, we can follow reason rather than be mere victims of whatever desires arise in us. This kind of free will is almost universally — and perhaps inescapably — recognised to be morally valuable. And this has resulted in some philosophers, most famously Immanuel Kant, thinking that it is possession of this kind of free will that transforms us from mere things into morally valuable persons who are now entitled to respect and goodwill and whose destruction would be bad.

If Kant and others are right about this, then it is significant where the moral value of the fetus is concerned. For fetuses fairly obviously lack the power of reason. However, it seems to me that possession of reason, valuable though it is, is not necessary for possession of moral value. For I can imagine the possibility that one day I will lack reason, and when I do my current reason assures me that I would still have moral value under those circumstances. Similarly, I can imagine encountering someone who lacks all reason — someone with advanced dementia, say — and when I do my reason tells me that I would still owe that person a degree of respect and goodwill, and that it would be bad to destroy them. If your reason concurs, then we have good evidence we are morally valuable *irrespective* of our possession of reason, rather than because of it.

PREFERENCES

What about the fact that we have preferences? There are things I want to do and be, projects I want to bring to fruition, places I want to go, states I wish to be in, and so forth. These are all preferences. Perhaps it is these that make me morally valuable? Again, there are some philosophers who think this is indeed the case. Contemporary philosopher Michael Tooley, for instance, believes that something can only be said to have a 'right to life' if it 'is capable of desiring to continue existing as a subject of experiences and other mental states'.[8]

Perhaps these philosophers are correct, in which case it would follow that if fetuses lack preferences (as seems likely), then they lack moral value. (And Tooley does conclude that fetuses — and even babies — lack a right to life.) But personally, I have my doubts. For I can imagine coming to lack any preferences; that is, I can imagine coming to be in the kind of state that Buddhists seek to achieve, a state of inner calm free from desire. And when I imagine this possibility, my reason assures me that I would still be morally valuable under those circumstances. And I think it would be bad to destroy meditating Buddhists who, because they are meditating, lack any preferences.

If your reason concurs, then it would seem that we are morally valuable *irrespective* of whether we have any preferences, rather than because we do. Again, this is not to deny the moral significance of our preferences, or to deny that they can affect dramatically what we are entitled to do to someone. It is just to note that our moral value does not seem to be due to our having preferences.

PLEASURE AND PAIN

What about our capacity to feel pain and pleasure? Is this the basis of our moral value? This view has had some important defenders. As the great Jeremy Bentham memorably expressed it: 'The question is not, Can they reason? Nor Can they *talk*? But, *Can they suffer?*'[9]

If Bentham is right, then this has important implications regarding the moral status of fetuses. For if it can be established that, at some point in their development, fetuses can feel pain, then this would be sufficient to establish their moral worth at that point.

But without denying the moral importance of pleasures and pains themselves, they do not seem to be the source of our moral value. For when I imagine being incapable of feeling pleasure or pain, my reason continues to tell me I would be morally valuable under those circumstances. I imagine your reason will tell you the same about you. Just imagine that the boffins invent a drug that, upon ingestion, makes one incapable of feeling pain or pleasure. Would taking it render you value-less such that destroying you would now not be bad? No, obviously not. So, we appear to be morally valuable *irrespective* of whether we can feel pleasure and pain, rather than because we can.

CONSCIOUSNESS

What about raw consciousness itself? After all, it is in virtue of being conscious that there is 'something it is like' to be me. And it is because you are conscious that there is something it is like to be you.[10] Our consciousness gives us a perspective onto the world that we, and we alone, occupy. Is it this profoundly strange feature of us that is responsible for our moral value?

Some would say so. But I am suspicious. I believe I am often unconscious (when I am asleep but not dreaming, for instance). Yet my reason assures me that I am still morally valuable during these times. Likewise, I believe others are often unconscious, yet my reason tells me it would still be bad to destroy them during these times. If your reason concurs, then we have good grounds for believing that our consciousness is not the ground of our moral value.

POTENTIAL

What about potential? Anything I actually have, I can potentially have. Perhaps I am morally valuable because I am *potentially* conscious, *potentially* rational, *potentially* useful, *potentially* valued, and so on. If so, then as a fetus also has all of these potentialities, it, too, would be morally valuable.

But on reflection I find this quite implausible. (See Mary Anne Warren, who thinks so, too.)[11] Not because potential cannot confer value on something — I think it can — but rather because it does not seem to be responsible for the degree of moral value we actually possess. Consider a beautiful oak tree and an acorn. The beautiful oak tree is plausibly a morally valuable thing, and wantonly destroying it would be bad. An acorn is a potential beautiful oak tree. Now, perhaps wantonly destroying an acorn is bad, too, but any badness it has pales by comparison to the badness of destroying the tree. So, the moral value of the oak tree cannot plausibly be said to reside in its 'potential' to be an oak tree, for that is something it has in common with the acorn.

Or consider a wonderful painting and a canvas and some pots of paint. The wonderful painting plausibly has some moral value such that wantonly destroying it would be bad. The blank canvas and the pots of paint are potentially a wonderful painting. Yet destroying them seems nothing like as bad as destroying the painting.

Note, as well, that I am potentially many bad things. I am potentially a cruel and heartless murderer (as are you). I am potentially someone who deserves to come to great harm. But clearly my potential to be these things does not mean that I actually have the worth of a cruel and heartless murderer, or actually deserve to come to great harm. So when it comes to the moral value I actually appear to possess, I do not believe that my potentials are its source.

Your reason may not have concurred with mine all the way to this point. But if it has, then I think the conclusion we should draw is that our moral value appears not to be grounded in any of our features. Rather, our moral value is something we seem to possess immanently or intrinsically. That is, it is I, the object that bears all of the features listed above, who is morally valuable. The features themselves may, in many cases, have moral value in their own right and may even add to mine. But they are not the ultimate source of my value (not all of it anyway) any more than they are the source of me.

To be clearer, note that I myself do not appear to be reducible to any of the features listed above. (And the same, I think, is going to be true of you as well.) That is, although I have uses, I am not a set of uses; I have relationships, but I am not a set of relationships; I have a set of physical features, but I am not a set of physical features; I have a history, but I am not a history; I have preferences, but I am not a set of preferences; I have conscious states, but I am not a bundle of conscious states; and I have potential, but I am not my potentials. These are all things I have, but none of them compose me.

It is this mysterious *I* — this *I* who has the features above yet who is not to be confused with any of them — who has moral value. This value can therefore be said to be *immanent* or *intrinsic*, because it does not derive from anything about me, but inheres in me. To put it more colloquially: I am morally valuable because I am morally valuable, and that's that. And the same, I think, is true of you as well.

Some may find this an unsatisfying conclusion. But note, if you think that our moral value derives from, say, our consciousness or some other feature, then to the question 'Why does consciousness (or whatever) have moral value?', you too will have to say, 'It just does, and that's that.' That is, you will have to insist that the moral value of consciousness (or whatever you ground our value in) is intrinsic.

So the notion of intrinsic value seems indispensable. The question is not, then, *whether* anything has intrinsic value, but *what* has intrinsic value. My own reflections above — and yours, too, if your reason has concurred — implies that *we* ourselves are among the things possessing intrinsic value.

The moral value of a fetus

So we — fully fledged adult humans — appear to possess our moral value intrinsically or immanently. Let's assume that is true, anyway. What does it imply where the value of a fetus is concerned? Well, it depends on what we, these bearers of immanent moral value, are. If we are our physical bodies (not a view I hold), then because our physical bodies were once fetuses, we would have to conclude that fetuses possess intrinsic moral value and that they possess it from conception. For it was at conception that there came into being an identifiable object, with a full genetic code, that developed into our present bodies. Our fetus was just our present body in its earliest stage. To insist we came into being at some other point would seem arbitrary. So, in the absense of good reason to think otherwise, if we are intrinsically valuable — and it seems we are — and are identifiable with our physical bodies, then fetuses have intrinsic moral value from the moment of conception.

Note, this would not follow if our moral value derived from our being conscious, or from our having preferences, or from being able to feel pleasure and pain. For then, although it would still be true to say that our physical bodies came into being at conception, it would *not* be true to say that our moral value began at that point. Our moral value would begin at the point at which we acquired the value-grounding attributes (something about which there is no consensus at present).

It would also not follow if, rather than being our physical bodies, we are something else entirely — an immaterial soul, say. Historically, this has been the most common view about what we are (and it probably remains the most common view among people generally, now and for time immemorial). Among philosophers it is known as 'substance dualism', because it is the view that there are two fundamentally different kinds of substance in the universe. There are physical substances, which have features such as size, shape, location, colour. These are investigated by the natural sciences. But then there are also size-less, shapeless, location-less, colour-less objects such as, well, *us*. These cannot be studied by the natural sciences. On this view, I am an immaterial entity and not my body at all. It is *my* body in that it is the material entity with which I am directly interacting. I am seeing, hearing, touching, smelling and tasting through it. But I am not identical with it any more than I am identical with my car when I am driving it.

Substance dualism is not a very popular view among contemporary philosophers. But that may change — it used to be the dominant view, and has enjoyed support from, among others, Plato, Descartes and Locke — and it has never been decisively refuted. It is, then, possibly true. And in fact, one of the reflections in the previous section seems to imply its truth. For if we are morally valuable irrespective of whether we have a physical body — as seems to be the case — then the simplest explanation of this is that it is because we, the bearers of moral value, are not our physical bodies.

But anyway, let us imagine that substance dualism is true and that we are immaterial entities temporarily residing in physical bodies. Well, then it is our souls that bear intrinsic value, not our physical bodies. And so the fact that our physical bodies began to exist at conception would not entail that our souls came into being at that time. In turn, this would mean that fetuses are not necessarily intrinsically valuable from conception, unless, that is, the soul enters at that point. That is to say, the relevant question where the value of the fetus is concerned, if substance dualism is true, is when the soul enters it.

On this matter, just as with the matter of when the fetus acquires consciousness or can begin to feel pain, there is no consensus. For instance, in the medieval period *quickening* — the point at which the woman can feel the independent movements of the fetus — was thought to indicate the arrival of the soul. But that is a crude guide, and is hardly conclusive evidence either way, for it seems entirely possible that a fetus could move by itself without there being a soul present, and entirely possible for a soul to be present in an unmoving fetus.

The fact is, detecting when a soul is present in a physical body is going to be as fraught with difficulties as detecting when consciousness is present or when pain can be felt. For just as there is no scientific instrument that can detect souls, there is no scientific instrument that can detect consciousness — or conscious states such as pain — either. The best we can do is simply infer their presence on the basis of the presence of certain physical states or systems. Whatever indirect evidence there may be for the presence of consciousness in a fetus — detectable brain waves, for instance — will also be indirect evidence for the presence of a soul. So, if we are souls rather than bodies, then the question of when the fetus possesses moral value becomes relevantly analogous to the question of when the fetus possesses other features, such as consciousness. These, unfortunately, seem to be matters that are destined to remain unresolved.

So, where the moral value of fetuses is concerned we are in a rather unhappy and frustrating situation. If the above reflections are right, we can reach no certain conclusion about when fetuses come to have moral value. If we are our physical bodies, then if we are intrinsically valuable the fetus will have intrinsic value from conception. However, it is at present an open question whether we *are* our bodies. Substance dualism — the view that we are not our bodies, but are immaterial souls — has not been refuted. Indeed it has not even been established with certainty that the view that we are our bodies is coherent: some philosophers deny that it is even possible that conscious states could be states of a physical thing. So, the fact is that at present we cannot reliably conclude that the fetus has moral value from conception.

Perhaps, instead, moral value arises with consciousness or the capacity to feel pain, or the capacity to form preferences — possibilities that I personally find dubious, but that many endorse. Well, in that case the fetus will possess moral value at the point in its development when it acquires these features. But again, it is at present an open question when exactly this is, for the features in question are not ones we can reliably detect.

Finally, perhaps we — the bearers of intrinsic moral value — are immaterial souls temporarily resident in our bodies. In that case fetuses will have moral value from the point at which the soul is present. However, we cannot at present establish with certainty when this is the case, any more than we can reliably establish when consciousness arises. Thus, frustratingly it looks as if we are going to have to conclude that it is simply unclear when, in the process of fetal development, a fetus acquires intrinsic moral value.

Note, however, we probably do have to conclude that fetuses acquire intrinsic value at some point in their development. This is because otherwise the irrelevance of location means that we will be forced to conclude that newly born babies lack intrinsic moral value. If you agree that newly born babies have moral value — and it seems self-evident to me that they do — then the irrelevance of location means that you should agree that a fetus that is just about to become a newly born baby has intrinsic moral value as well. Thus, fetuses must acquire moral value at *some* point. The problem is that there is little prospect of us being able to determine with any reliability exactly when.

Given the indeterminate nature of this conclusion, what should we do? Well, for the sake of argument — and it really is only for the sake of argument, for only *one* view canvassed above has this upshot

— let us assume that fetuses have moral status from the moment of conception. In other words, let us assume that from conception a fetus has the same basic intrinsic moral worth as one of us. What follows? Does it follow — as New Zealand law currently seems to assume — that abortions are almost always immoral and are only justified under the most extreme circumstances?

Thomson's violinist

We are now assuming — purely for the sake of argument — that from conception the fetus has the same intrinsic moral value as one of us. Surely, if fetuses have the same intrinsic moral value as you and me, then their destruction is only going to be justified under the most extreme circumstances — circumstances in which another person's physical and mental health are in jeopardy?

Let us test that thesis. Imagine the following scenario conceived of by philosopher Judith Jarvis Thomson:

> You wake up one morning and find yourself back to back in bed with an unconscious violinist. A famous unconscious violinist. He has been found to have a fatal kidney ailment, and the Society of Music Lovers has canvassed all the available medical records and found that you alone have the right blood type to help. They have therefore kidnapped you, and last night the violinist's circulatory system was plugged into yours, so that your kidneys can be used to extract poisons from his blood as well as your own. The director of the hospital now tells you, 'Look, we're sorry that the Society of Music Lovers did this to you — we would never have permitted it if we had known. But still, they did it, and the violinist now is plugged into you. To unplug you would be to kill him. But never mind, it's only for nine months. By then he will have recovered from his ailment, and can safely be unplugged from you.[12]

Is it not obvious that you may unplug yourself? It would, as Thomson says, be 'very nice of you' if you stayed.[13] But the idea that you are morally obliged to stay and would be doing something very immoral if you left just seems, well, incorrect. Certainly my reason says, and says loud and clear, that you are perfectly within your rights to unplug yourself, even though this means that the needy violinist — someone who is as intrinsically valuable as the next person and is wholly innocent — will die.

Note, there is no suggestion that the violinist lacks intrinsic value, or that your value exceeds that of the violinist. No, the violinist has intrinsic moral value and his death will be a very bad thing. The point, though, is that, bad though it is, it does not entail an obligation for you to give him nine months of your life.

We can now apply this lesson to fetuses. Fetuses are intrinsically morally valuable (we are assuming). And they need the use of a woman's womb if they are not to die, something that would be very bad. Nevertheless, this does *not* entail that the woman is morally obliged — at nine months of great inconvenience and pain to herself — to grant the fetus the use of her womb for that time. True, it is not the fetus's fault that it depends on a woman's womb for its survival. But then it was not the violinist's fault that he depends on your kidneys for his survival. If you are morally entitled to unplug yourself from the violinist, then it would seem that women *are* entitled to abort fetuses from their wombs, *even if the fetus has the same intrinsic moral value as one of us.*

Note as well, you do not have to show that your physical or mental health is seriously jeopardised by your staying for nine months before you are entitled to unplug yourself from the violinist. Indeed, to make such a demand would be utterly unreasonable. Even if staying plugged into the violinist for nine months would in no way jeopardise your health — mental or otherwise — you are clearly still entitled to leave, and it would be those who might try to prevent you doing so who would be in the wrong.

It might be objected that this analogy is not perfect, for in Thomson's violinist case you have been kidnapped. Thomson's violinist case is, then, more closely analogous to a case of pregnancy by rape, in which one is forcibly impregnated, rather than the more usual case of voluntary sexual relations that happen to result in impregnation. This is true. But it still implies that it can be morally permissible for a person to abort a fetus if rape is responsible for its presence in you. Plus we can easily adjust the scenario so that it becomes more closely analogous to the more usual cases of pregnancy. And when we do, unplugging seems to remain something one is quite obviously entitled to do.

Imagine, for instance, that you are on your way out to what you believe will be a fun evening at the cinema. You are running late, however, and need to take a short-cut down an alley way if you are to arrive at the cinema on time. You know that the alley in question is one in which the Society of Music Lovers hang out, and that they occasionally kidnap people who walk down it and plug their kidneys into those of a needy musician. You decide, nevertheless, to take this risk. You get unlucky, and wake up to find yourself plugged into a needy violinist. Once again, the doctor explains the nature of your situation. May you unplug yourself?

Well, speaking personally, my intuitions are clear: yes, of course you may. Again, very generous of you if you stay for nine months, but there is no moral obligation for you to do so. And certainly it would be the doctor — and not you — who would be being unreasonable and immoral if he insisted that you must stay unless or until you can show that your staying will seriously jeopardise your mental and physical health beyond the ways in which this kind of procedure can normally be expected to jeopardise them. Yet this case seems relevantly analogous to a case in which someone wanted to have sex, but found themselves without protection and decided to run the risk of pregnancy and got unlucky.

If that is correct — that is, if the analogy holds up — then it seems that in the vast bulk of cases of pregnancy for which abortions are sought, there would be nothing immoral about these abortions. Indeed, the case implies that New Zealand law is seriously immoral in insisting that those who wish to abort under these circumstances must demonstrate that their mental and physical health is seriously in jeopardy (beyond what could normally be expected in a pregnancy) before they are allowed to do so.

Another variation: imagine you find out that there is a violinist who, for blood-type reasons, needs the use of your kidneys (no one else's will do) for nine months if he is to live. You positively decide to give him the use of them. However, after you arrive and get plugged in, you have a change of heart and decide you would rather leave. Now, my own intuitions say that you are perfectly within your rights to do so. Indeed, even if you have a change of heart after, say, eight months of being plugged into him, I think you are entitled to leave. (Although at this point it seems a little unseemly to do so, but not so much that you must stay.) After all, it was generous of you to plug yourself in *at all*. Certainly, it strikes me as immoral to insist that you stay unless or until you can demonstrate that staying would jeopardise your mental or physical health more than could normally be expected in the course of this kind of procedure. Again, if your intuitions are anything like mine, then it would seem that New Zealand law is currently immoral, and that the consultants are therefore right not to adhere to the spirit of it.

Perhaps my intuitions about some of the cases above are not shared by everyone. Thomson herself thinks her thought experiment — and numerous others she provides — leaves open that 'there are *some* cases in which the unborn person has a right to the use of its mother's body, and therefore *some* cases in which abortion is unjust killing'.[14] I think that may be correct. However, I am inclined to think that given the burdensome nature of pregnancy and birth, very few abortions are going to qualify as unjust killings, or at least as unjust killings that anyone is entitled to prevent from occurring. For there seems to be a real limit to how much altruism morality can demand from us, and hours of torturous pain seems to be beyond that limit under most circumstances.

For example, imagine once again you have tried taking the short-cut to the cinema and, being unlucky again, you awake to find yourself plugged into another violinist. This time the doctor informs you that you are needed for only a short while — a matter of hours, not months. However, the violinist will die unless either your stomach is slit open or you push something the size of a melon through your vagina (or, if you do not have one of those, imagine that preserving the violinist's life requires that something the size of an apple needs to be forced down your penile urethra). What now? Are you morally obliged to agree to one of those things happening? Would it be okay to insist that you do these things unless or until you can show that they will jeopardise your physical and mental health beyond what they could normally be expected to do? Well, I do not think so. I think you are perfectly entitled to unplug yourself and run away under those circumstances. If your intuitions concur, then I think this gives us good reason to think virtually all abortions are ones it is morally permissible for a person to have.

Now imagine that because of the way you have been hooked up to the violinist you are unable to unplug yourself. Indeed, you need the help of someone who specialises in unhooking people from violinists, otherwise you will almost certainly do yourself a serious injury. Should such third parties be prevented from being able to offer you their assistance unless or until they certify that they believe your mental or physical health is seriously at risk, beyond what could normally be expected in the course of being plugged up to a violinist? Well, I think quite obviously that would be outrageous. *Of course* a third party should be allowed to help you, even if neither your physical nor your mental health was in jeopardy. Indeed, it seems to me plain enough that it would be positively immoral to prevent them from offering their help. If that is correct, then this just underlines that the laws on abortion currently on the books in New Zealand are positively immoral.

Relationships

I noted earlier that, although we are embedded in networks of relationships to others, these relationships are not plausibly the basis of our moral value. Nevertheless, relationships can be morally valuable, and can also dramatically affect what we are morally entitled to do to another. Here's another example to illustrate, this time one originally conceived by the philosopher Robert Nozick.[15]

> I am temporarily stuck at the bottom of a deep and narrow well, and an innocent person is falling towards me. I have in my possession a vaporiser. I know that if I do nothing, then the person will land on me, killing me. However, my body will break their fall and they will survive unscathed. On the other hand, I could vaporise them before they reach me.

It is clear enough to my reason that I am morally entitled to vaporise them. It would be very nice of me to lay down my life for theirs, but I am under no moral obligation to do so. It is not that I think I am intrinsically more valuable than they are. After all, I believe they would be morally entitled to vaporise me if our roles were reversed. It is just that they have come to stand in a life-threatening relationship to me, and this has generated in me an entitlement to vaporise them. (An entitlement I would not have in other situations — vaporising people is seriously wrong in the main, of course.)

The same would be true, I think, if a crate containing, say, 10 tiny innocent people was falling towards me. I could lay down my life, knowing that my body will cushion the crate sufficiently that the 10 tiny people will survive unscathed, or I could vaporise the crate. I think — and I suspect your intuitions will agree — I am entitled to vaporise the crate. Again, it is not that I think I am morally more important than 10 tiny people, for again I think that if I was in the crate with nine others falling towards a person, that person would be entitled to vaporise the crate. It is the life-threatening relationship that is doing the moral work and rendering permissible something — the destruction of 10 innocent lives — that would be extremely wrong in other contexts.

But what if it is my partner who is falling towards me, and I know this? What now? Well, now I think I probably ought to take the hit. She's my partner; I owe her that. I am not, in this scenario, entitled to vaporise her. Legally, I may be. Morally, I am not. And clearly, in this case, it is the relationship in which I stand with her that is making this difference, for there is no other difference between this case and the others. There is no difference in her intrinsic value and mine, or anyone else's. I certainly do not believe her moral value eclipses that of 10 people. And if she was falling towards someone else, then they would be entitled to vaporise her. It is because — and only because — she is falling towards me, her partner, that I am morally obliged to take the hit. So, the relationships we stand in relation to others can alter — and alter dramatically — what we are morally entitled to do.

Returning to fetuses. Those who conceive fetuses are causally responsible for the existence of the fetuses in question. That is a kind of relationship, one of production. Plus, the fetus is *in* someone, and that person — the woman — comes thereby to develop a relationship with the fetus that is inside her. If relationships can affect what we are morally entitled to do to another, might not these relationships affect what the woman may do to the fetus?

Without denying the possibility that they may do so, I think further reflection on variations of Thomson's violinist case implies that they do not actually do so — or do so sufficiently — in the relevant cases. For instance, imagine once more that you wake up plugged into the violinist. This time, however, the doctor informs you that he is your long-lost son whom you put up for adoption several decades ago and have had no contact with since. Are you entitled to unplug? Or is the doctor now entitled to make you stay — and have you ultimately pass a melon through your vagina or slit open your stomach — until or unless you can show that staying will imperil your mental or physical wellbeing beyond what could normally be expected?

I think the fact the violinist is your son does make a moral difference. That is my intuition, anyway. Yet not so much of one that you are not entitled to unplug. Plus the differences cut both ways. The violinist — unlike a fetus — is already invested in a life. The violinist is analogous, in some ways, to a person who is partway through watching a film. They are invested in the plot and want to know what is going to happen next. By contrast, the fetus is analogous to someone who is, at best, watching the trailers. The main feature has yet to start, and they are in no way invested in it. If the main feature does not start, this is not of a piece with stopping the film that the violinist is partway through viewing. The latter is much worse than the former.

To put it another way, the violinist's life is up and running, and is therefore something he has an interest in continuing. The fetus's life, by contrast, has not really started yet. This is not to deny that depriving it of its life is still bad. It is just to note that if — as my intuitions say is the case — one is entitled to unplug from the violinist who is your long-lost son and is invested in a life, then *a fortiori* one is entitled to unplug from a fetus who is your son but has yet to become invested in a life.

One more observation. I was once a fetus and I am someone's son, and speaking on behalf of the fetus I once was, I would *never* want my mother to be made to go through nine months of great discomfort and hours of torturous pain in order to bestow a life upon it — a life it had yet to start really living, a life yet to be *this* life — if she had at any point not wished to. I think that is going to be true of most of us. Just imagine *you* need the use of someone else's kidneys and you awake one morning to find that someone has taken it upon themselves to plug you into your mother's kidneys and is now insisting that your mother must stay where she is — and ultimately have her stomach slit open or a melon passed through her vagina — so long as you remain hooked up to her. Wouldn't you be outraged at their temerity and insist they leave your poor mother alone and unhook you from her? And that's *now*, when you are invested in a life that you, hopefully, very much wish to continue.

This, I think, just underscores the ethically unobjectionable nature of virtually all abortions. After all, on one view of respect, we respect another when we treat them in ways to which they would have consented were they rational and fully informed. Well, I am now rational (to some degree) and far more informed than I was as a fetus. In this more rational and informed state I approve, retrospectively, of my mother aborting the fetus version of me, had she ever wanted to (and disapprove — in the strongest terms — of anyone having the effrontery to deprive her of that choice). If that is true of you, too, then chances are most abortions are likely to be precisely what the person who otherwise would have been brought into existence would have wanted. This suggests — and this will come as a surprise to many

— that *not* allowing the woman the choice to abort fails not only to respect her, it also fails to respect the fetus.

What about the ongoing relationship that woman may come to have with the fetus developing within her? Well, although it may be a very important and valuable relationship, I believe there are good grounds for being suspicious that it is of a sort capable of affecting radically what one's obligations and permissions are in respect of it. Return once more to the violinist. This time, imagine that it is a violinist you have read about in magazines and such like. Although you have never met at a personal level, you have seen him on TV. You are, then, abundantly well aware of his existence; however, he is totally unaware of yours. You have feelings and beliefs about him, but he has none about you. And now you have woken up to find yourself plugged into him. He is now physically present to you — he is lying on the bed next to yours and his kidney is now joined to yours — but he is unconscious, so you still cannot make him aware of your existence or interact with him at a personal level. Now, in some sense you have a relationship with the violinist. And it may even be said to be a very important and significant relationship. But does the existence of this relationship mean that you are now obliged to stay hooked up? Well, again my intuitions are clear: no, of course you may leave.

Perhaps it would be different if the relationship was not so asymmetric. For instance, when I imagine that the violinist was my close friend or partner, then, I think, the relationship I stand in relation to them does operate to make my staying morally obligatory. (Although even now I still think I would be *entitled* to leave — and that others are permitted to help me do so.) But if he is not yet my friend or partner, then, even if I know that he could become my friend or partner were he to live, my reason says that the absence of the actual relationship makes it morally permissible for me to unplug.

I stress again, this is not to deny the significance of asymmetrical relationships. There is no suggestion in what I have just said that the asymmetrical relationship a woman may come to have with a fetus is irrational, or morally unimportant. It is just to note that such relationships do not yet seem capable of generating obligations and permissions in the way that symmetrical relationships do.

Dangers normally attendant upon childbirth

Finally, I want to look at the 'not being danger normally attendant upon childbirth' clause in the current law. It means that whatever dangers — no matter how great they may be — that are normally attendant upon childbirth are not ones that can serve to make an abortion legal. I think that upon a bit of reflection it becomes clear that this clause is radically unfair on those who are pregnant. As should be clear by now, I think the whole law on abortion is unfair — indeed, seriously immoral — but this clause is especially worrying. For note, there is no limit to the dangers normally attendant upon childbirth.

Historically, the risk of dying due to pregnancy was estimated to be approximately 1 in 100. But advances in medicine have meant that childbirth is nothing like as dangerous as it used to be, at least in New Zealand. (Needless to say, in many parts of the world it is as dangerous as ever.) Yet it is entirely possible that this could be reversed. That is, it is entirely possible for pregnancy to become incredibly dangerous. As the current law stands, this will not matter. For instance, if it became normal for, say, 90 per cent of pregnancies to result in maternal death, then the 90 per cent risk of death that you are running by being pregnant would not be allowed to serve as a justification for an abortion, for it would now be a risk 'normally attendant upon childbirth'. That, I suggest, is wholly unreasonable and makes no real sense.

It means that at present — where the normal risk of dying attendant upon childbirth is very low — if your pregnancy posed a 90 per cent chance of killing you, an abortion would be permitted (for now the risk to your physical health is great, and exceeds that normally attendant upon childbirth). If, however, the risks normally attendant upon childbirth happen to increase so that now 90 per cent will end in the death of the pregnant person, this risk to your health — which is the same as before — will *not* serve to justify an abortion.

Conclusion

Currently the law in New Zealand forbids abortions under all but the most extreme circumstances. Yet abortions are performed in New Zealand with as much regularity as they are in countries — such as the United States and Canada — in which there is a right to abortion. Interestingly, then, there exists a radical mismatch between the law and practice on this issue. The law assumes a very conservative position on abortion, in which the fetus is assumed to have a significant moral status, and its destruction is assumed to require weighty justification. By contrast, many others — including, it would seem, many of the certifying consultants — believe either that the fetus does not have a significant moral status, or that it does, but its destruction does not require that a woman meet the very demanding conditions laid down in the law.

What I have tried to show, above, is that there exists a good, although far from decisive, case for thinking that the fetus has a significant moral status from conception. However, by contrast, the case for thinking that a woman needs to meet the conditions outlined in the current law before being allowed an abortion is, in my view anyway, very poor. Numerous thought experiments strongly imply that, even if the fetus enjoys the same moral status as one of us, it is well beyond the demands of duty to undergo a pregnancy and birth in order to keep it alive.

Furthermore, if my reason is anything to go by, it seems positively immoral — under most imaginable circumstances anyway — to prevent those who wish no longer to bear the burdens of pregnancy and birth to escape them, or to insist that they must bear them until or unless they present an extreme and unusual threat to their health that would not otherwise attend pregnancy and childbirth.

---

1 Quoted in Amy Dixon, 'Authorisation of Abortion for a "Serious Danger to Mental Health": Would the Practice Stand Up to the Judicial Test?,' *Victoria University Law Review* 43 (2012): 289–320 at 290.

2 Ibid.

3 Quoted in Susan Sherwin, 'Abortion: A Feminist Perspective,' in *Social Ethics: Morality and Social Policy*, ed. Thomas A. Mappes and Jane S. Zembaty (New York: McGraw-Hill, 2002), 53–59, at 54.

4 Don Marquis, 'Why Abortion is Immoral,' in *Social Ethics: Morality and Social Policy*, in ibid., 22–28, at 24.

5 Michael Tooley, 'Abortion and Infanticide,' in *Applied Ethics*, ed. Peter Singer (Oxford: Oxford University Press, 1986), 57–85, at 60–62.

6 Annette Baier, *Postures of the Mind: Essays on Mind and Morals* (Minneapolis: University of Minnesota Press, 1985), 84.

7 Bertrand Russell, *The Analysis of Mind* (London: Allen and Unwin, 1921), 159–160.

8 Tooley, 'Abortion and Infanticide,' at 69.

9 Quoted in Peter Singer, 'All Animals Are Equal,' in *Applied Ethics*, ed. Peter Singer (Oxford: Oxford University Press, 1986), 215–228, at 221.

10 See Thomas Nagel, 'What Is It Like To Be a Bat?' *The Philosophical Review* 83(4) (1974): 435–450.

11 Mary Anne Warren, 'On the Moral and Legal Status of Abortion,' in *Social Ethics: Morality and Social Policy*, ed. Thomas A. Mappes and Jane S. Zembaty (New York: McGraw-Hill, 2002), 14–22, at 19–20.

12 Judith Jarvis Thomson, 'A Defence of Abortion,' in *Applied Ethics*, ed. Peter Singer (Oxford: Oxford University Press, 1986), 37–56, at 38–39.

13 Ibid., 39.

14 Ibid., 49.

15 Robert Nozick, A*narchy, State and Utopia* (Oxford: Basil Blackwell, 1974), 34.

About the contributors

Stephen Chadwick received a British Academy scholarship in 1994 to undertake a PhD in social and political philosophy at Aberdeen University. He went on to complete an MA in social work at the University of Hull, and subsequently worked for many years with drug users, professional sex workers and people with physical disabilities. Stephen has been teaching applied ethics at Massey University since 2006. In addition, he has taught the ethics of war to officers of the New Zealand Defence Force and facilitated sessions for nurses on bereavement support. He is also one of New Zealand's premier astronomical photographers and has written two books on the subject. Stephen is the current secretary of the New Zealand Association of Philosophers.

Stephen Duffin is a lecturer at Massey University, where he has taught critical thinking for the past 20 years. He also teaches courses on environmental ethics and the philosophy of religion. Aside from his publications in these areas, he is also the author of *Reason in the Real World* (Dunmore Press) and, with William Fish, *Tū Arohae: Multidisciplinary Critical Thinking* (Massey University Press). Stephen lives on a lifestyle block, and his hobbies include playing guitar and piano and trying to master the Arabian oud.

Gerald K. Harrison is a philosophy lecturer at Massey University. He teaches a variety of courses on ethics, as well as a course on great Western philosophy. Gerald finds every aspect of morality fascinating, and is especially interested in what morality is, in and of itself. He lives in Palmerston North with his partner, Julia, and a cat of questionable character.

Vanya Kovach spends half of her working time teaching ethics and, most recently, philosophy for children, in the undergraduate programme of the Discipline of Philosophy at the University of Auckland. Her central interest is in philosophy in the community, which she currently pursues; the other half of her working time is primarily in the areas of philosophy for children (through Philosophy for Children New Zealand) and professional ethics. Vanya has a long-standing interest and involvement in palliative care ethics.

Nick Munn is a senior lecturer in Philosophy at the University of Waikato, where he teaches ethics and political philosophy. He works on virtual worlds, which requires him to spend a lot of time online, dutifully examining how people behave in immersive online spaces such as the *World of Warcraft* (a hard task, but someone has to do it). He also works on democracy and enfranchisement, and hopes to see the franchise expanded and improved.

Tim Rochford is Chair of Te Rūnanga o Makaawhio, the body that represents the hapū of Kāti Māhaki of Te Tai Poutini the South/West Coast of Te Wai Pounamu (the South Island of New Zealand). Tim has sat on Te Rūnanga o Ngāi Tahu for many years, and works for Te Puni Kōkiri (Ministry of Māori Development) as a senior policy analyst, and has worked in Treaty of Waitangi settlements, social and health policy for Māori in government, and academic institutions.

Vanessa Schouten completed her BA and MA at Victoria University of Wellington and her PhD at Princeton University. She works mainly in the area of sexual ethics, with a focus on questions to do with consent: what it means to consent, and when and why consent matters. She has been teaching at Massey University's Albany campus since 2015.

Natalya Tamariki is a registered nurse, and currently works in Kaupapa Māori Adult secondary mental health services in the Waikato. Previously she led Ngāti Whātua Ōrākei's Whānau Ora service in Ōrākei, Auckland, where she grew up. Natalya is of Ngāti Whātua o Ōrākei and Cook Island heritage. She lives in Raglan with her husband, Otto, and daughter, Kalani.

Krushil Watene is a senior lecturer in philosophy at Massey University and was previously a postdoctoral research fellow at the James Henare Māori Research Centre, University of Auckland. She completed her PhD at the University of St Andrews, Scotland, in 2011. Krushil's main areas of research are contemporary moral and political philosophy. Her work also extends to the areas of development ethics, and she is also committed to indigenous and Pasifika people's perspectives. Her current research focuses on the contribution of indigenous philosophies to contemporary global challenges. Krushil grew up in Otahuhu (South Auckland), and belongs to the Ngāti Manu, Te Hikutu, Ngāti Whātua Ōrākei and Tongan communities.

Marcel Zentveld-Wale MA is a senior tutor at Massey University's Centre for Defence and Security Studies, and a doctoral student of philosophy at the University of Auckland. He holds academic qualifications in political science, philosophy, classical studies and economics from Massey University and Victoria University of Wellington. He has taught on a range of subjects, from philosophy, politics and international relations, to conflict, strategic and security studies, both at Massey University and at the New Zealand Defence Force and Royal Brunei Armed Forces command and staff colleges. Marcel has a particular interest in the ethics of security, especially as it applies to the issue of terrorism.

Index

E

F

G

H

I

J

K

L

M

N

O

P

R

S

MASSEY UNIVERSITY PRESS

For more information about our books please visit
www.masseypress.ac.nz